IMAGES
of America

AROUND SELINSGROVE

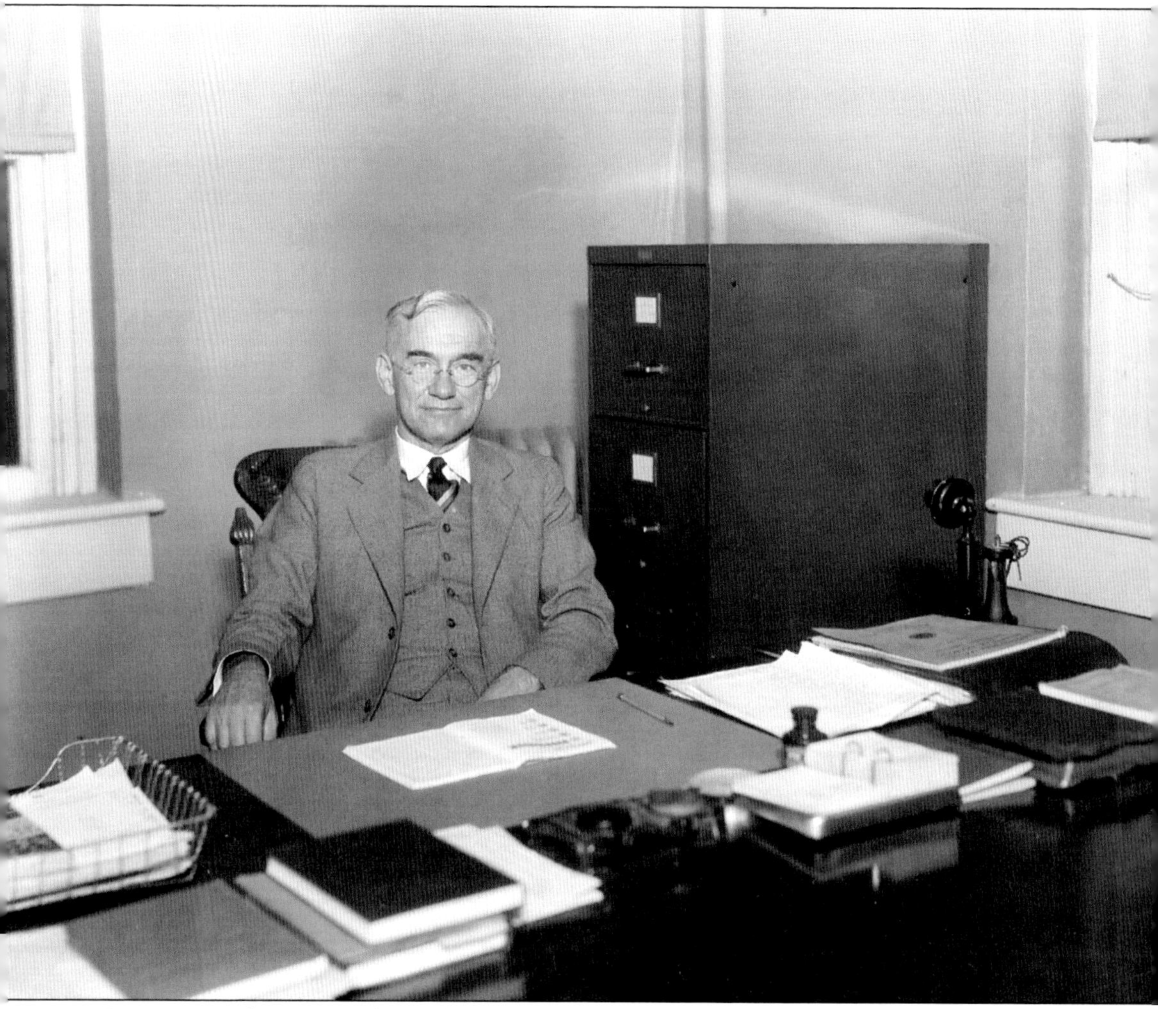

Previous Snyder County books by Arcadia Publishing were only able to pay verbal tribute to Dr. George F. Dunkleberger. Now, a photograph has been discovered, and it is a pleasure to include it in this volume. Dunkleberger published his highly-valued *The History of Snyder County* in 1948. It has been an important research tool for this and other books. William M. (Billy) Schnure's *Chronicles of Selinsgrove* also was invaluable. Dunkleberger is pictured in his dean's office at Susquehanna University in the 1930s.

On the cover: Please see page 99. (Courtesy of the Snyder County Historical Society.)

IMAGES
of America

Around Selinsgrove

Jim Campbell

ARCADIA
PUBLISHING

ISBN 978-0-7385-5711-3

Published by Arcadia Publishing
Charleston SC, Chicago IL, Portsmouth NH, San Francisco CA

Printed in the United States of America

Library of Congress Catalog Card Number: 2007940070

For all general information contact Arcadia Publishing at:
Telephone 843-853-2070
Fax 843-853-0044
E-mail sales@arcadiapublishing.com
For customer service and orders:
Toll-Free 1-888-313-2665

Visit us on the Internet at www.arcadiapublishing.com

To the people of Selinsgrove who literally make the community "an ideal place to live, work, and worship," as signs proclaim upon entering many areas. Your caring and involvement make it more than a slogan—it is the truth.

Contents

ACKNOWLEDGMENTS

As with three previous Snyder County books published by Arcadia, many have been most cooperative. They are listed as follows: Randy Arbogast, Karen Athey, Diane Aumiller, Pam Aungst, Lloyd and Shirley Bailey, Nelson Bailey, Vivian Beaver, Maryon "Booty" Beck, Bill Bingaman, Eunice Boden, Dick Bogar, Mary Bolig, Art Bowen, Carl and Shelva Brouse, Earl Brown, Barbara Brownlee, Gail Burd, Lee Burgard, Carolyn Burns, Brenda Campbell, Eva Conrad, Ray Conrad, Brian Cornwell, Kathy Dalton, Ronnie and Irene Day, Don "Homer" Ernst, Karl Fahnestock, Charles K. Fasold, Ralph Fisher, Chet Gaugler, Rudy Gelnett, Laird Gemberling II, Max Gemberling, Susan Gift, Lonnie Groce, Dave Gross, Sherrill Grosse, Scott Harro, Sally Hayhurst, Dick Herbert, Ruth Herman, Ted Herman, Judy Hickman, George Hummel, Bob Hunter, Tanna Kasperowicz, Jimmy Kauffman, Helen Keiser, Jim Keiser, Jane Kessler, Lorraine Klingler, Dave Lauer, Max and Ann Leitzel, Heidi Metzger, Holly Metzger, Barry Miller, Dale Miller, Ken Miller, Don Musser, Todd Myers, Ron Nornhold, Glenda Pyle, Ann Rainey, Sid Ranck, Jean Rathfon, Ed Rhoads, Jim Rutkowski, Dwight Saxton, Betty Schlingmann, Jane Schnure, Jim Schnure, Cara Schreck, Barry "Buzz" Siegfried, Diane Smith, Neal and Sharon Smith, John Snyder, officers past and present of the Snyder County Historical Society, Doug Sprenkle, Carol Sundling, staff of Susquehanna Bank, staff of Susquehanna University Library, Scott Tanner, Jim Taylor, Dave Troutman, John Troutman, Erin Vosgien, Bob Walker, Gene Walter, Cal Witmer, Ken Wochley, Bob Yerger, and Rick Zeckman.

All who gave generously of their photographs, many from treasured family albums, are gratefully acknowledged here, along with those who gave of their knowledge and time in an equally generous manner.

INTRODUCTION

The facts, the figures, the dates, and the numbers about Selinsgrove and the other communities of eastern Snyder County are known.

In 1713, George Gabriel established a settlement "at the mouth of Penn's Creek." That, of course, would be where Selinsgrove is today. It became known as Gabriels Plantation, and is generally thought to be the first white settlement on the west bank of the Susquehanna River. This was well before the area was part of Northumberland County, which was formed from portions of what were the only three original counties—Bucks, Chester, and Philadelphia—in "Penn's Woods" (as Pennsylvania translates from the Latin local students learned from Miss Phoebe Herman).

The dream Shikellamy had is known, whereby Conrad Weiser, the very influential interpreter who controlled much of the settlement of Selinsgrove and surrounding area, handed over his prized Pennsylvania, or Kentucky (as the firearms erroneously became known), rifle to the Onondaga chief. Not to be outdone when it came to dreams, Weiser related his nocturnal vision that had Shikellamy presenting Weiser with the Isle of Que, which at the time was a true island and not the peninsula that it is today as a result of the relocating of the flow of Penn's Creek. Wisely, after the exchange, Shikellamy solemnly said, "Let's neither of us dream no more." As with New York's early Dutch settlers supposedly obtaining Manhattan Island from Native Americans for $24-worth of trinkets and beads, Weiser is deemed to have gotten the better of the deal. One can only speculate as to whether either man actually had the dream he related.

The Penn's Creek massacre of October 16, 1755, which was commemorated gaily in Selinsgrove in 1915, began near New Berlin, but continued along Penn's Creek eastward toward Selinsgrove for 10 miles. Gen. Edward Braddock's defeat and subsequent death during the French and Indian War is what sparked the uprising—the first within the bounds of the Commonwealth of Pennsylvania. In the spring of 1756, Deputy Gov. Robert Hunter Morris dispatched Col. William Clapham north to quell the disturbance. His unit was known as the Augusta Regiment, and they were to establish an outpost (Fort Augusta) at Shamokin, as Sunbury was then known. Naturally, Clapham's troop passed very close to Selinsgrove on the Susquehanna River, if not actually through it.

Meeting in 1771, the Pennsylvania General Assembly, the governing body of the commonwealth, declared and designated the Susquehanna a "public waterway." In the days when any roads in the area were little more than Native American trails, this was important to the settlers "at the mouth of Penn's Creek." The river, as it is simply known to many, was perhaps the best if not the only means of transportation.

In May 1776, a Swiss soldier of fortune captained an independent corps per orders of Gen. George Washington. To Washington, the captain was probably just another much-needed officer. But he was much more significant. He was Anthony Selin. After Revolutionary forces under Washington accepted the surrender of the British at Yorktown, Virginia, in 1783, Selin resigned his commission and moved to the area that would and still does bear his name—Selinsgrove—although at the time it was not so named. Selin opened the first hotel in the town. A year later, he and Simon Snyder opened a store in Penn Township, and Selin was elected to represent the area in the general assembly.

In 1808, Snyder was elected to the first of his three terms as governor, the only person to so serve. The state capital at the time was Lancaster. What may not be as widely known is that in 1816, Snyder, respected for his leadership during the War of 1812, received a significant number of votes for the office of vice president of the United States. That was the year that James Monroe was elected president. A year later, Snyder retired to his stately limestone mansion on North Market Street in Selinsgrove—a still-standing building that now houses the Selin's Grove Brewing Company.

A cornerstone was laid on October 19, 1828, for a Roman Catholic church on the Isle of Que. It was to accommodate the many Irish immigrant laborers who worked on and maintained the Pennsylvania Canal. This was also the year of the first attempts to incorporate Selin's Grove (as it was then known and spelled) as a borough. Opposition from Penn Township residents scuttled the proposal.

There is a good reason Susquehanna University is located in Selinsgrove. Community visionaries saw the benefit of an institution of higher learning and led the drive for local support that raised $22,500 to bring the Missionary Institute (as it was known when first chartered in 1858) to town. The successful fund-raising led to Selinsgrove Hall being named in honor of the community, which officially became a borough on September 24, 1853. Chapter 4 is devoted solely to Susquehanna University, as the school celebrates its sesquicentennial.

The first of two great fires consumed much of downtown Selinsgrove on February 21, 1972. The second conflagration occurred on October 28, 1874. In all, 54 businesses and residences were lost in the blaze. The Dauntless Hook and Ladder Company was formed on November 20, 1874. Better known as the Hookies, the volunteer fire company still protects and serves the community.

Sigfried Weis opened a store at Market and Pine Streets in 1884. The family business grew into a huge chain of "pure food" markets.

In 1902, perhaps the most elegant building in Selinsgrove, Seibert Hall on the Susquehanna campus, was dedicated on November 25.

The long-running Sunbury and Selinsgrove Electric Railway Company, or S&S trolley, went out of business at 12:00 p.m. on December 31, 1934. Some Selinsgrove residents rode the trolley one last time to Sunbury for the midnight New Year's Eve movie at the Strand theater. How did they get home? Well, the Buffington, Kessler, and Wilhour (BKW) Coach Line came into existence at 12:01 a.m. on January 1, 1935, and was on hand in the wee hours of the morning to return the theatergoers to town.

Otto F. Kuehnart, a native of Germany, purchased the B. Edmund Silk Mill on April 27, 1938, and began operating as the OK Hosiery Mill. The building in the vicinity of Spruce and High Streets was converted into apartments after the mill ceased operations.

These are the facts and the figures—some well known, and others not so well known. But the true story of Selinsgrove and the surrounding community is the people who made and are making the area what it is—a unique and wonderful place to live. A community that was comprised mostly of Pennsylvania Germans and Pennsylvania Dutch nevertheless welcomed many diverse groups into the community fold. These groups blended into the community and made the community bonds, already strong, even stronger.

This book is dedicated to the countless folks who made and are still making Selinsgrove and its suburbs both a typical and unique part of the nation—small town America.

One

HOMETOWN

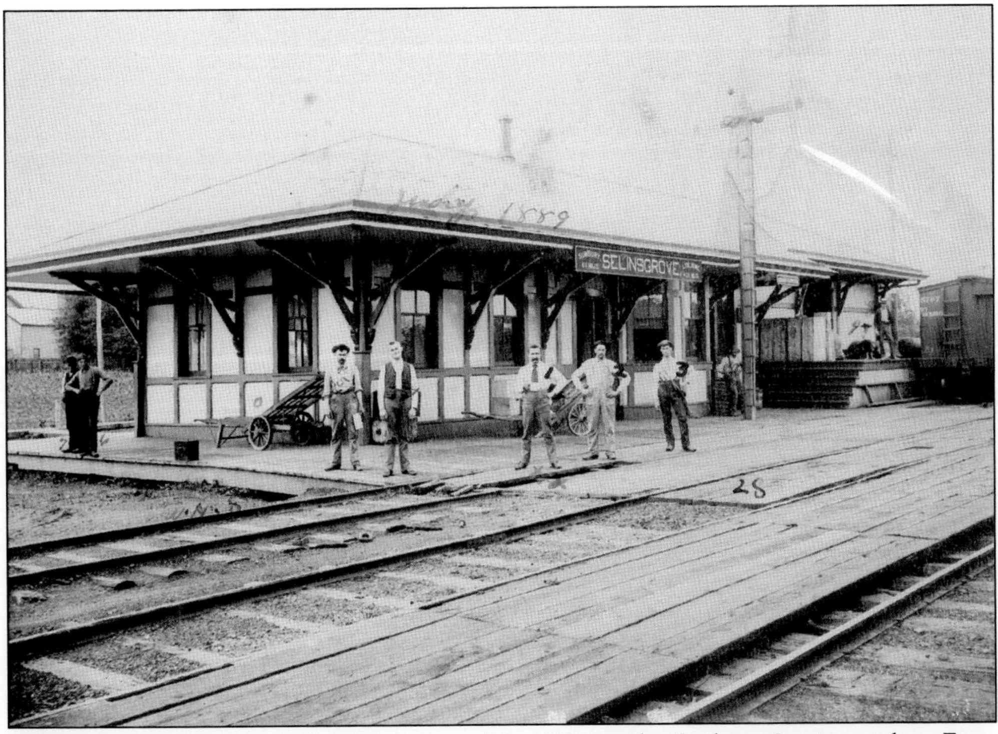

The railroad running through Selinsgrove in July 1889 was the Sunbury–Lewistown line. From left to right, the men at the station are Henry Gaugler, Charles Fisher, George Reigle, G. B. Arnold, A. W. Smith, M. A. Miller, D. E. Kreamer, Harvey Romig, Edgar Miller, and H. P. Miller. Smith held the important post of station agent. Trains ran frequently through town into the 1960s. They still occasionally do, going as far west as the Kreamer Feed mill.

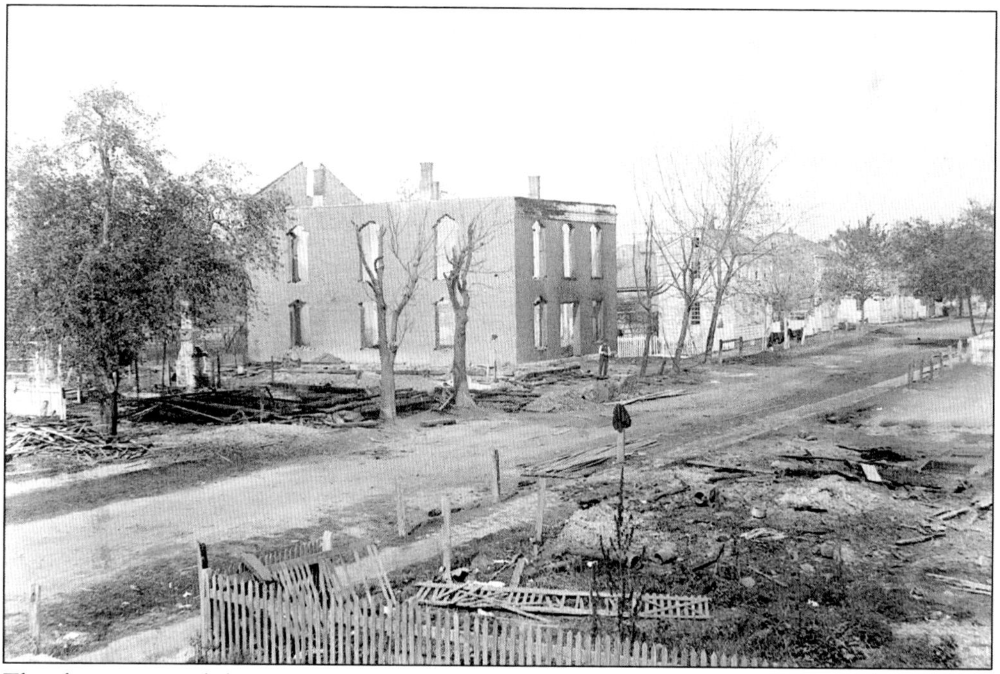

The devastation of the October 30, 1874, fire is clearly evident in this Roshon and Richie photograph. The foreground is the southeast corner of Water and Pine Streets looking north. The brick building—severely damaged, but still standing—is the Methodist church. Completely lost in the blaze was Bergstresser's tannery to the left of the church.

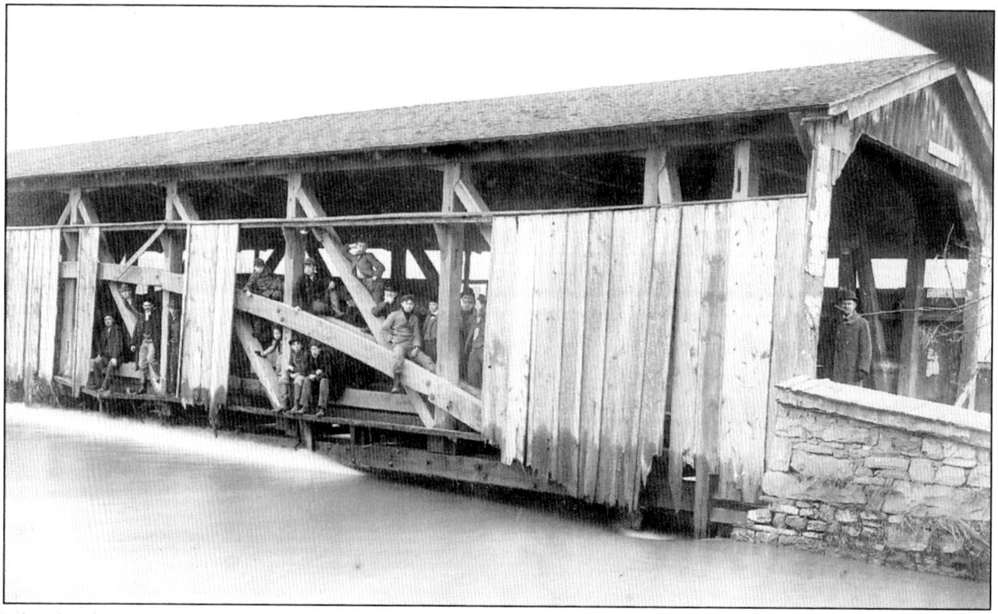

This bridge over Penn's Creek, connecting the town and the Isle of Que, serves as a nesting place for some of Selinsgrove's more daring residents. Because the bridge was removed in 1902, it is known that the high water is from one of the following floods: 1889, 1894, or 1900. The flood that led to the removal of the Pine Street bridge in 1902 completely washed away the Bough Street bridge.

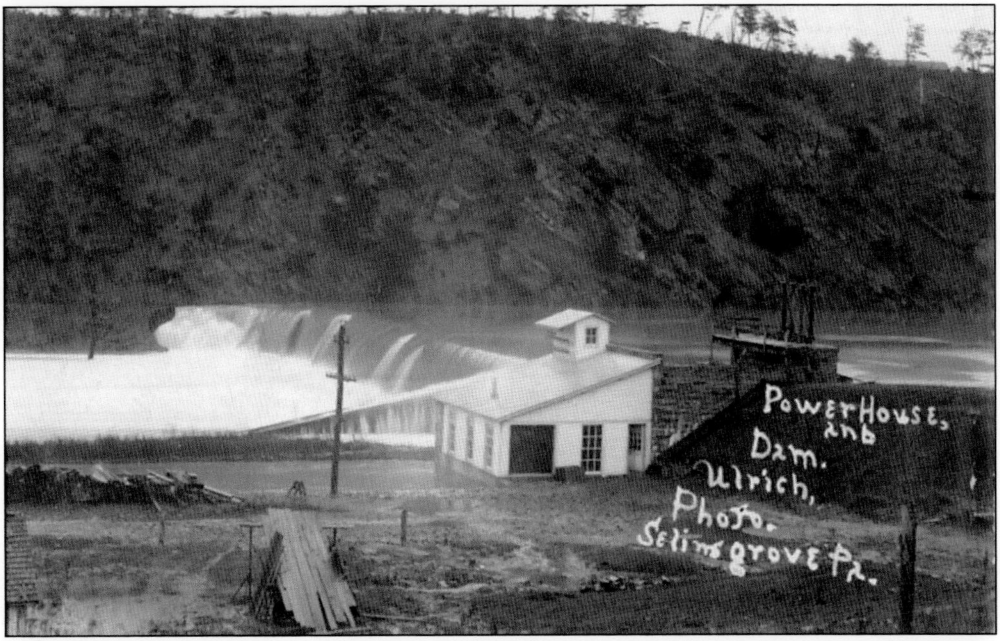

R. L. Ulrich, with his trusty view camera, was still documenting life in Selinsgrove in 1908 when this real-photo postcard was produced. The power dam, only recently dismantled—although out of service for decades—was located south of town on Middle Creek. It provided electrical power for, among other things, the Sunbury and Selinsgrove Electric Railway Company (S&S) trolley line and Rolling Green Park.

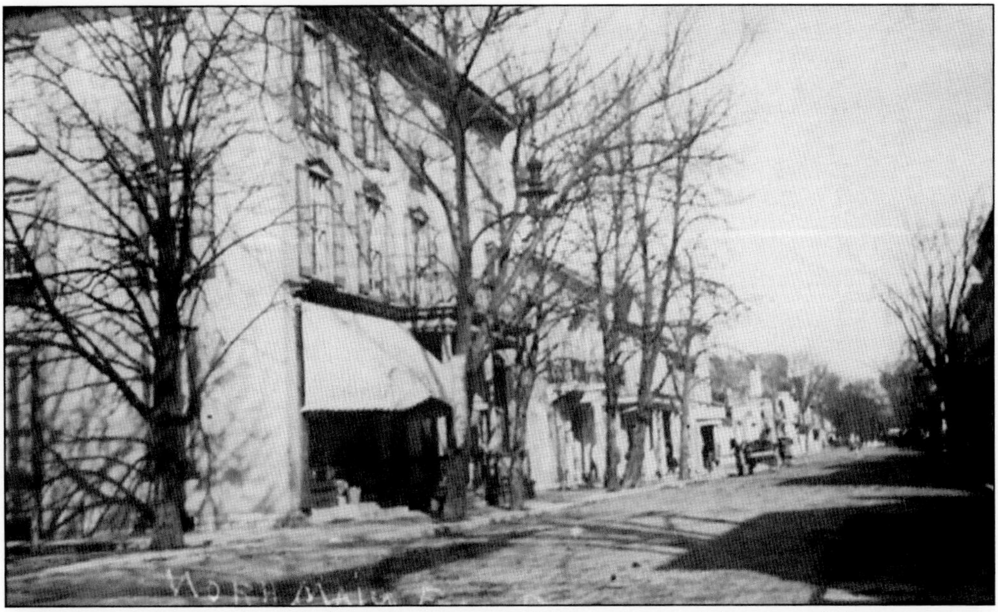

Another real-photo postcard, this one is imprinted "Pleasant St., Selinsgrove." At one time, it was unknown if it was actually the proper name of a street or the description of said street. It states, "North Main [Market] from Pleasant St." Note Main/Market Street is paved with bricks and the fountain stands in the middle of the square at the intersection of Pine and Market Streets. This dates the card to approximately 1912.

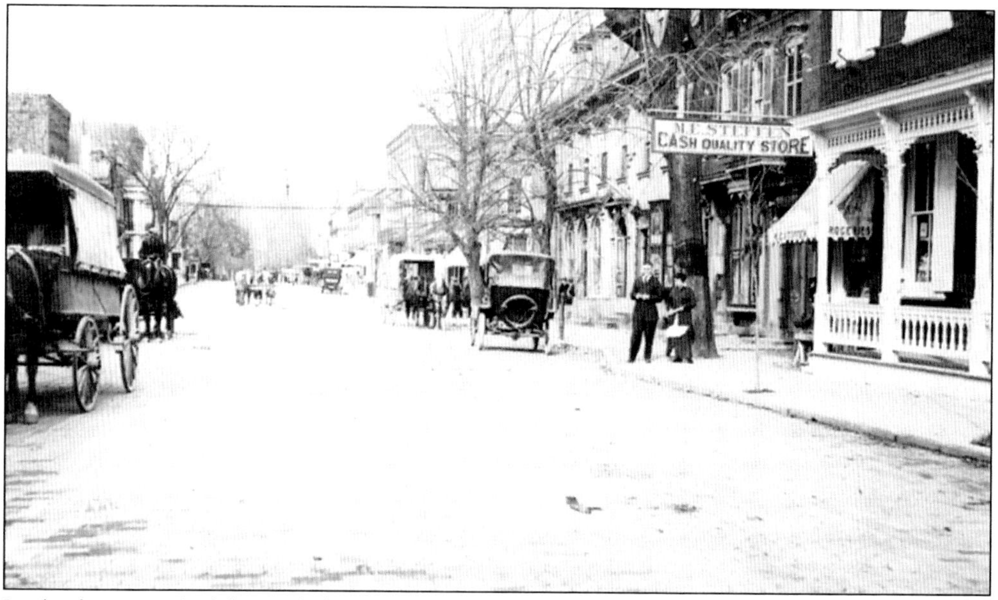

In the foreground of this real-photo postcard is the M. E. Steffen grocery store. Steffen and his wife are seen standing beneath the store's sign. The location is the east side of the first block of South Market Street. Later Russell Learn operated a similar store there. A feature of Learn's was two or three stationary stools where shoppers rested while he filled their orders from his bins and shelves. This scene can be dated to 1914 thanks to the fountain, which existed from 1910 to 1925.

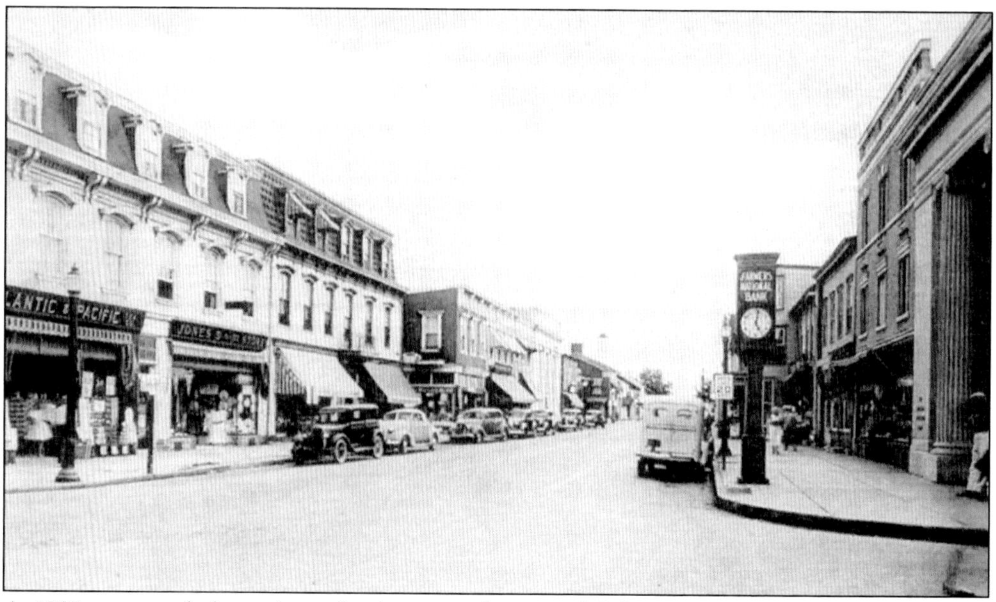

A 1930s postcard shows how the business district of Selinsgrove was evolving. An A&P replaced a previous business on the east side of the first block of South Market Street. The Farmer's National Bank moved from North Market Street to the southwest corner of Pine and Market Streets. It become the Snyder County Trust Company and eventually—after several changes—First National Bank. The landmark clock still stands, although it has been changed to Snyder County Trust Company.

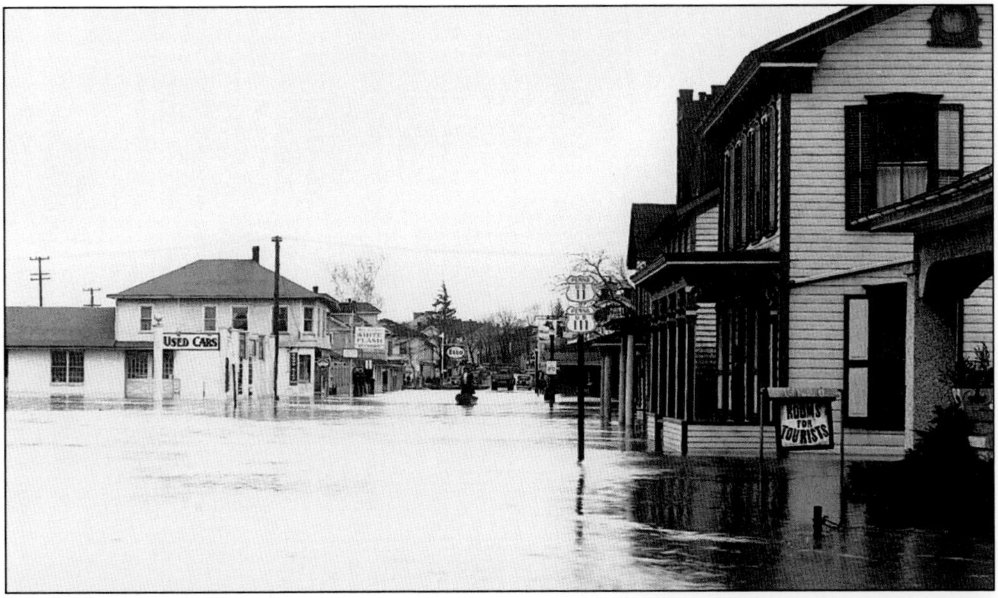

The spring flooding of March 1936—thought to be the mother of all floods by Selinsgrove residents until Hurricane Agnes struck in 1972—wreaked havoc on much of the nation. The town suffered as much as any. This photograph was taken at the intersection of Penn and Market Streets. Notice how traffic has stopped at the railroad crossing at Spruce Street and a man is standing in a rowboat near Market and Mill Streets. Note too that Routes 11 and 15 are designated 11 and 111.

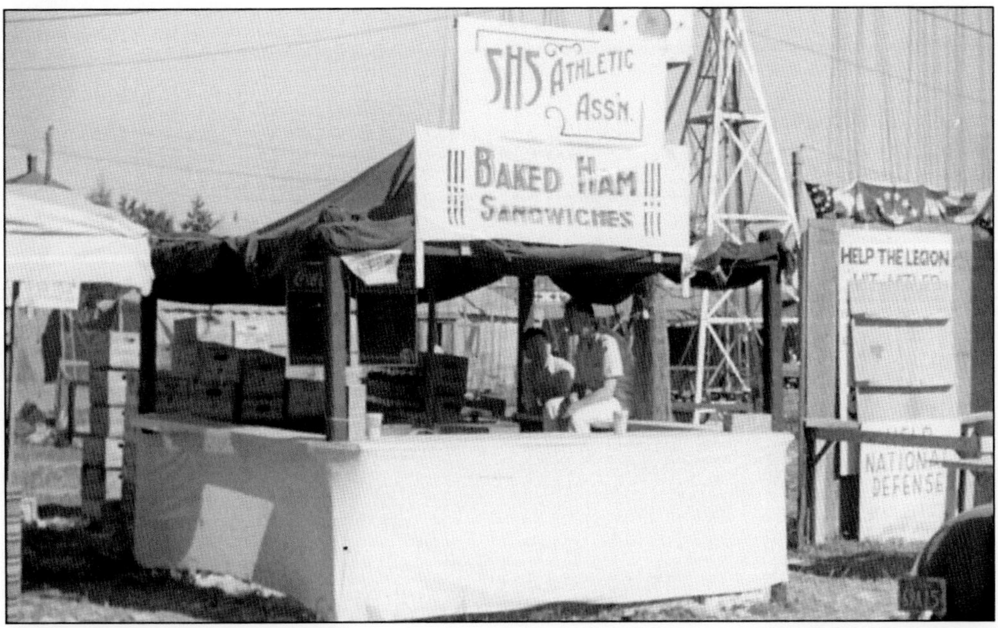

Harold Follmer (nearest the camera), a longtime principal at Selinsgrove High School, was one of those manning a food stand at the Selinsgrove Night Fair in July 1941. Coca-Cola (note the neatly stacked cases) and baked ham sandwiches were the specialty—if not the only menu options—of the stand, which benefited the Selinsgrove High School Athletic Association. The neighboring stand, before the United States' official entry in World War II, already suggests "Hit Hitler."

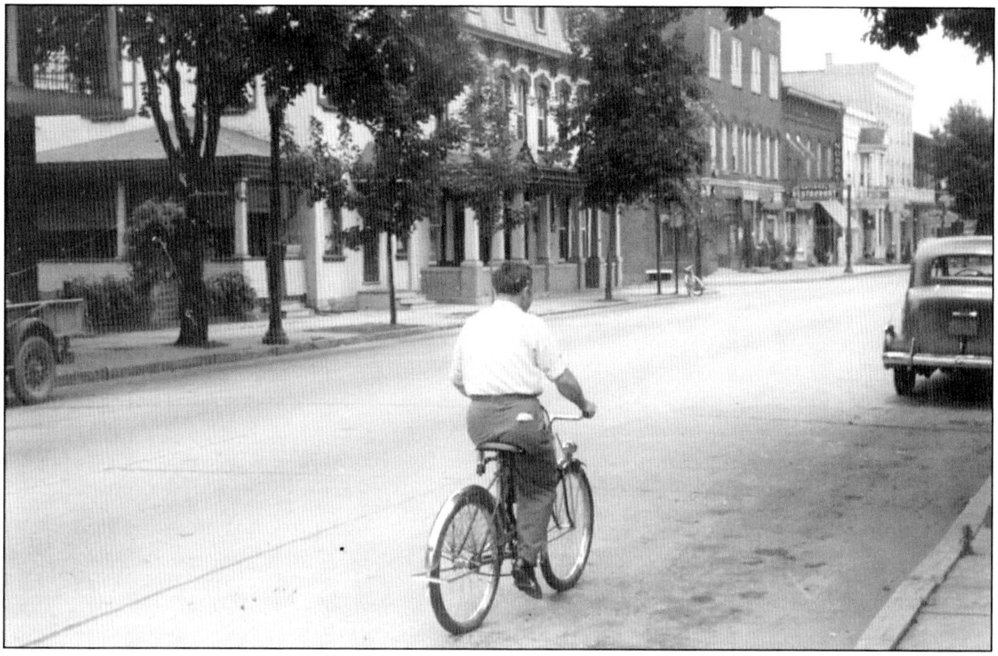

There is something about a tree-shaded small-town street in summer that evokes feelings of nostalgia. Add a longtime Selinsgrove High School teacher/administrator to the scene and one cannot help but long for the good old days. Pedaling south on the second block of North Market Street on a quiet July day in 1942 is Albert Potteiger, enjoying his summer off from school.

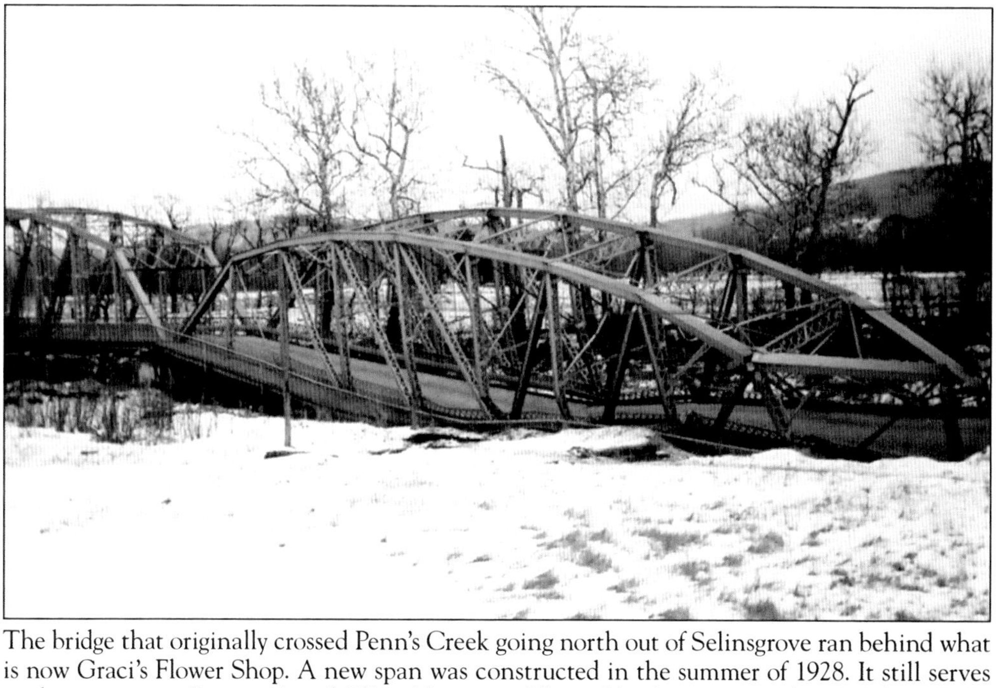

The bridge that originally crossed Penn's Creek going north out of Selinsgrove ran behind what is now Graci's Flower Shop. A new span was constructed in the summer of 1928. It still serves as the gateway to Routes 11 and 15's golden strip. The red bridge, as it was known then, came off second best in a confrontation with a passing bulldozer on February 4, 1943. Repairs were quickly made, and the flow of traffic reached its prior volume.

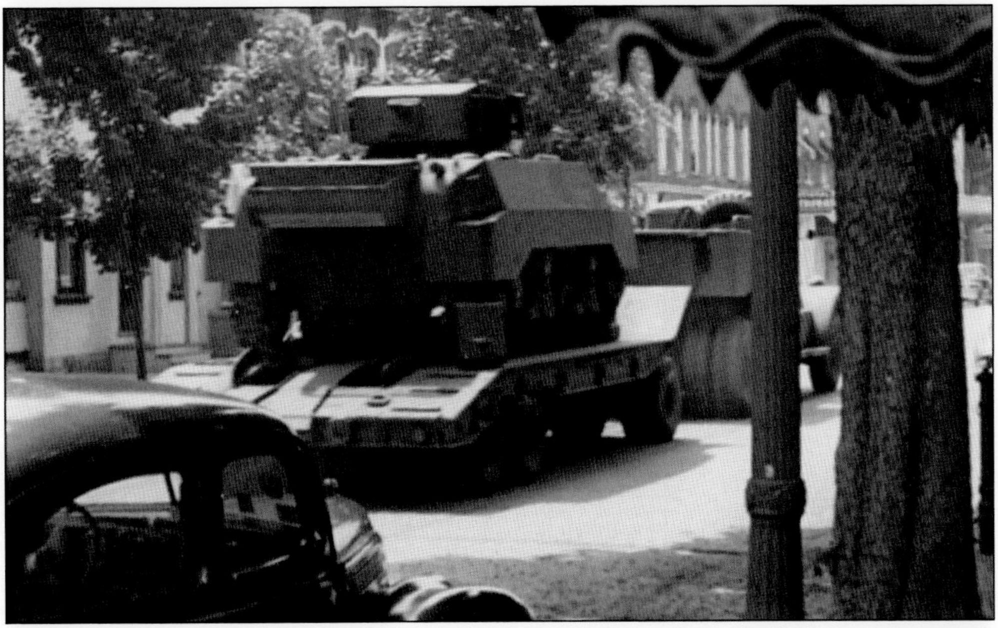

There was no doubt the nation was at war in July 1943. To reinforce the feeling, a 17-ton tank passed through town. The armored vehicle was coming from Berwick, where it was repaired at the American Car and Foundry (ACF) plant. During World War II, ACF converted from its normal business of making railroad cars to producing and repairing tanks as part of the war effort—just as so many other industries did.

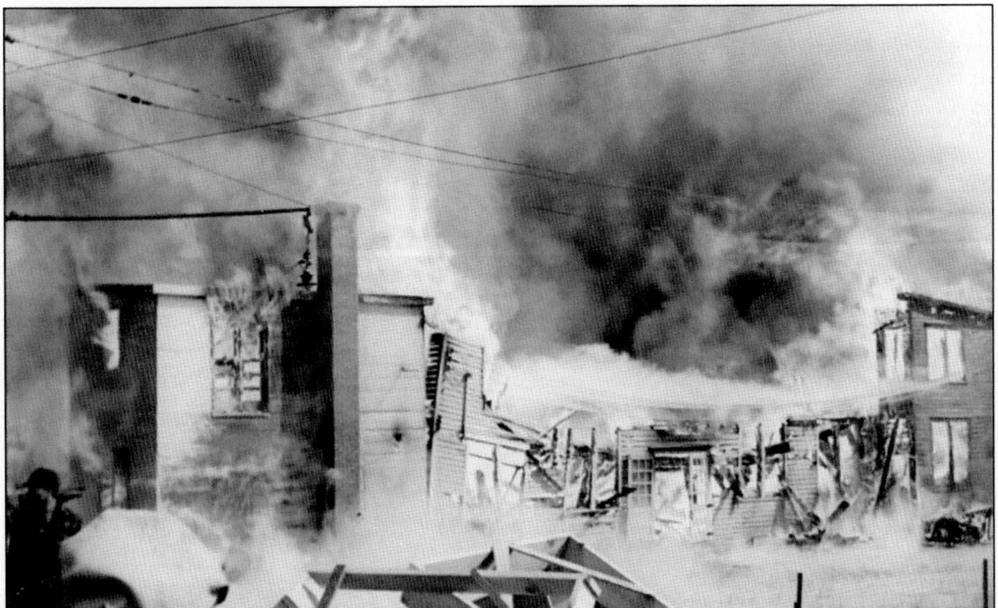

Fire, especially in the days when many buildings were of wooden construction, was a hazard that was never too far away. On Saturday, April 11, 1944, a spectacular blaze destroyed the Bogar Lumber Company on North Water Street. As devastating as the fire was, the Bogars rebuilt and quickly reopened for business and remained in operation for many years.

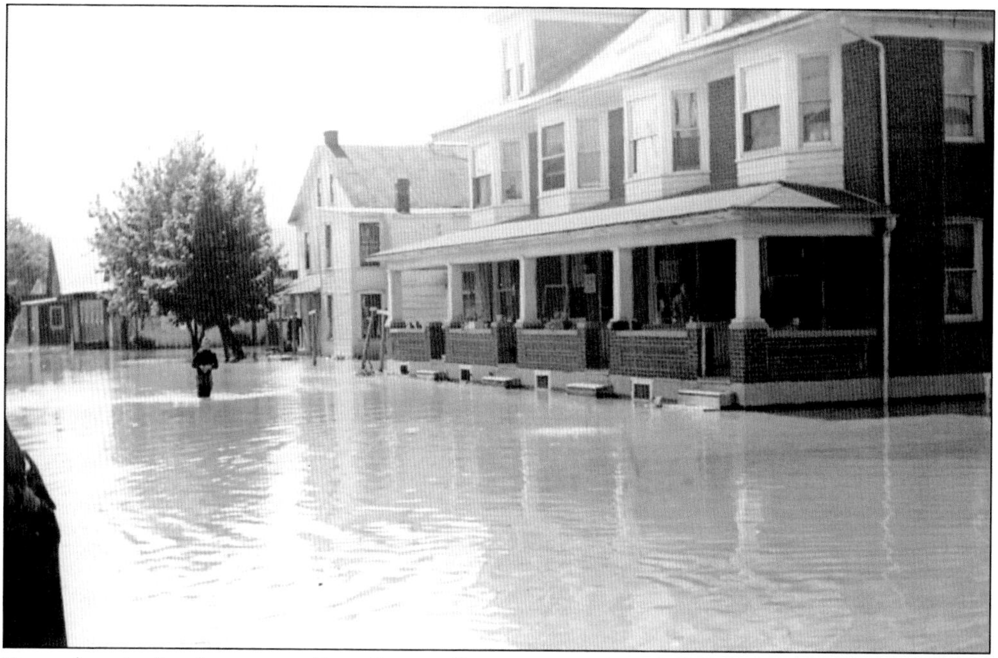

Knee deep in flood water on East Spruce Street, an unidentified Selinsgrove resident gives a gauge as to the depth of the high water. Each spring, Selinsgrove and other communities on the Susquehanna River experience elevated river stages. Mostly the river stays within its banks. This was not the case in 1946, just 10 years after a previous disastrous flood.

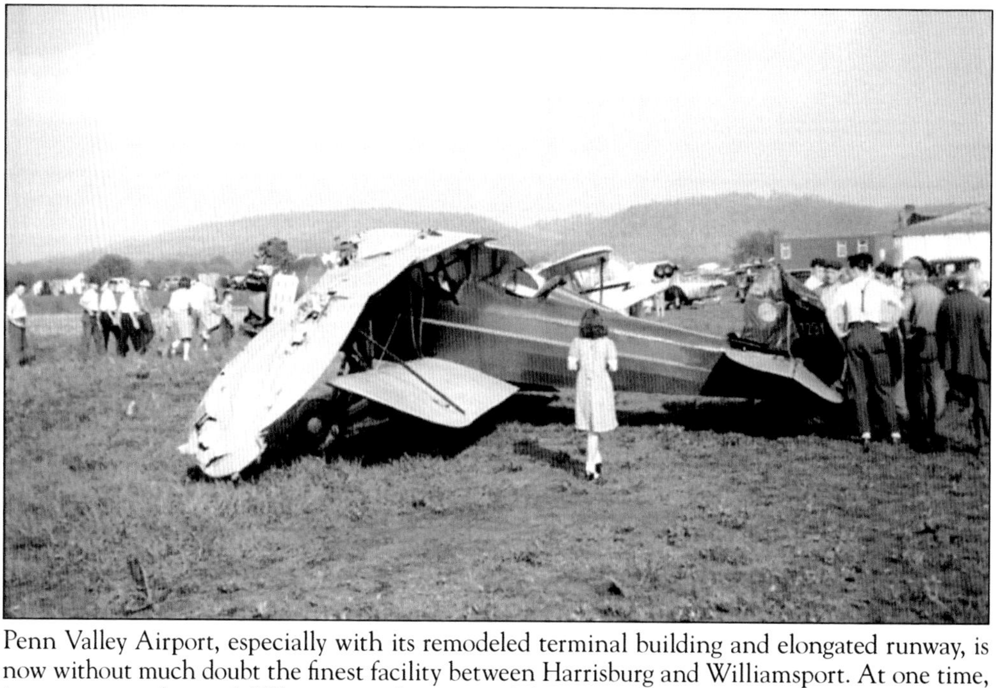

Penn Valley Airport, especially with its remodeled terminal building and elongated runway, is now without much doubt the finest facility between Harrisburg and Williamsport. At one time, it was not so advanced. When it was known as Selinsgrove Airport, it was stuck by what was described as a "mini-cyclone" on Sunday, May 18, 1947. The damaged plane in the foreground is a Bird model biplane. It was a top-of-the-line craft at the time.

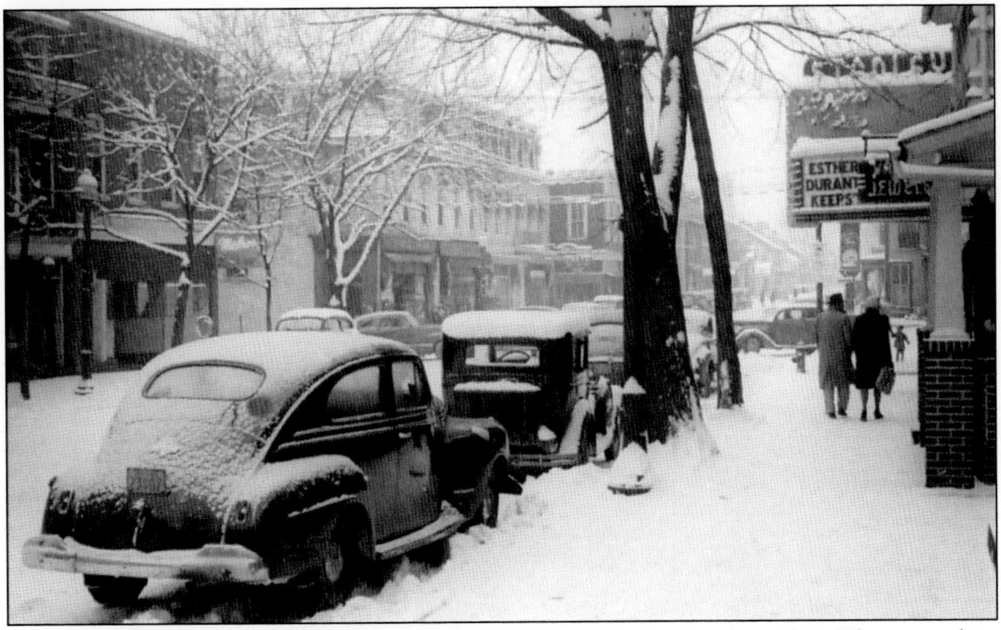

Several inches of freshly fallen snow blanket Market Street in January 1948. The snow does not appear to be much of a hindrance to pedestrian or vehicular traffic. The marquee of the Stanley theater advertises an Esther Williams–Jimmy Durante film, *This Time For Keeps*. Also seen is the sign for Max Valsing's jewelry store, a landmark for decades. Note how many cars are prewar models.

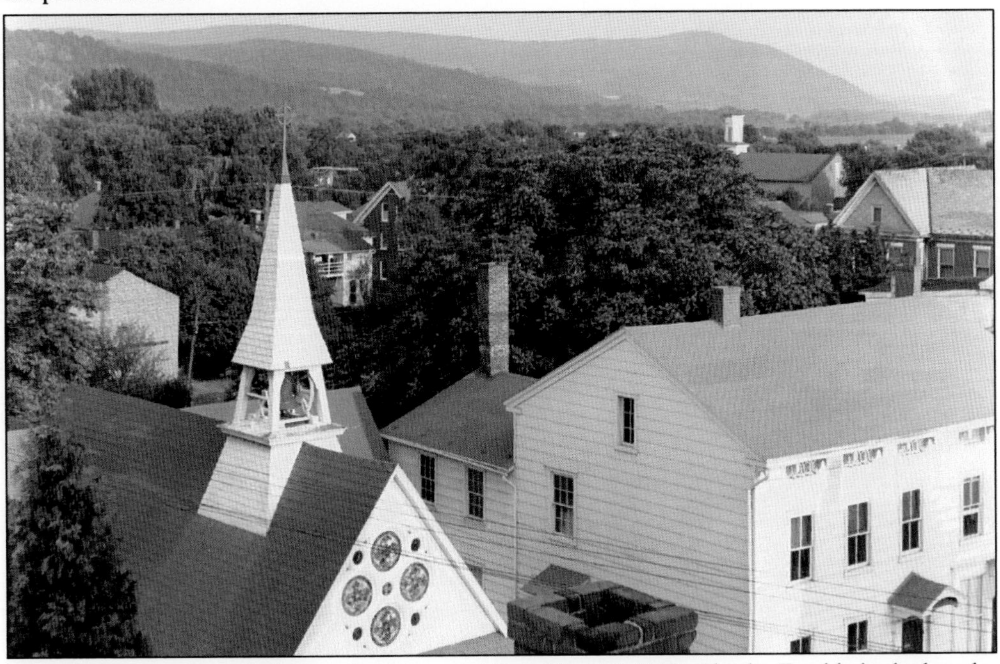

On a fine spring day, which was also Memorial Day, May 30, 1948, Charlie Fasold climbed to the cupola of the Noetling building, where he resided with his wife, Kathryn, and infant son, Bo, and snapped this serene photograph of Selinsgrove. Poking higher than the other rooftops are the steeples of the Episcopal and Methodist churches. Mahanoy Mountain is visible in the background.

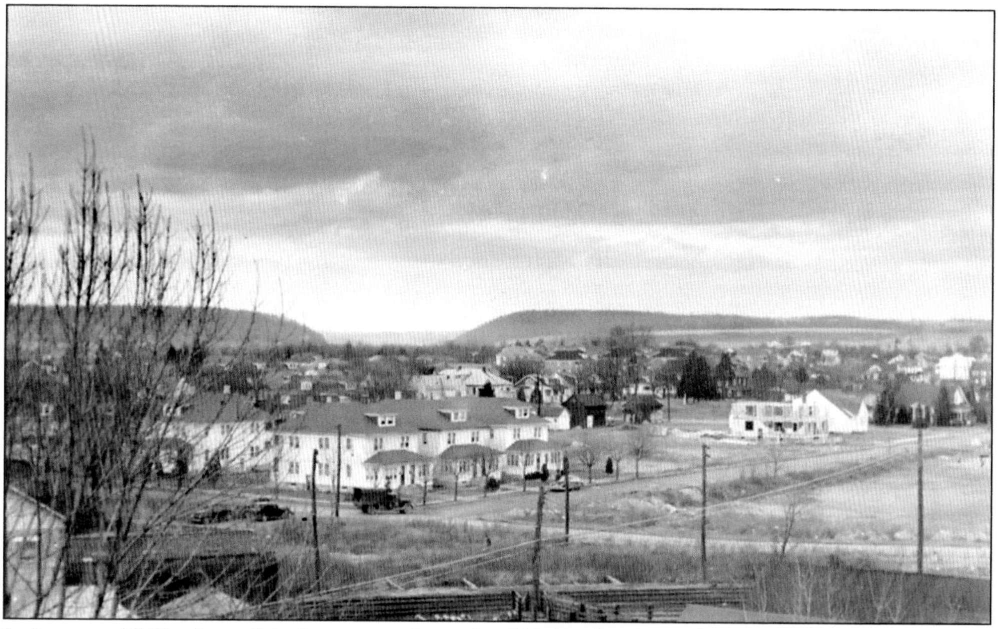

In January 1949, when this shot was taken, the 300 block of North High Street (west side) as it intersects with West Spruce Street was just beginning to be developed. Note the partially constructed building near the upper corner. The vacant lot is the Moose Playground, which was much livelier when school was out for the summer. The land in the foreground (across Spruce) was eventually occupied by the Loyal Order of Moose (LOOM) building.

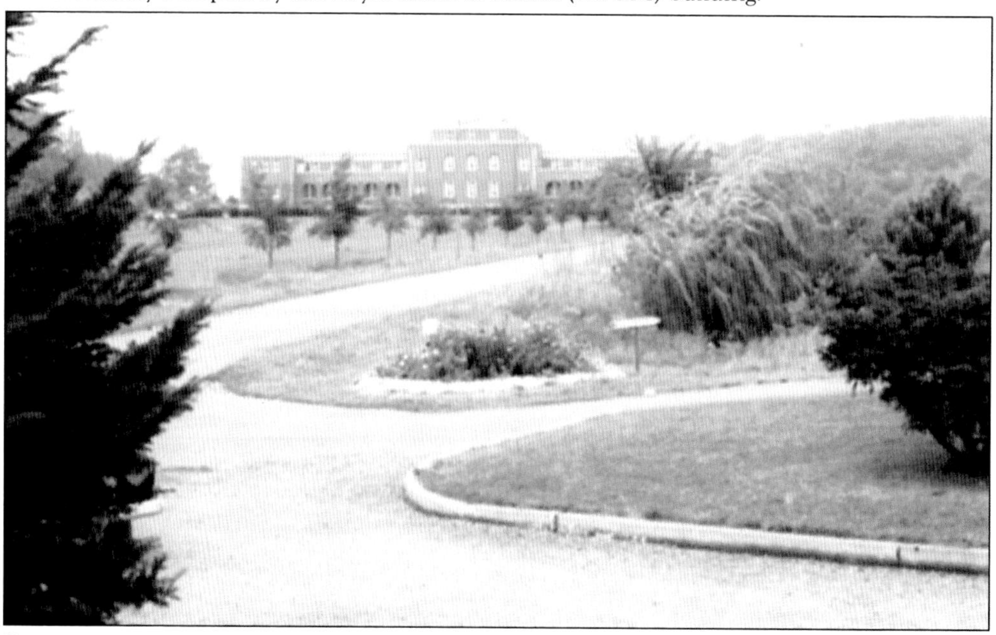

Since its opening on August 9, 1929, on 1,400 acres in Penn Township as the State Colony for Epileptics, the Selinsgrove Center, as it is now known, has been an integral part of the community. Not only has it provided care for those in need but it has also provided hundreds if not thousands of employment opportunities for area residents. Viewed is the original administration building in the summer of 1949.

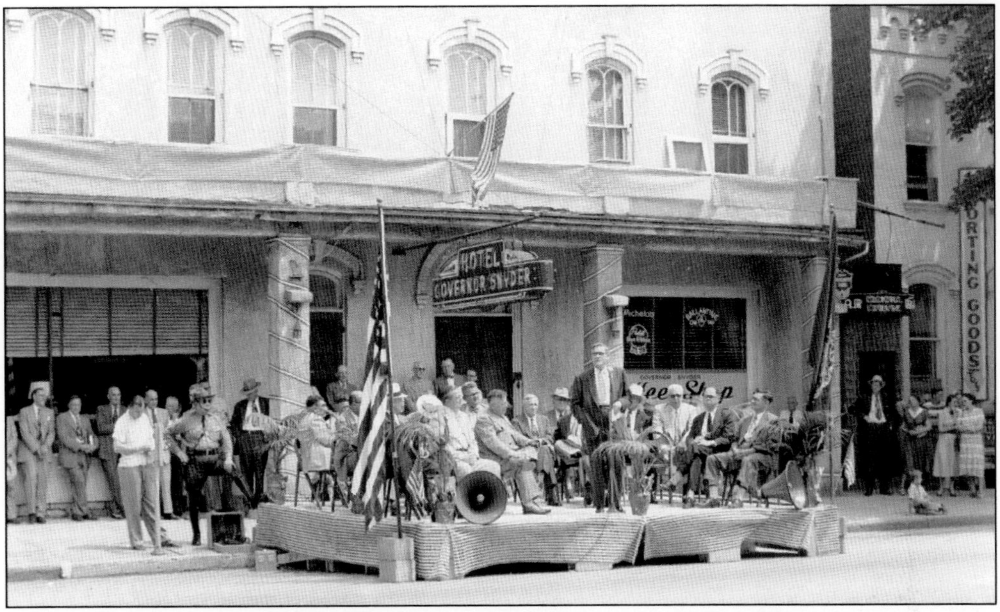

Just as the Selinsgrove bypass, and the hoped-for Routes 11 and 15 golden strip bypass, were looked forward to with great anticipation, the opening of the new Susquehanna Trail was a great event. The dedication ceremony took place in June 1951. The speakers' platform is loaded with local and state dignitaries, including Gov. John S. Fine, as much speech-making was the order of the day. This event took place in front of the Hotel Governor Snyder on North Market Street.

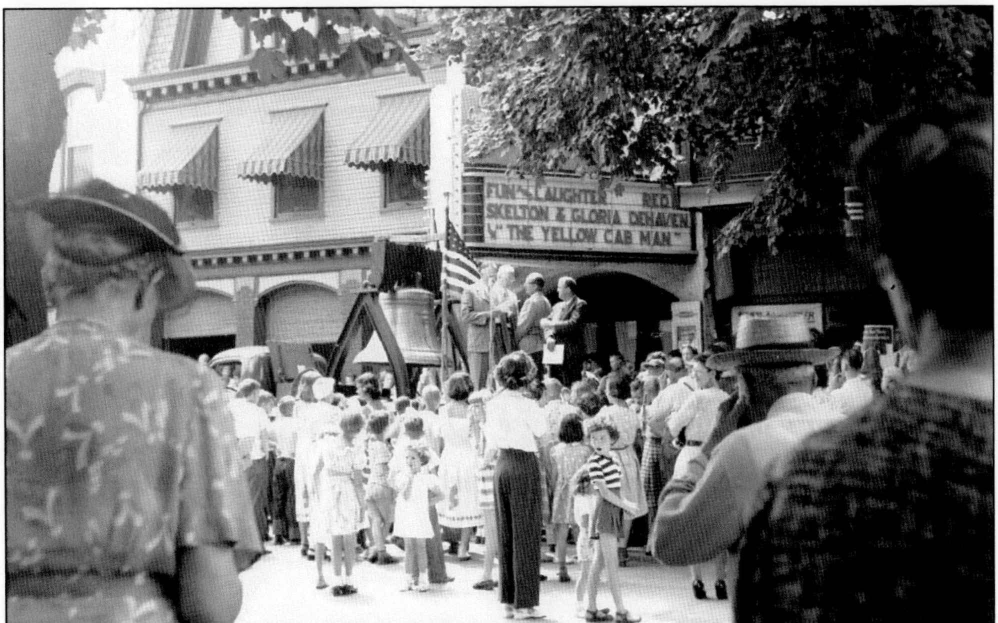

North Market Street in front of the Stanley theater was where a flatbed truck, bearing an actual-size replica of the famed Liberty Bell, parked on Saturday, July 1, 1950. On a nationwide Independence Savings Bond tour, the bell stayed in town just 45 minutes before moving on. During that time, the Selinsgrove High School band, directed ably by Ray Fulmer, played appropriate patriotic music.

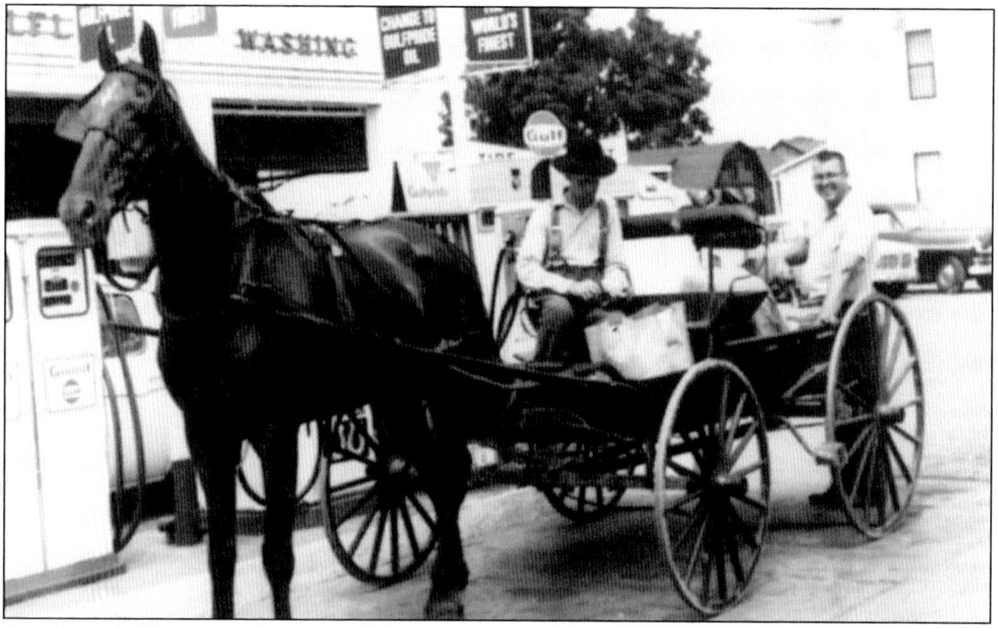

Amish and Mennonite horses and buggies are, and have been for years, common sights in Selinsgrove. Banks and stores provide hitching posts or rails for them. It is not known what this horse and buggy is doing at Troutman's Gulf Service at the corner of Market and Sassafras Streets in the late 1960s, but it is a safe bet that the owner of the rig did not tell Dave Troutman (right) to "fill 'er up."

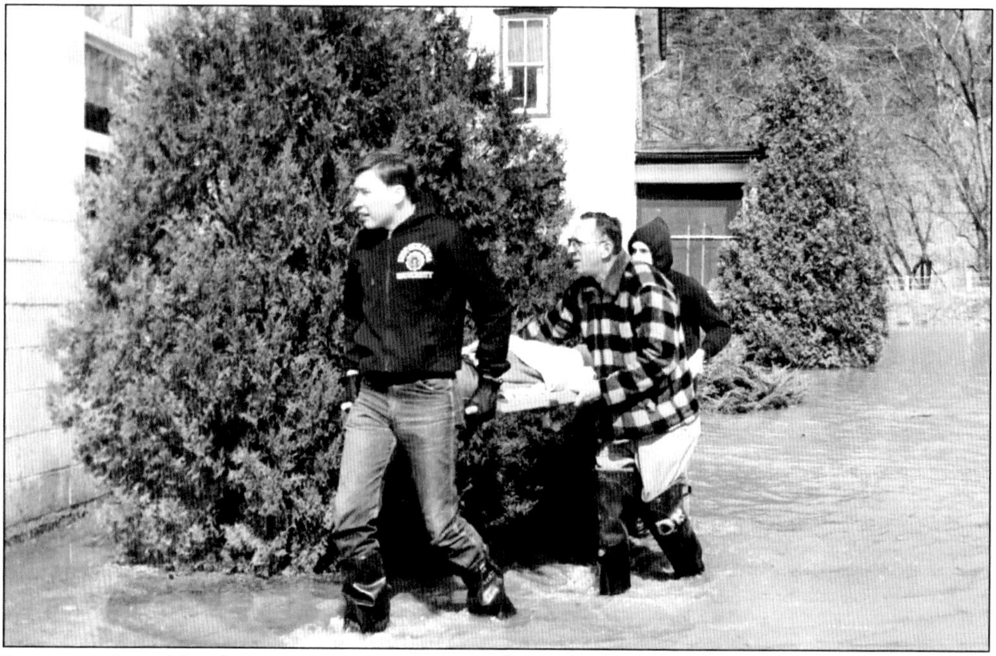

In times of trouble, the town was not separate from the gown. Selinsgrove and Susquehanna University are one community with one goal: to help where help is needed. During high water in 1972, Susquehanna student Ken Terhune and Dauntless Hook and Ladder Company officer George Haas evacuate a flood victim from a nursing home south of town.

Two

CITIZENS

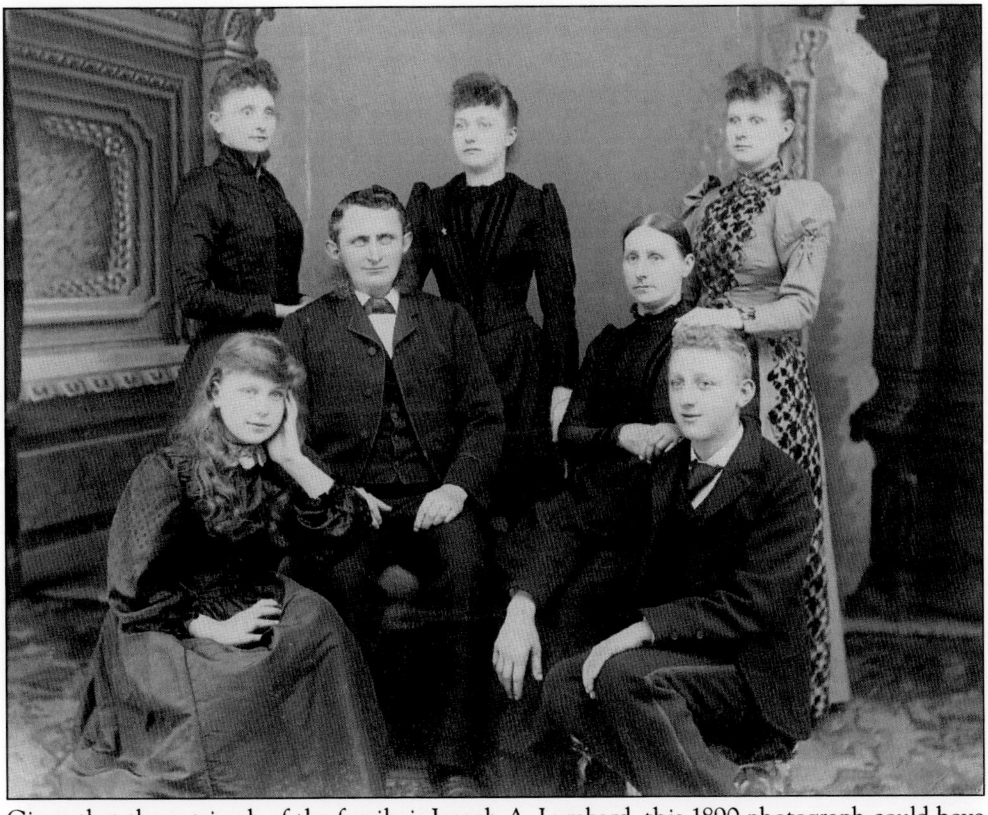

Given that the patriarch of the family is Joseph A. Lumbard, this 1890 photograph could have found its way to the section honoring veterans. Lumbard served with "Our Boys," Selinsgrove's Company G of the 147th Pennsylvania Volunteer Infantry, and sustained combat wounds at Gettysburg. He was also part of Gen. William T. Sherman's March to the Sea. Lumbard later was editor of the *Snyder County Tribune*. Shown from left to right are (first row) Ethel and George; (second row) Lumbard and his wife, Sarah; (third row) Lucy, Maude, and Anna.

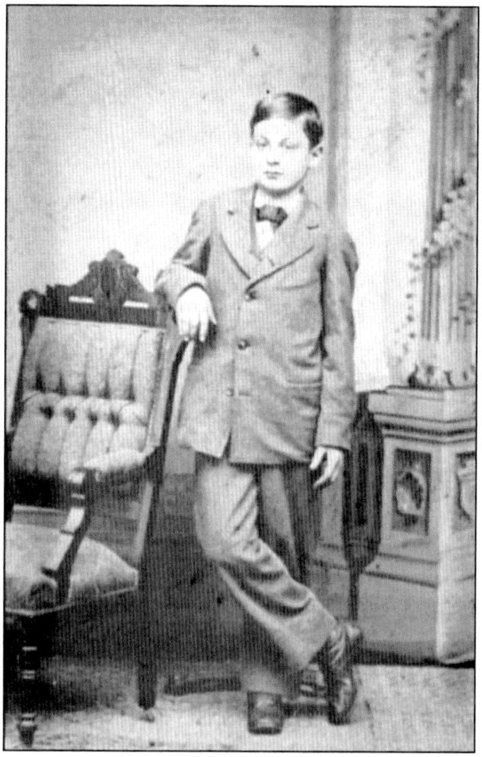

A. Ira Gemberling grew up to be a well-respected businessman. Gemberling's dairy milk built strong bones and healthy bodies for generations of Selinsgrove youth. Here, in an R. L. Ulrich photograph, young Gemberling, born in 1870, is sporting his first pair of long trousers—always a big moment in a young man's life. The photograph dates to 1882, when he was 12 years old.

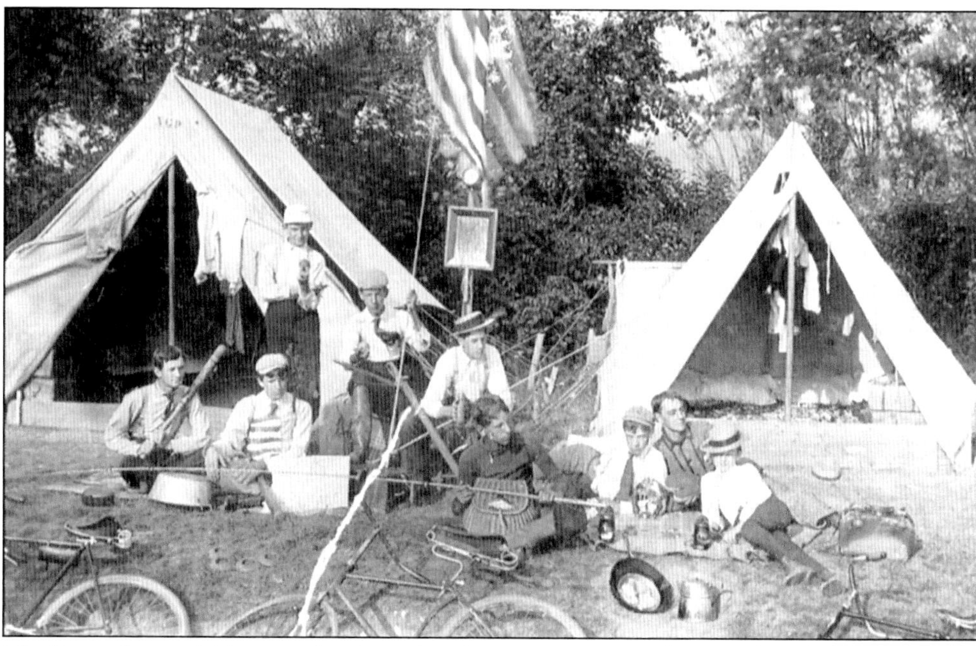

The Susquehanna Rifles were first introduced via a captivating photograph in *Snyder County* in the Images of America series in 2004. In this July 14, 1895, photograph, the boys' outdoors club pose again. Cyril Haas, an officer, is behind the camera. He snapped his fellow rifles without weapons. From left to right, they are George Marks, William Phillips, Howard Doebler, John Schoch, Bruce Burkhart, George Schoch, Ralph Wagenseller, Billy Schnure, and Silas Schoch.

The accomplishments of Dr. Robert Potteiger and his family have been documented in previous Arcadia Snyder County books. The veterinarian, whose son Robert Jr. also became a respected veterinarian, is shown in an Ulrich studio portrait with man's best friend. The photograph is from the dawn of the 20th century. The livery stable and dog kennels are gone, but the Potteiger House is a quaint bed-and-breakfast at 8 West Chestnut Street in Selinsgrove.

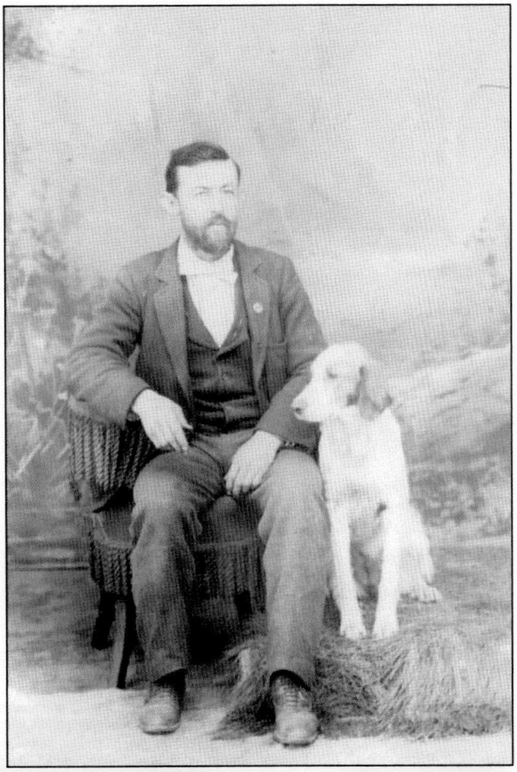

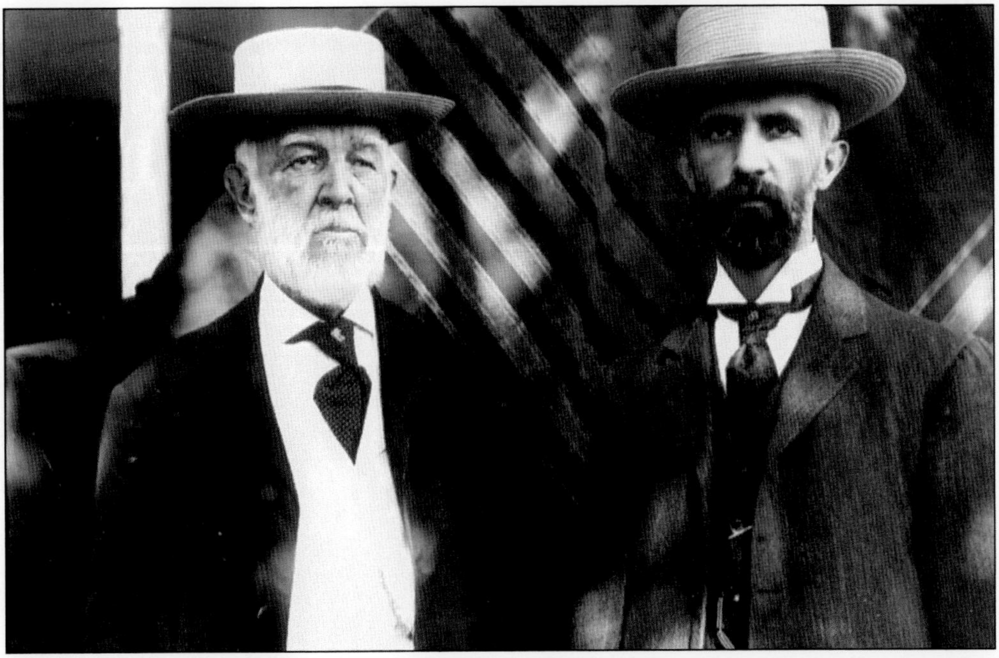

What has evolved into M&T (Manufacturers' and Traders') Bank began as the First National Bank of Selins Grove. For years the North family was associated with the financial institution. Shown here in 1910 are Calvin North (left) and his son Roscoe. At first, the bank merged with Tri-County National Bank, then with Northern Central Bank, and eventually with M&T.

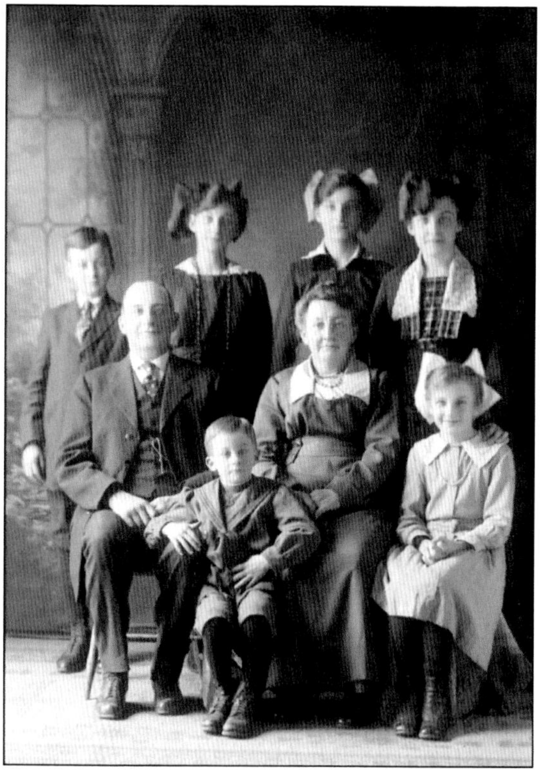

A. Ira Gemberling grew up to be quite a businessman—with a dairy bearing his family name—and family man. Shown in 1919 from left to right are (first row) A. Ira; Sephares; Gemberling's wife, Clara; and O. Naomi; (second row) Edgar, Ida, C. Mildred, and Laura. In addition to being a dairyman, A. Ira, along with his family, was active in St. Paul's Reformed (later United Church of Christ) Church.

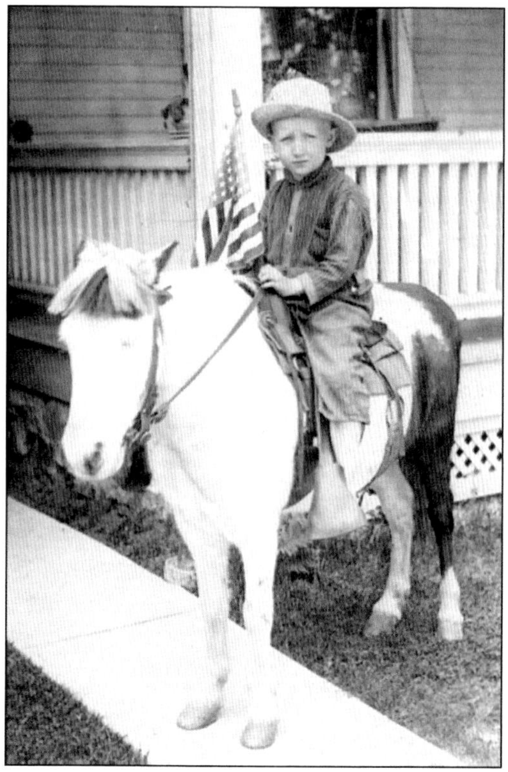

In the first decades of the 1900s, a tradition in much of the country was having children photographed on an obedient pony. Usually, the pony and the photographer were just passing through town. In this instance it was 1922. The six-year-old patriotic equestrian is Francis "Rudy" Gelnett in front of his South Market Street home. Although handy with a guitar, Gelnett did not become a singing cowboy but a talented musician, never the less.

Looking like a Bessie Peace Guttman calendar illustration or the cover of a Bobbsey Twins book come to life with their period sundresses, knee socks, and Mary Jane shoes, Doris (left) and Muriel, the daughters of Ralph and Mae Carter of Selinsgrove, are pictured. The little girls were photographed in 1925 at an unidentified studio.

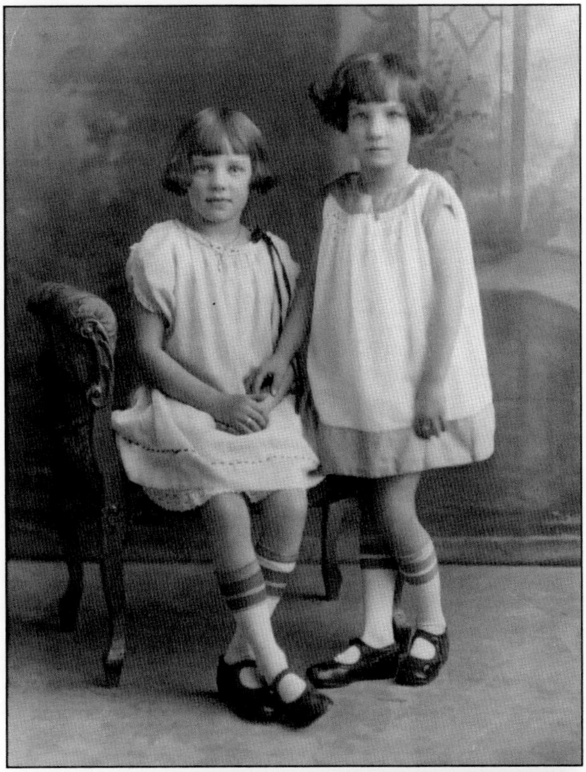

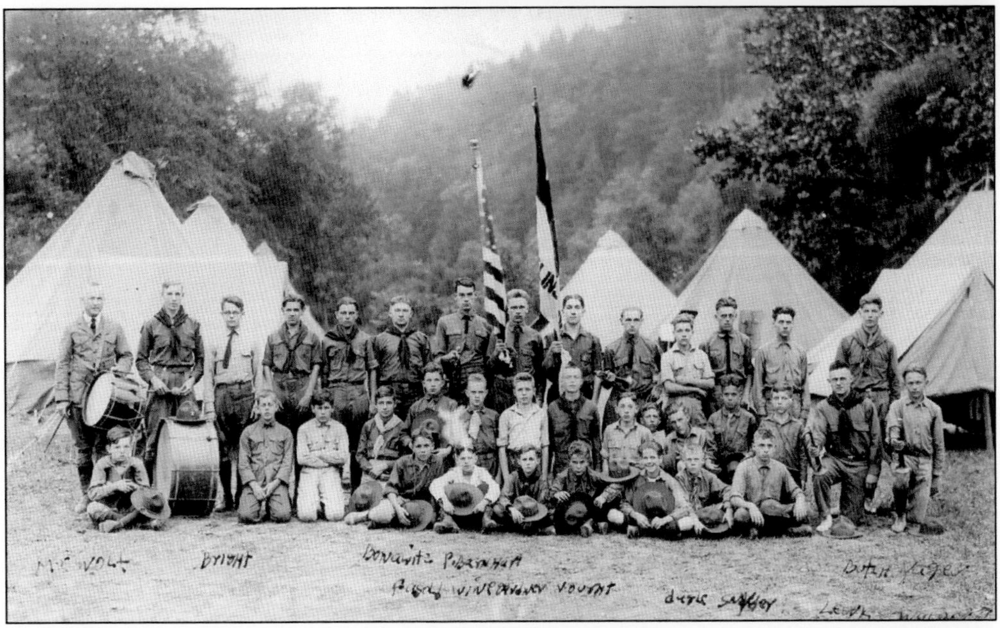

It is not known for certain if the 1880s Susquehanna Rifles were indeed the precursor to Selinsgrove's scouting movement. This group is Troop 19 from town, pictured at camp (perhaps Karoondinha) in the 1930s. The local Boy Scouts of America (BSA) was organized by Edgar Wingard and other civic-minded adults shortly after World War I. Some names appear on the picture, but positive identification has not been made.

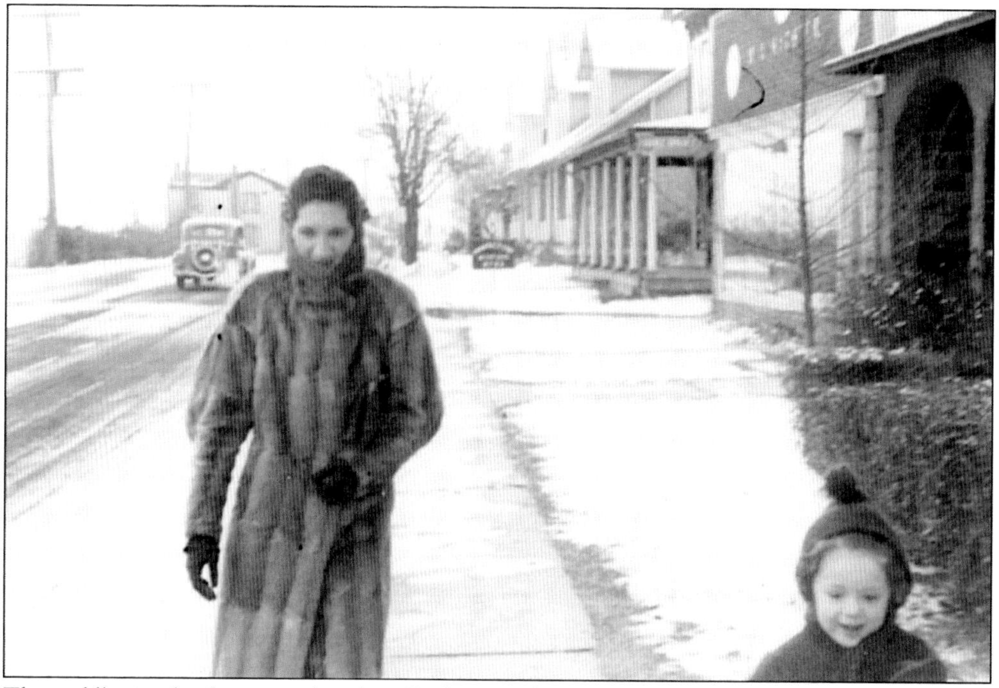

The toddler in the foreground is Ann Richter at about age three in 1938, racing ahead of her mother, Roberta (Bobby) Richter, wife of Fred Richter Jr., on a blustery winter's day. The business to the right of the frame is an automobile parts store that followed an early Chevrolet agency begun by Fred Richter's father, Fred Richter Sr. The locale is the west side of the 300 block of South Market Street in Selinsgrove.

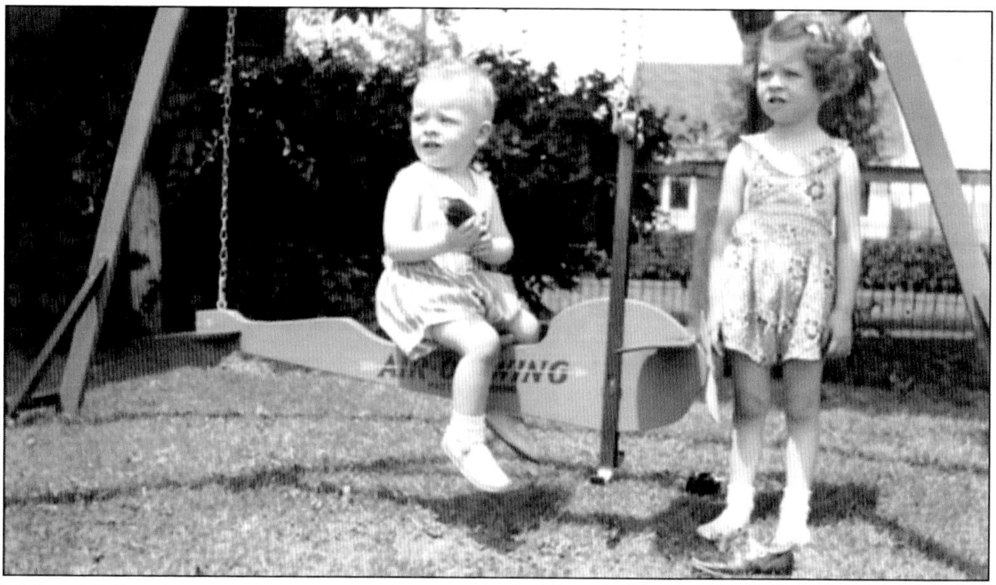

This 1938 photograph shows three-and-a-half-year-old Carol Campbell and her one-and-a-half-year-old brother cleared for takeoff. It would be nice to say the Air-O-Wing plane pilot grew up to be an astronaut—or even a barnstorming crop duster. However, he apparently lacked "the right stuff" and pursued a more earthbound career.

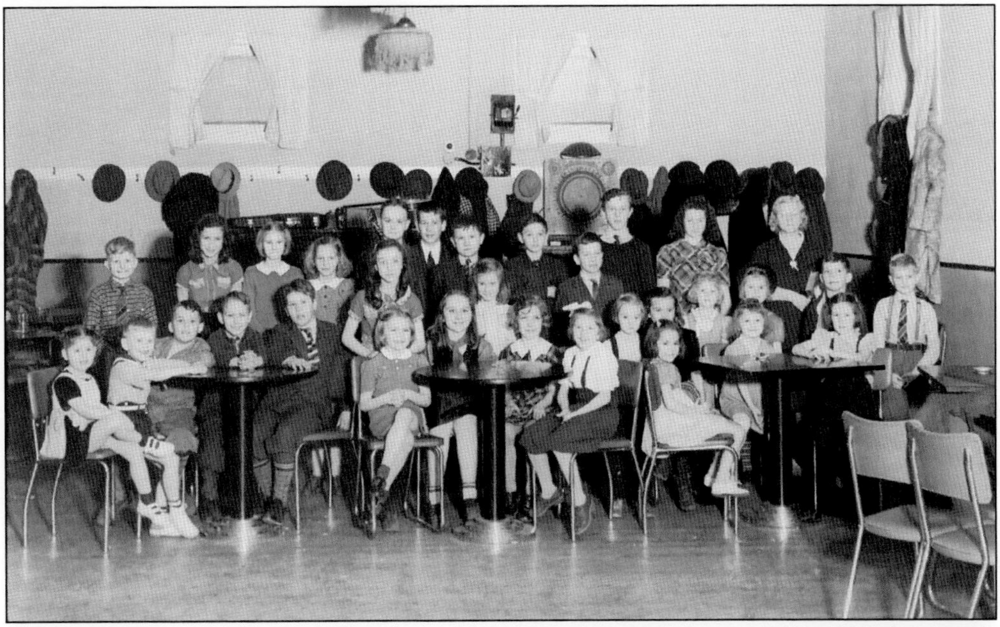

The LOOM has been a long-standing fraternal organization in Selinsgrove. This 1938 photograph was taken before moving to newer lodgings at Spruce and High Streets. A group of youngsters is being treated by Moose members. Not all are identified, but Jack Steffen and Ronnie Day are third and fourth from the left at the left table, and Dick and Ed Day are third and fourth in the group of boys in the middle of the back row.

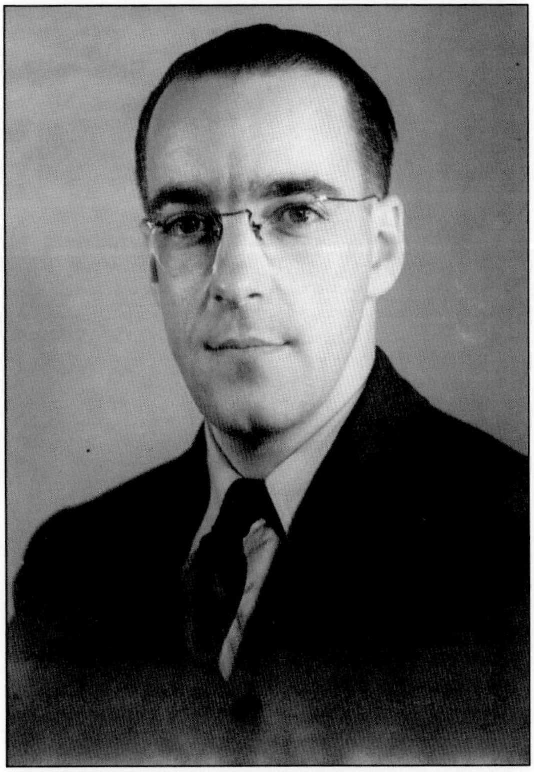

Generations of pupils remember Charlie Fasold as a conscientious teacher and administrator. He served the Selinsgrove School District long and well. What may not be so well known is his ability behind a camera. His documentary skills are evidenced in thousands of photographs, many of which have been used in this and prior Arcadia Snyder County books. This photograph was taken by someone else in 1941.

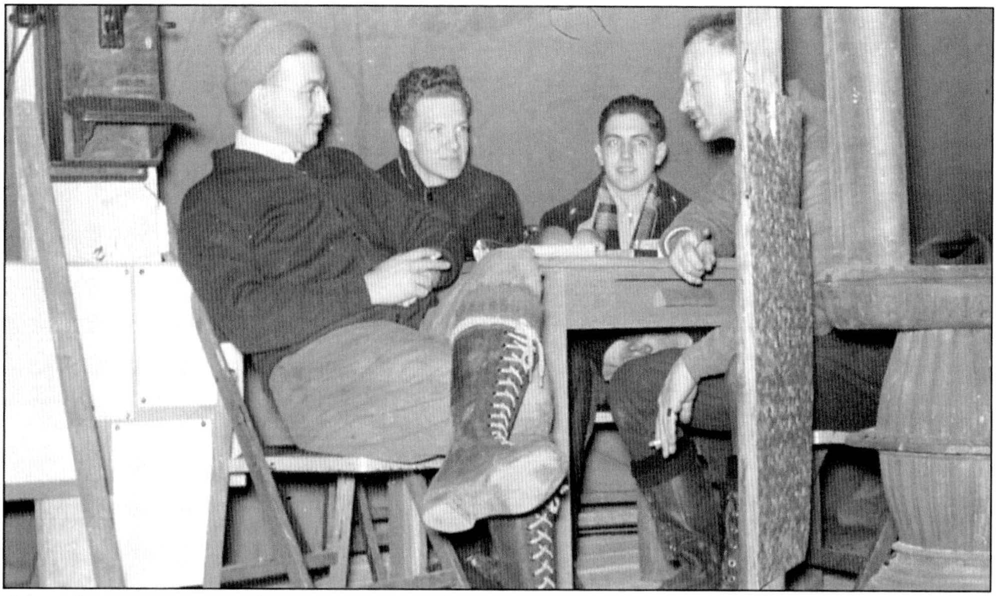

After the events at Pearl Harbor on Sunday, December 7, 1941, Selinsgrove, like every other community, beefed up security. In a tent on the high school campus, civil defense officials set up an observation post to identify and report all aircraft. Note the oaken, hand-cranked telephone. Shown just days after the Japanese sneak attack, from left to right, are Willard Maginnis, Jack Hummel, Donald "Dick" Leach, and Harold Follmer. Follmer bagged three German planes as a World War I pilot.

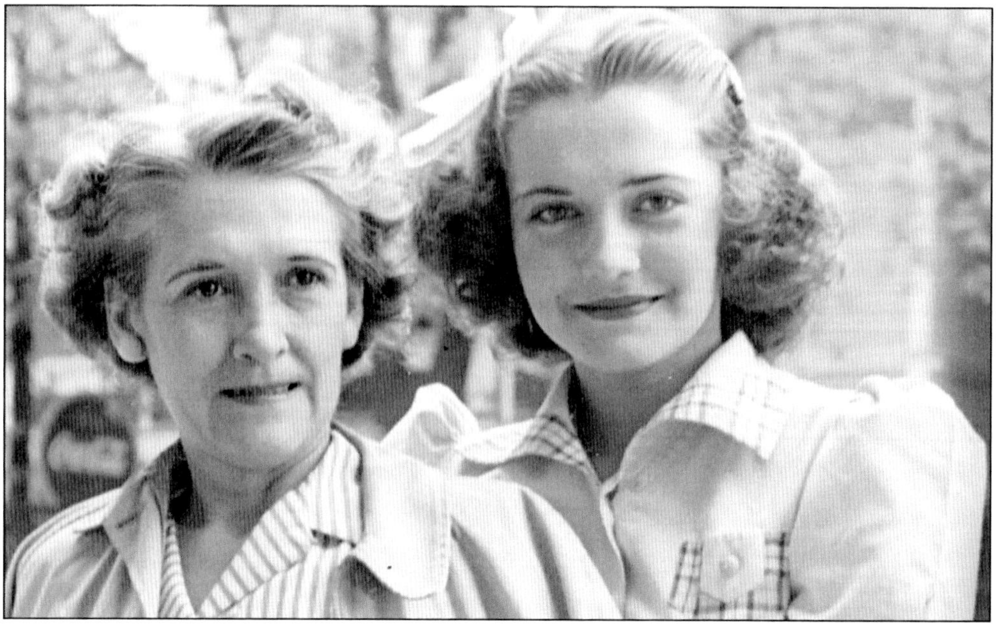

On April 27, 1942, Edna "Sweetie" Raudenbush (right) with her mother, also Edna, posed for this photograph. The elder Edna served many years as Selinsgrove's school nurse. Sweetie, as talented as she was pretty, was a "girl singer" with many of the region's bands, including some well beyond Selinsgrove. The attractive pair is the wife and daughter of Jim Raudenbush, long associated with the automobile business in town.

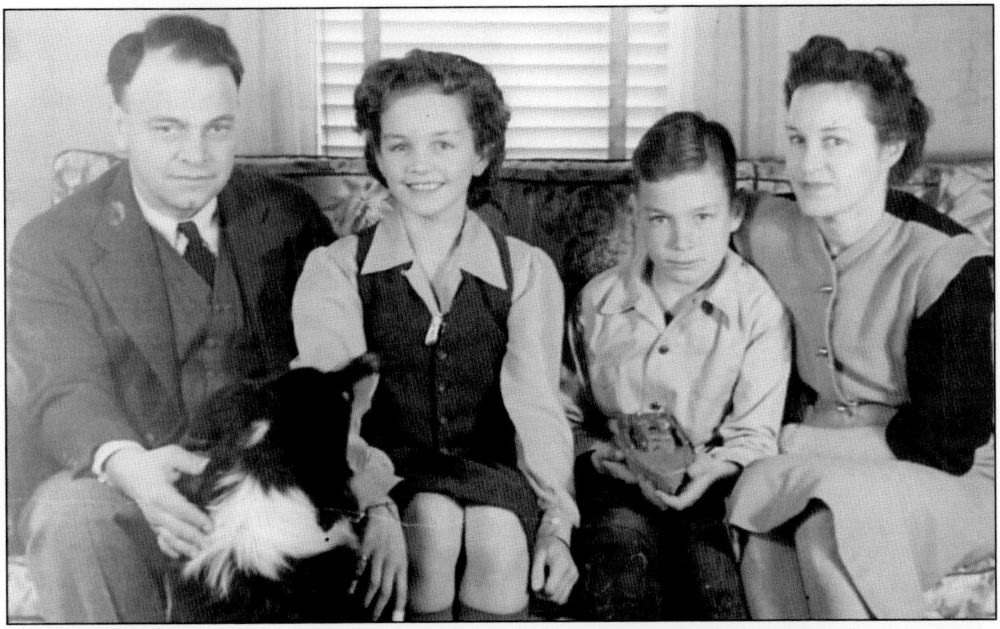

In March 1943, Dr. Harry Clark (left) and his family, including their faithful collie, posed for a portrait. Jane "Oakie" and Davis are seated between the dentist and his wife, Lydabelle. Davis is holding a model navy PT boat. This is a harbinger of things to come. After graduation from high school in 1950, Davis was appointed to the U.S. Naval Academy. Later graduating from Annapolis, he was commissioned and became a career naval officer.

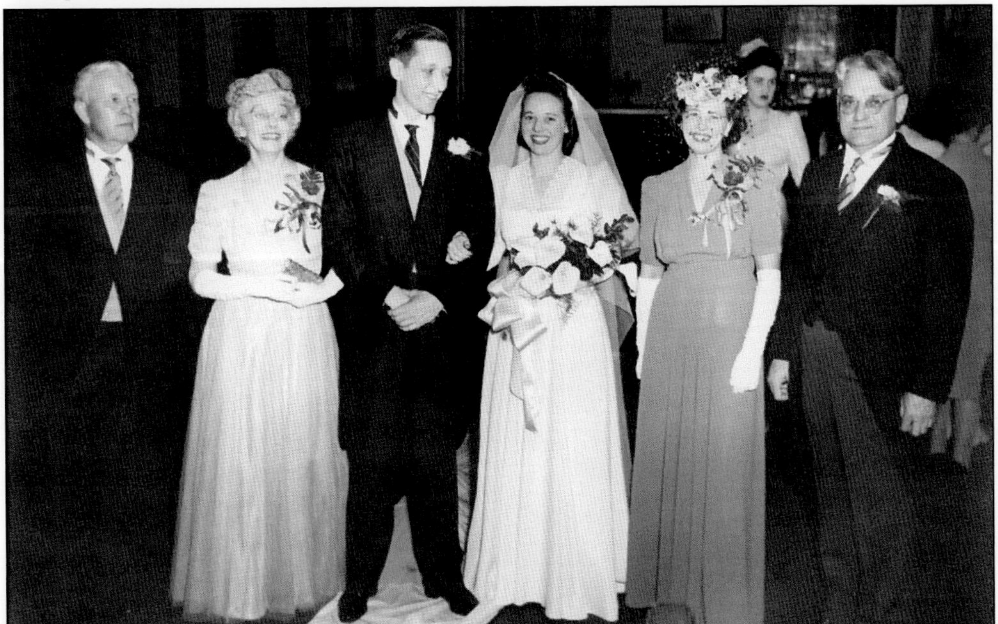

The wedding party is formally attired at the nuptials of Doris Carter and Bernard Beck on April 17, 1943. From left to right, the party consists of Dr. Herbert and Gladys Beck, the parents of the groom; Bernard; Doris; and Mae and Ralph Carter, the parents of the bride. The wedding took place at a church in Berwick before the couple became Selinsgrove residents.

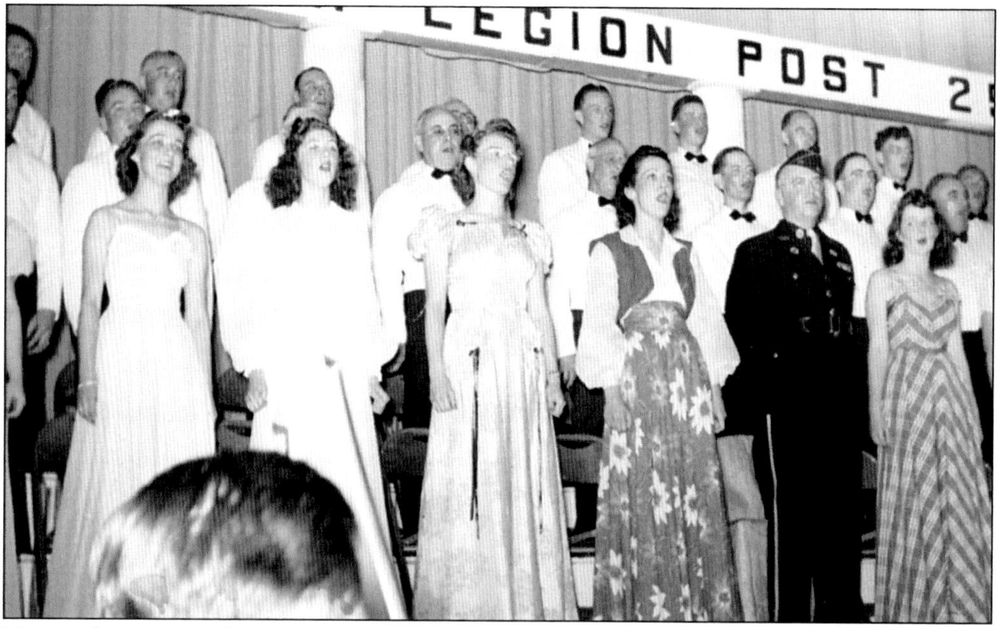

Variety shows put on by the American Legion Victory Post 25 were a staple on the Selinsgrove entertainment scene for over a decade, lasting into the 1950s. This is a large, mixed chorus of residents around 1946. From left to right in the first row are Mary Jane Fritz, Jane Feeher, unidentified, Faye Hummel, Henry "Doc" Mowles, and Peggy Winner. The stage show always included a medley of patriotic songs and took place in the high school auditorium.

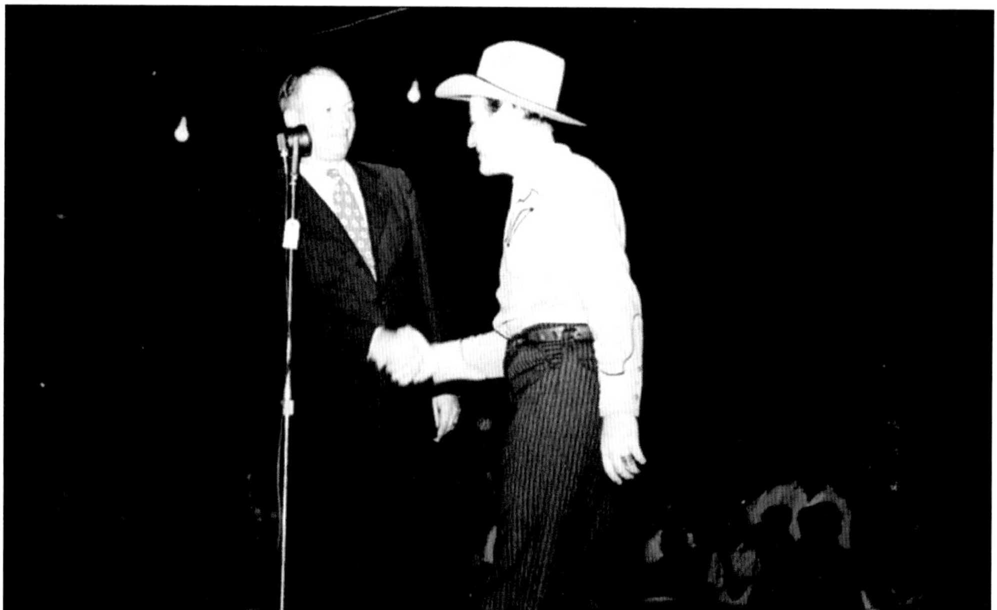

The annual Selinsgrove Night Fair, advertised as "Pennsylvania's Largest Free-Gate Night Fair," was a much anticipated and well-attended event each summer from the 1930s through the 1950s. Roland Fisher (left) was one of the driving forces behind the event. Here he is shown in 1946 shaking hands with cowboy singer Dick Thomas, whose No. 1 hit "Sioux City Sue" made him a household name at the time.

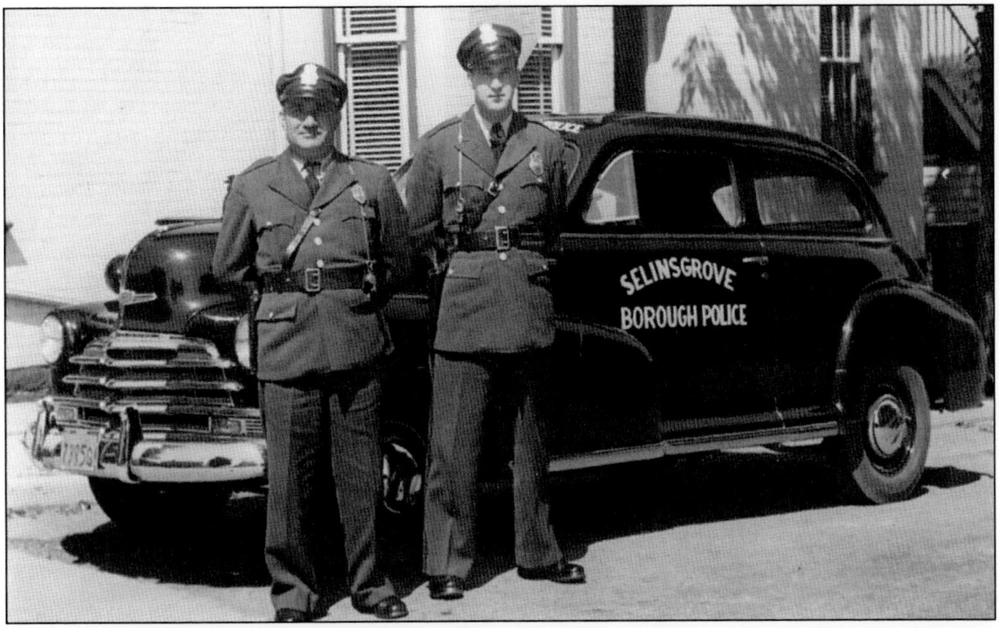

Selinsgrove residents of the 1940s and 1950s now often reflect on how efficiently "Ez and Charlie" kept law and order in the town. Of course, they meant Ezra Kemberling and Charlie Gemberling. Until May 1947, they did so without benefit of mechanization. At that time, the borough purchased its first cruiser, a 1948 two door from Kepler Chevrolet, which submitted the low bid of $1,042.75. Times have changed in more ways than one.

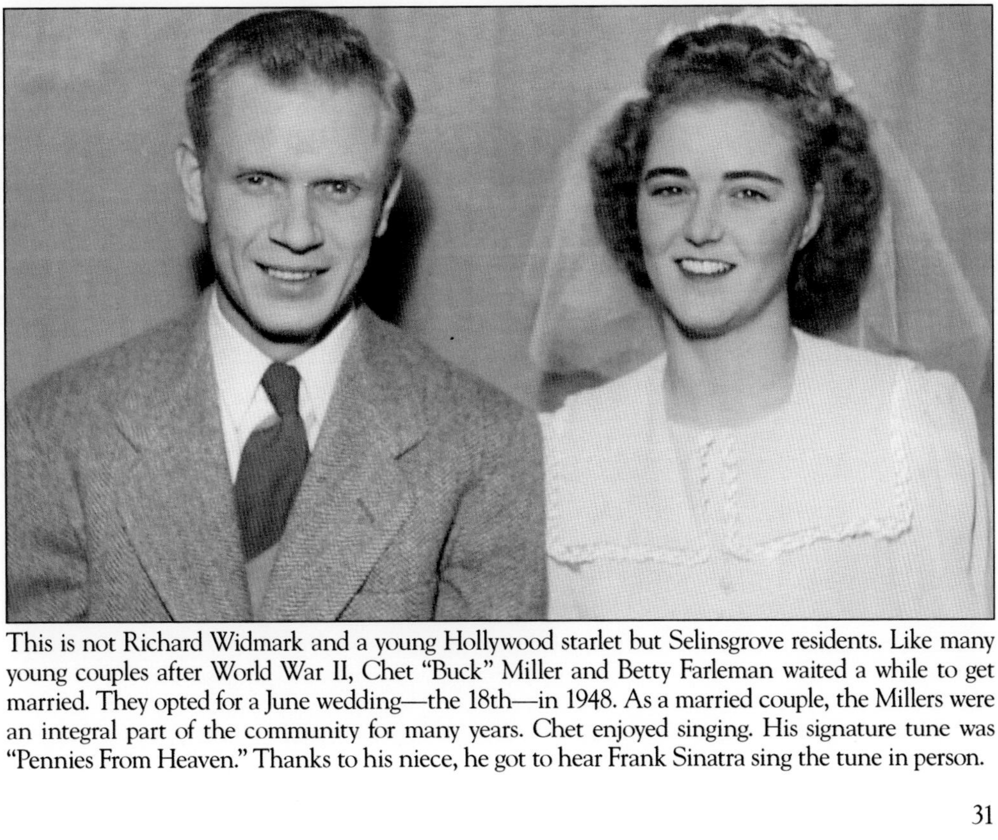

This is not Richard Widmark and a young Hollywood starlet but Selinsgrove residents. Like many young couples after World War II, Chet "Buck" Miller and Betty Farleman waited a while to get married. They opted for a June wedding—the 18th—in 1948. As a married couple, the Millers were an integral part of the community for many years. Chet enjoyed singing. His signature tune was "Pennies From Heaven." Thanks to his niece, he got to hear Frank Sinatra sing the tune in person.

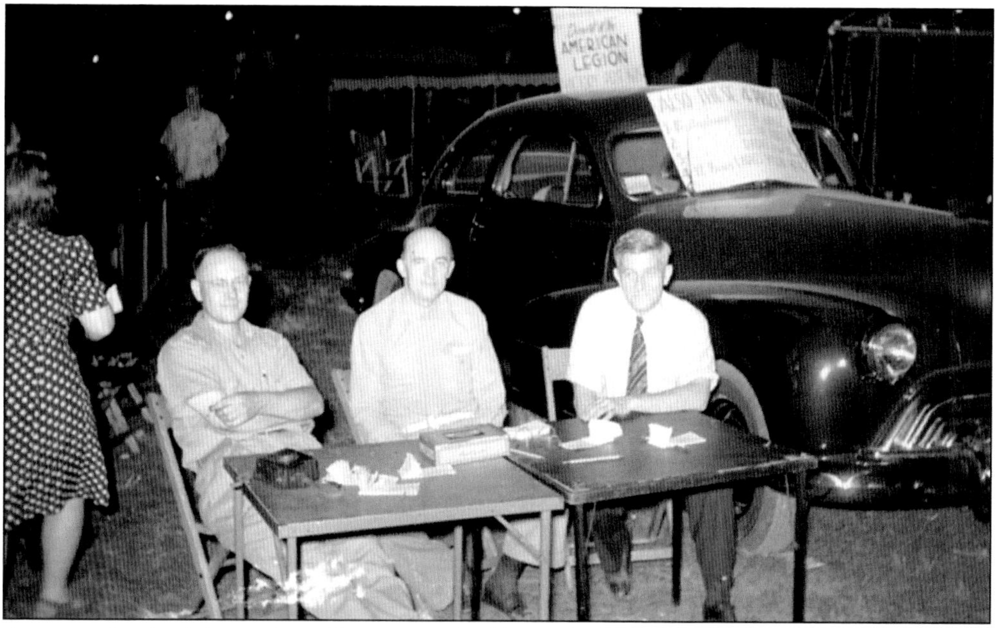

American Legion Victory Post 25 set up card tables at the Selinsgrove Night Fair to sell chances at 25¢ each on a new 1948 Oldsmobile from the Arbogast and Son agency. Harry Arbogast is shown at the left. Receipts and raffle stubs were kept in a Phillies cigar box. While the 1948 Oldsmobile was the grand prize, Westinghouse appliances and a dozen pairs of ladies' nylon hose were other valued prizes. The identities of the other two men have not been determined.

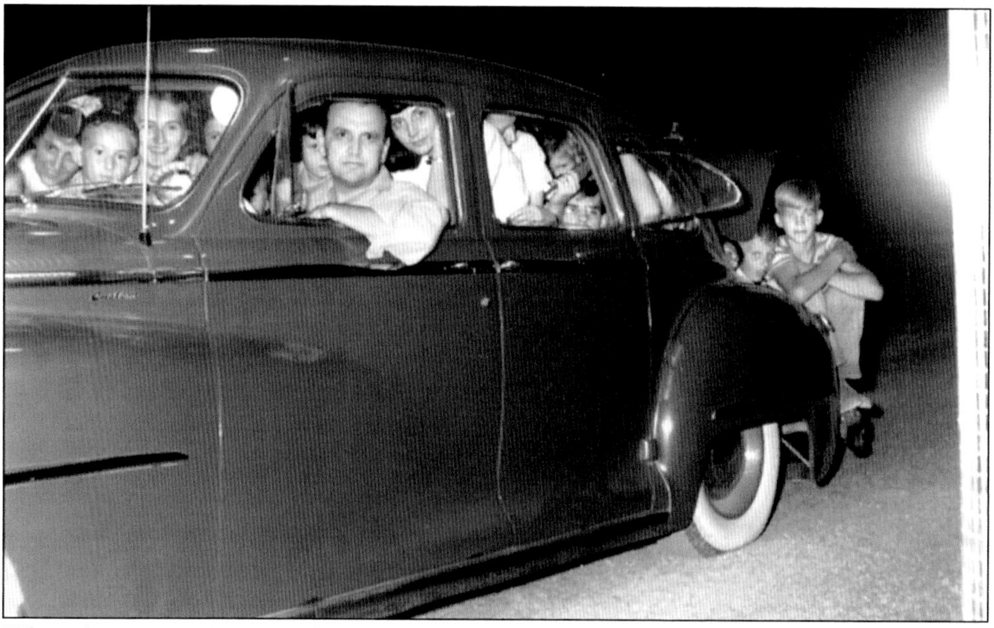

When the Nu-Way Drive-In theater opened in 1948, about where Wal-Mart is now, it quickly became a movie mecca. Buck-a-Car nights drew unusually large crowds, regardless of what was showing. A car full with passengers cost only $1. On August 11, 1949, Walt Good crammed his 1938 DeSoto with family and friends and took the most-in-a-car prize. He fit 36 people—12 adults and 24 children. Cost-wise, that was 2.7¢ per person.

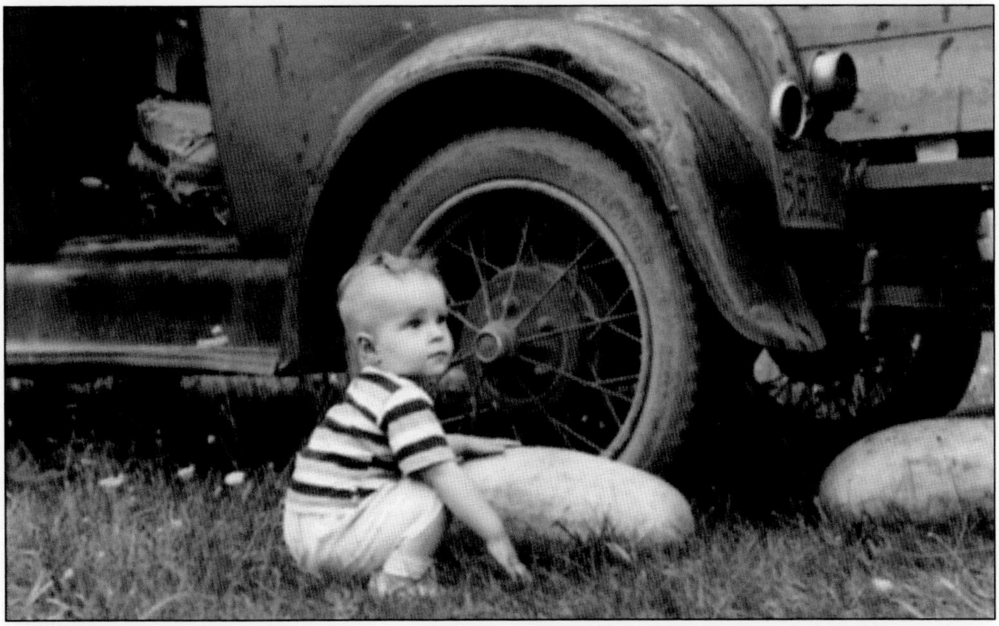

The watermelon picnic, sponsored by LOOM on the fraternal organization's playground, was a big deal in the postwar 1940s. Here, in 1949, Bo Fasold (at about age 18 months) is contemplating how to attack a large melon. Many older youngsters were not faced with such a dilemma; they just dove right in, so to speak. The backdrop is Bob Shadle's modified Model A Ford. A box replaced the trunk lid, allowing it to serve as a pickup truck.

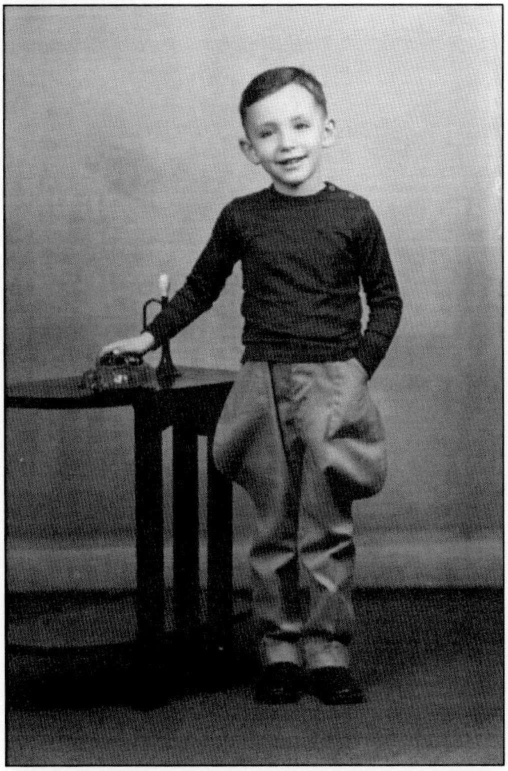

This preschool youngster wearing jodhpurs is Bob Burd. Burd's adult career was involved in banking, but his involvement went well beyond that. First and foremost, he was totally involved with his close-knit family, including his wife, Gail; his children, Bill, Matt, and Missy; their spouses; and his grandchildren. That total involvement carried over to church, community, school (especially sports programs), and his many friends. Not knowing Burd was missing out on something very special.

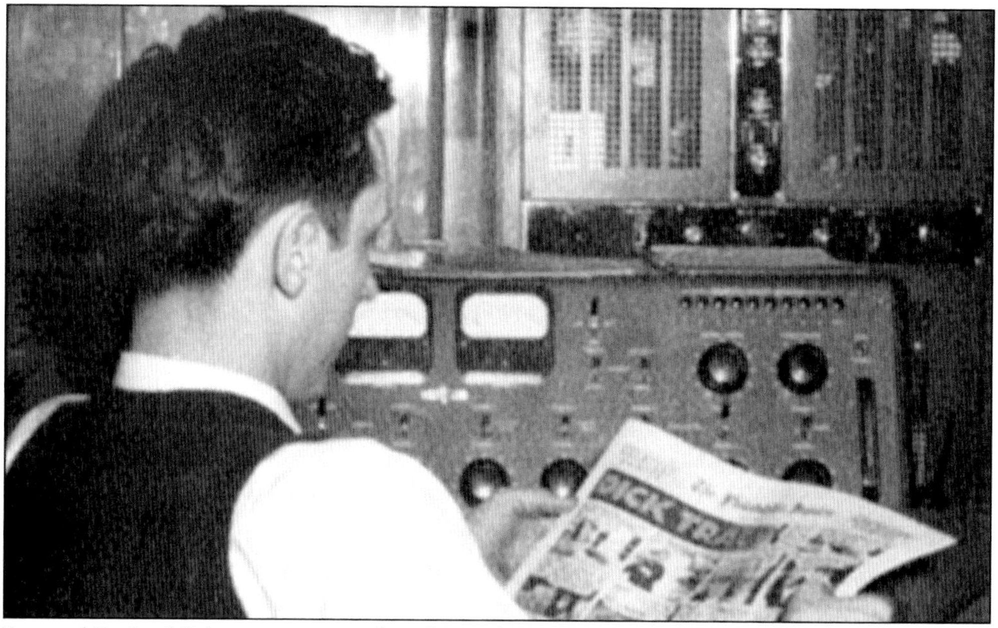

Bernard Beck of Selinsgrove was a first-class radio engineer at WKOK in Sunbury, "located at the site of historic Fort Augusta," as the station identification proclaimed. Beck is pictured at the board on a quiet Sunday in 1950. Because WKOK, which signed on the air on May 17, 1933, as the area's first commercial station, carried much of the CBS network's programming, Beck had time to keep one eye on the dials and one on the *Philadelphia Inquirer*'s Dick Tracy comic strip.

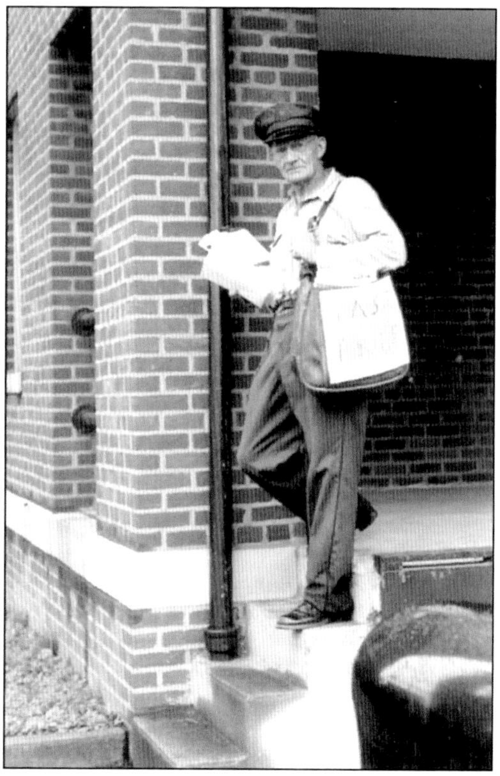

Mail carriers take their credo, "Neither rain, nor snow, nor dark of night shall keep this carrier from the swift completion of his [or her] appointed rounds." In Selinsgrove, mail was once delivered twice a day all over town. There was also another business delivery. Many carriers were treated as family and vice versa. They also tended to make their appointed rounds for years, if not decades. Shown here is George Luck on his last trip, as stated on his mail pouch. He served from 1922 to July 31, 1950.

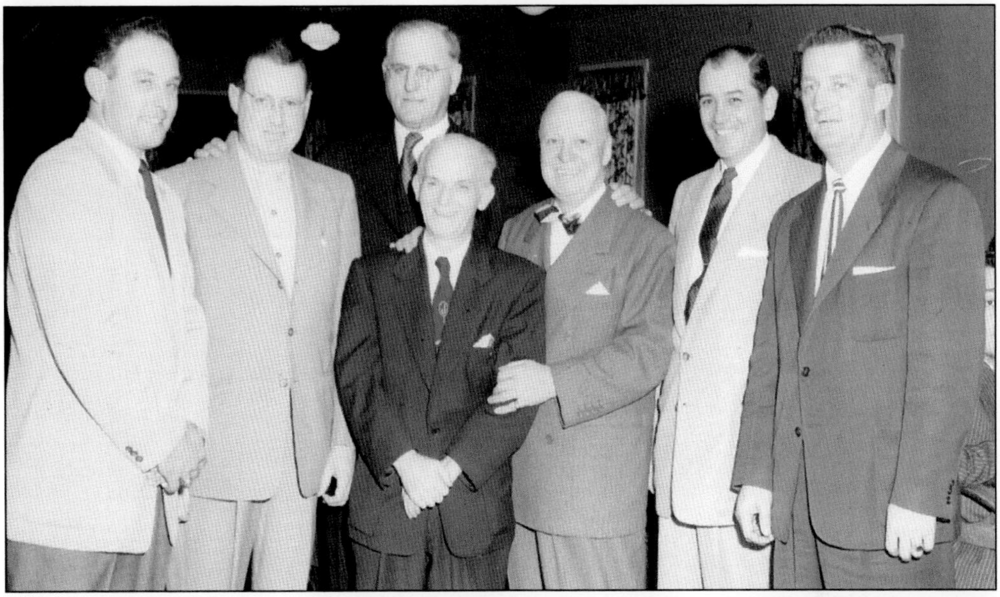

Everett "Cuffy" Bolig (third from the left, rear) was a man who took pride in Selinsgrove. He was a community activist all of his adult life. As a longtime Western Union telegrapher in the Pennsylvania State University football press box, his sports connections read like a who's who. Picking up the phone was all it took to secure a speaker for a local event. While not all are identified in this 1951 photograph, Gene Woodling, a New York Yankees outfielder (far left), and Penn State assistant Sever Toretti (second from right) are recognized.

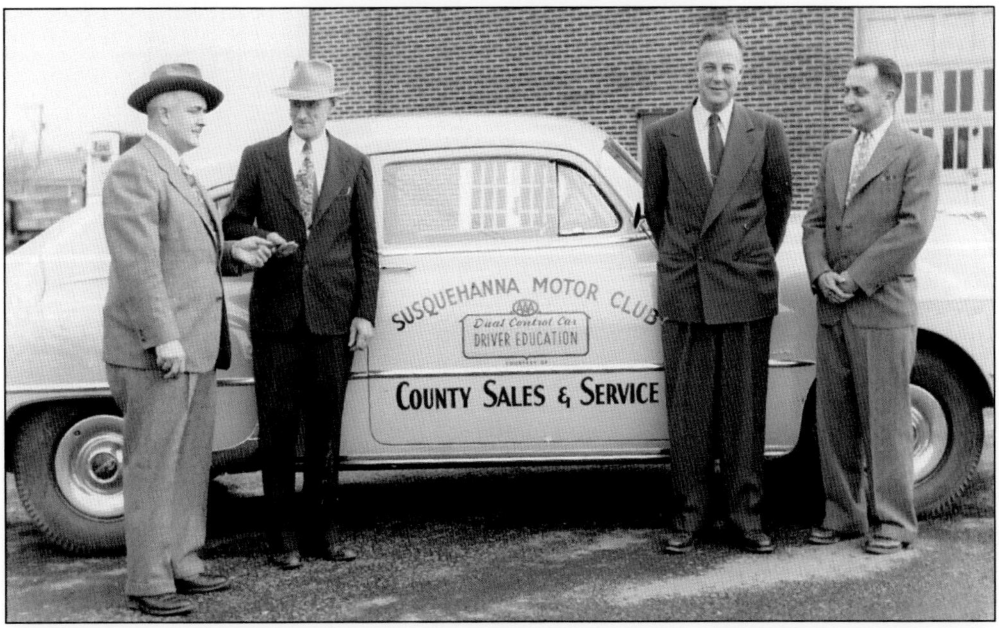

The American Automobile Association, better known as AAA or "Triple A," generously took part in providing dual-control cars to area high schools for their driver-education programs. County Sales and Service (Pontiac, Cadillac, and GMC trucks) dealership owner S. Graydon Ranck (far left) turns over the keys to a 1951 Pontiac. Ray Fulmer (second from the right) is the Selinsgrove High driver-education instructor. The other men mostly likely are AAA connected.

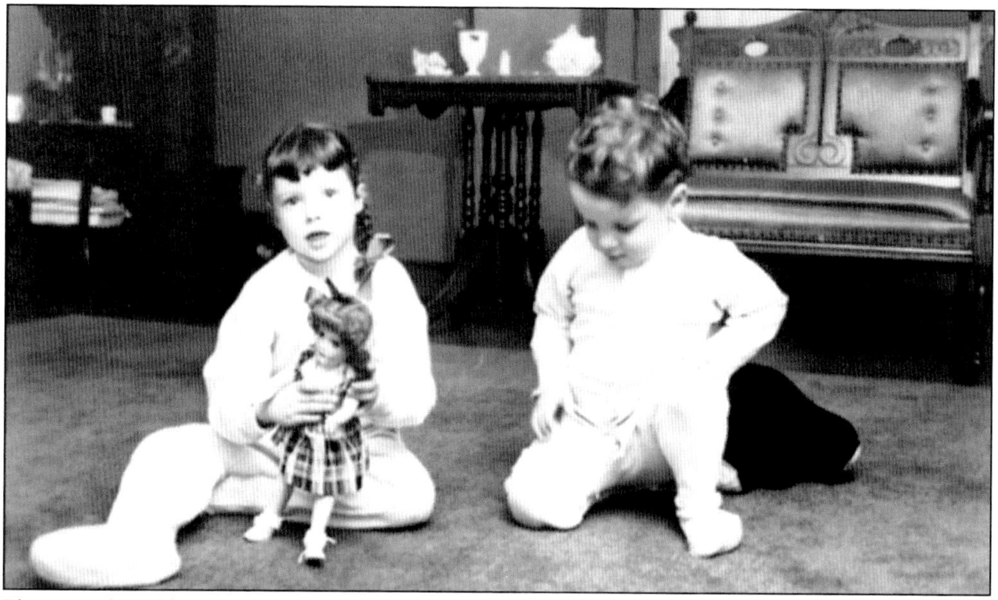

Photographic Christmas cards were all the rage after World War II and beyond. A different generation of photograph cards is very popular today—the kind one can make on a computer. In 1952, Bob and Muriel Trow of Selinsgrove sent this card, featuring daughter Megan (left) and son Harper. The Dr. Denton–clad tots are about three years and one year of age.

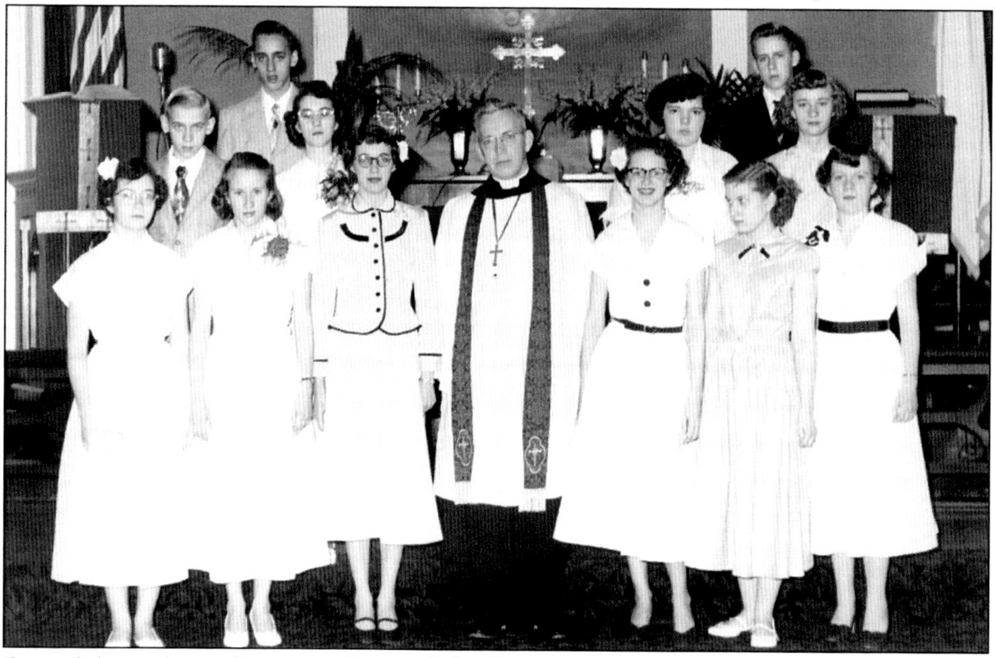

One of the early confirmation classes of the Reverend Eugene Steigerwalt, successor to the Reverend Sam Frost at First Lutheran Church in Selinsgrove, was the class of 1950. Confirmands shown, from left to right, are (first row) Virginia Steigerwalt, Joan Shetterly, Dianna Schafer, Reverend Steigerwalt, Diane Miller, Roberta Frost (the reverend's daughter), and Claudette Bedeaux; (second row) Ralph Fisher, Maryn Mae Starr, Lorraine Kelly, and Diana Fisher; (third row) Dick Fisher and George Snyder.

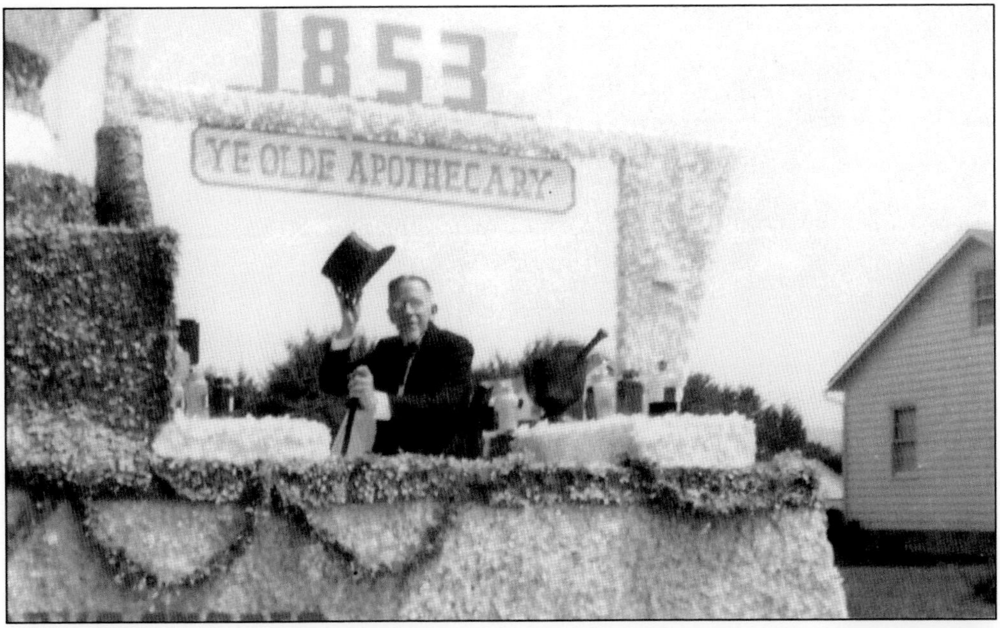

A large parade was part of the Selinsgrove centennial celebration on Saturday, August 22, 1953. Many businesses sponsored elaborate and decorative floats. One such float was entered by the Rea and Derick Drug Store chain. Riding on the attractive float in appropriate centennial attire is longtime Rea and Derick pharmacist Harold "Doc" Glass amid authentic apothecary jars and bottles. Like other men, his chin whiskers indicate membership in Brothers of the Bush.

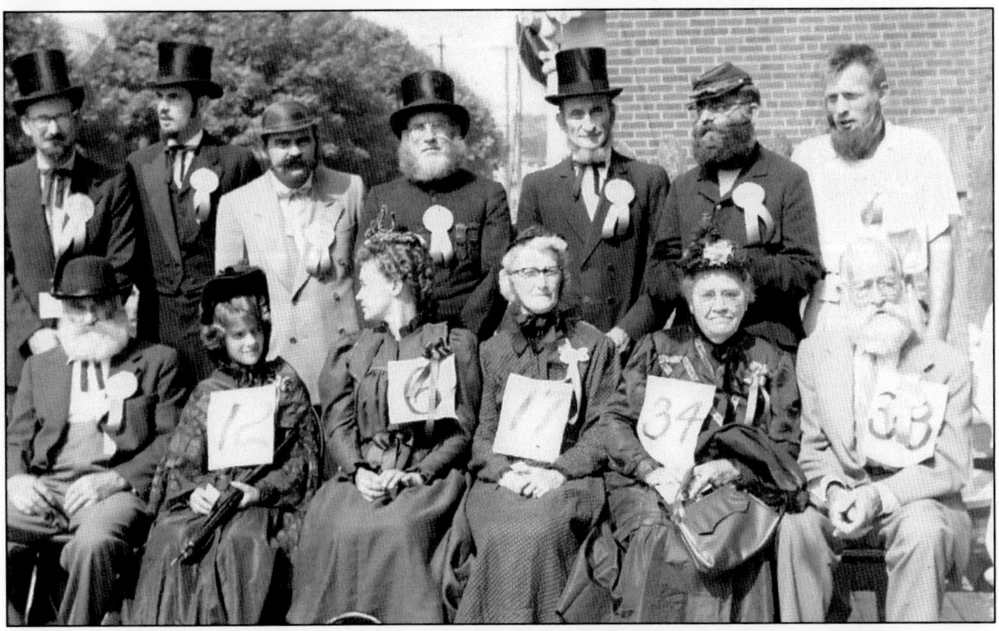

When Selinsgrove officially passed the century mark in 1953, a gala centennial celebration was staged. Pictured are participants of the Bonnets and Beards contest. From left to right, they are (first row) Wilson Page, Judy Shuker, Mrs. Calvin Pyers, Hazel Couldren, Mabel Clapp, and Madison Long; (second row) Warren Wolfe, Dale Musser, Harold "Pee Wee" Aurand, Harry A. Varner, Harry Row, John "Yank" Garbera, and Charles "Red" Fisher.

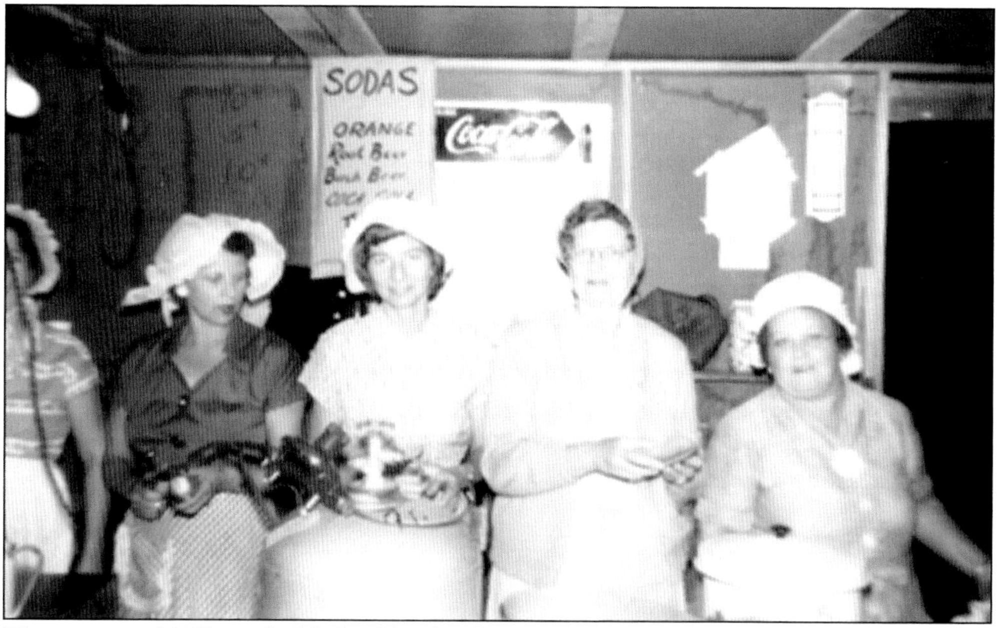

The summer of 1953 was highlighted by the observance of Selinsgrove's centennial. The entire community got behind the event. Everyone was into the spirit of the celebration. Celebrants were hungry and thirsty, and these four civic minded, bonneted ladies staffed a food stand to accommodate them. From left to right are Evelyn Campbell, Hazel Bingaman, Marie Bensinger, and Anita Harro.

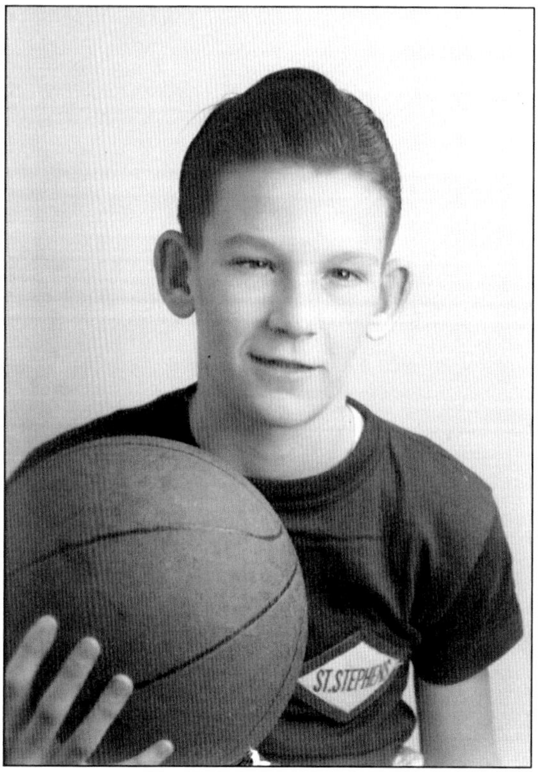

Thirteen-year-old Jim Rutkowski is shown in 1954 as a member of St. Stephen's eighth-grade team in the Shenandoah (sometimes pronounced Shen-doe) Catholic Youth League (CYO). He is one who came to town and made a lasting contribution. He was instrumental in bowling becoming a varsity sport at the high school. Rutkowski and his wife, Carol, have two sons, Jim Jr. and Steve, who were also stellar student athletes.

Jim Taylor, doing his best imitation of Harry "Rags" Gilmer (a University of Alabama and National Football League jump-pass specialist), is another of a considerable number of people who moved to Selinsgrove, stayed, and made an impact on the community. As a teacher and coach, Taylor and his family truly became part of the town. He is shown in 1954 as quarterback for the Lewistown (Pennsylvania) High School team. At Selinsgrove High School and Susquehanna University, his track and field successes became stuff of legend.

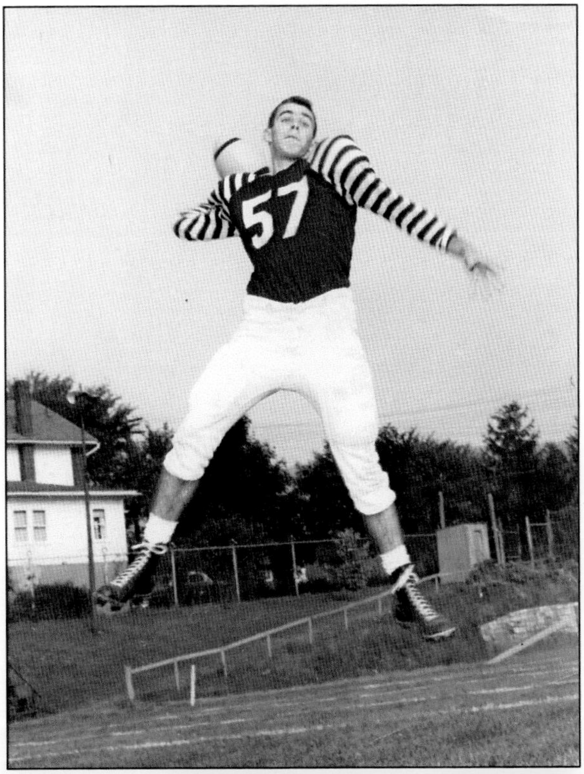

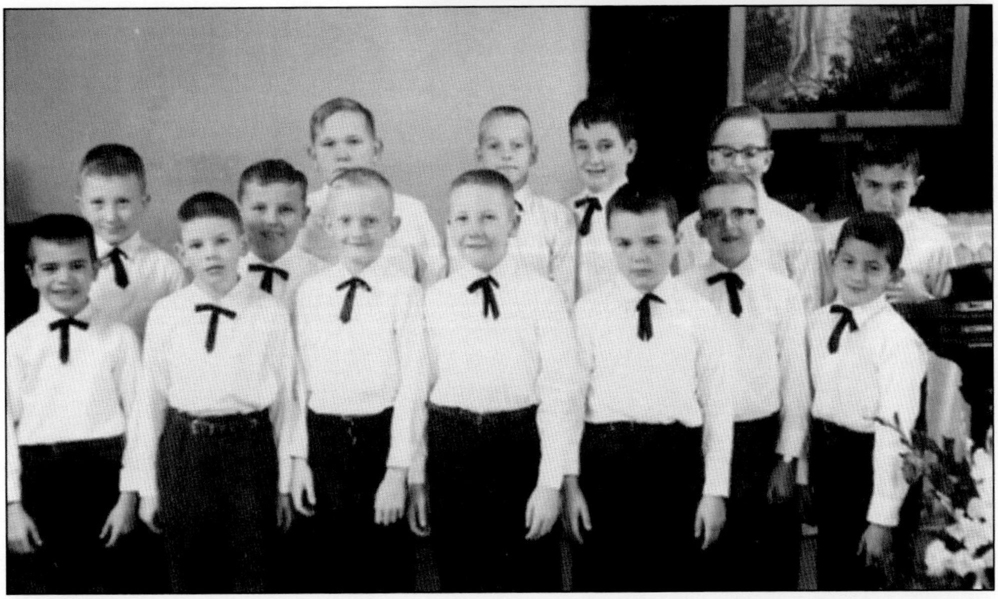

St. Paul's Reformed Church (now United Church of Christ) has been known for a long time for great cooks (Fasnact doughnuts, public turkey, and ham dinners) and outstanding music (several choirs, talented soloists, and stalwart organists and pianists). The boys' choir is shown in 1961. From left to right, they are (first row) Bobby Brown, Mike Aurand, Dean Jones, Scott Adams, Fred Mease, Laird Gemberling II, and Jim Renner; (second row) Dave Wagner, Tom Wagner, Bob Persing, Bob Rhodes, Kim Reichley, John Searer, and Don "Homer" Ernst.

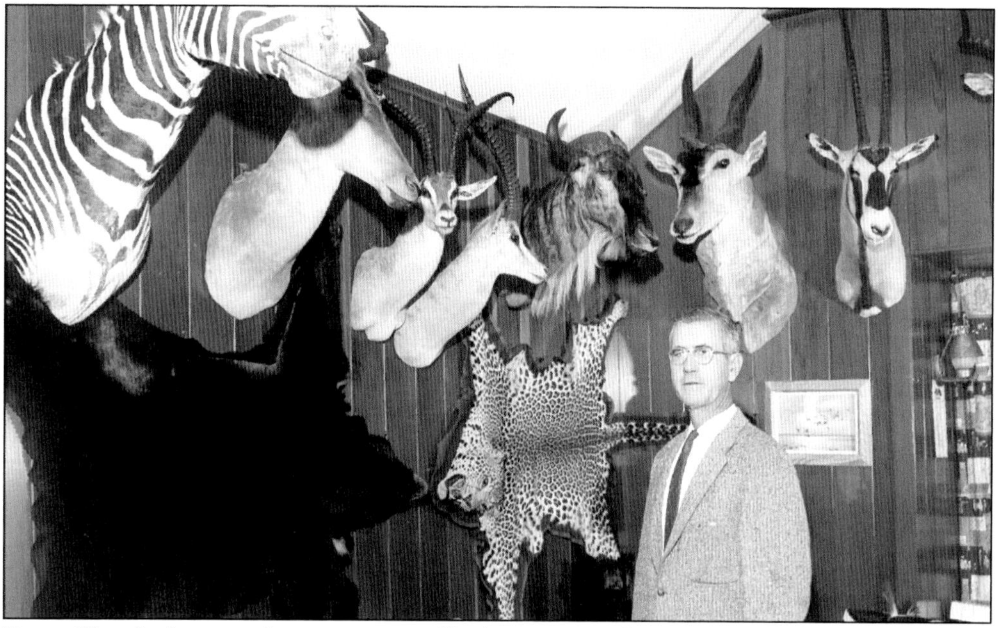

Simon Rhoads, shown with just a portion of his big-game trophies, hunted not only in many of the states making up the nation but also on other continents. Films of his African safaris enthralled countless area residents. He is pictured around 1963 in the trophy room of his Rhoads Avenue home with a considerable number of animals he bagged on the Dark Continent. The wall-mounted leopard was depicted at the time of its taking in a previous Arcadia Snyder County book.

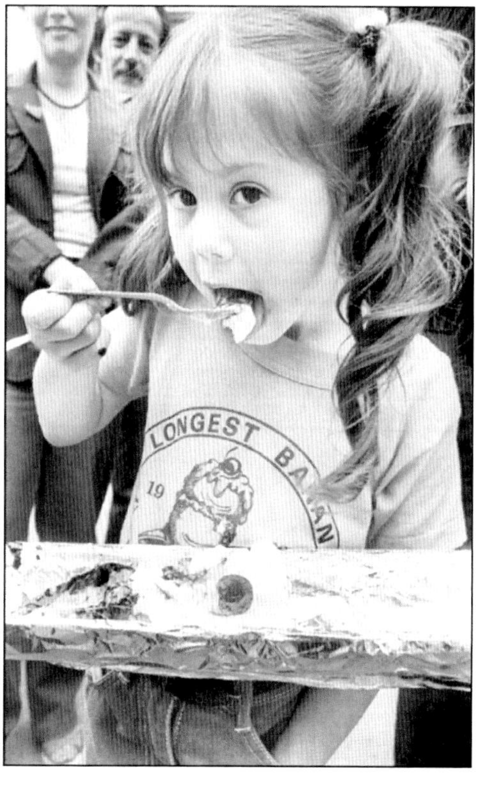

On May 1, 1982, a balmy Saturday, Selinsgrove entered the *Guinness Book of Records* for constructing and consuming "the world's longest banana split." The giant sundae, which was 8,006 feet in length, lined several blocks of Market Street. Shown is five-year-old Danielle Palmer, a local youngster, as she is about to sample the tasty treat. In 1988, the town restaged the event to reclaim the record, which was broken by another community. As is best known, Selinsgrove still holds the record.

Three

FLAG AND COUNTRY

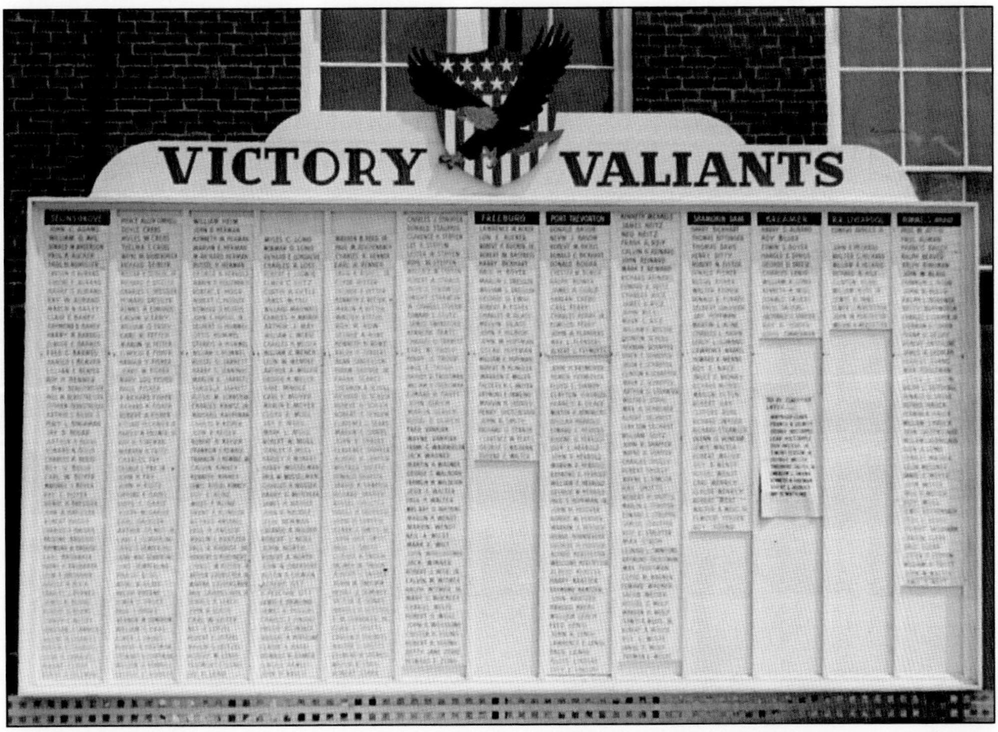

During World War II, any town of any size had—usually in a place of prominence—an honor roll of hometown veterans serving their country. Selinsgrove was no exception. As men and women left for military service, their names were added to the growing display tribute. Not only were Selinsgrove veterans honored, but those from all eastern Snyder County communities were listed. In the third column from the right, the names are recorded temporarily on paper, to be added permanently later.

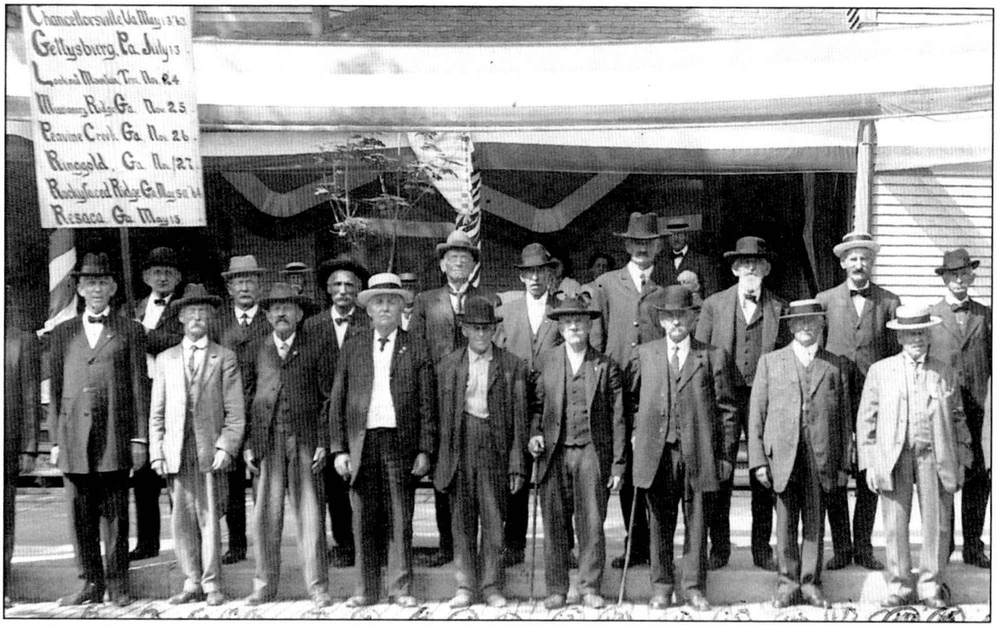

At the Charles Ulrich home at 8 North Market Street in Selinsgrove on October 13, 1912, surviving Civil War veterans, "Our Boys" of Company G, 147th Pennsylvania Volunteer Infantry, held one of their many reunions. The sign notes their campaigns from 1863 and 1864: Chancellorsville, Gettysburg, Lookout Mountain, Missionary Ridge, Peavine Creek, Ringgold, Rocky Face Ridge, and Resaca.

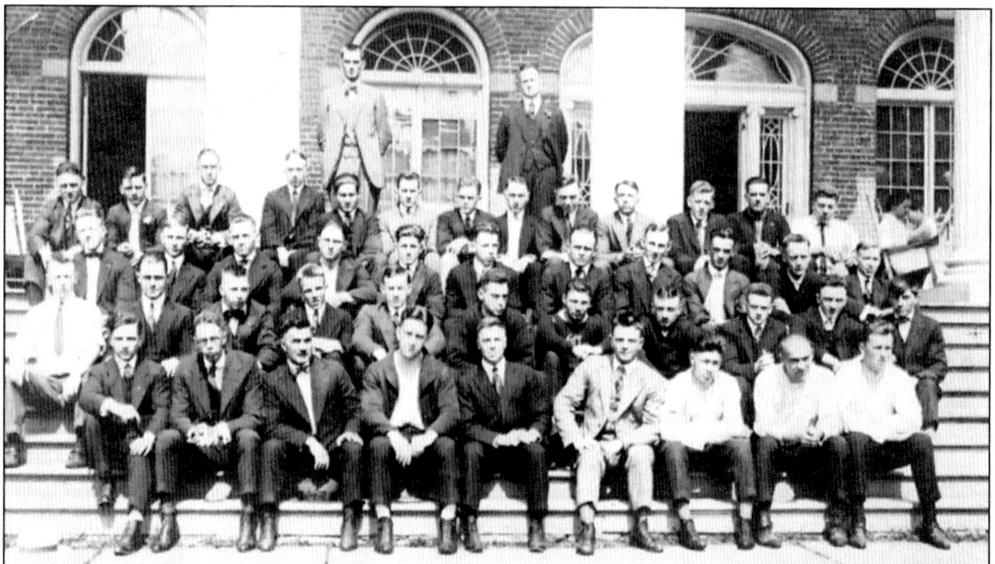

Susquehanna University provided soldier drivers for Section 574, U.S. Army Ambulance Corps (USAAC). The troops later trained in the Allentown area, sailed to England, and eventually saw service in France from March to November 1918. The USAAC performed honorably at the Marne, Chateau Thierry, and Verdun. Familiar names of drivers include Ralph Witmer, Ralph Woodruff, Burleigh Peters, and Nathan Danowsky. The group was also known as the "hospital unit" and "motor corps."

Everyday citizens have long supported American troops in the nation's conflicts. One way is for youths to don smaller versions of military uniforms. In 1919, young Charlie Fasold personally saluted those who served in World War I, which was called the Great War then. Most likely, he is suited up for Selinsgrove's gala welcome home celebration. Another photograph from the same time shows him shouldering a replica rifle.

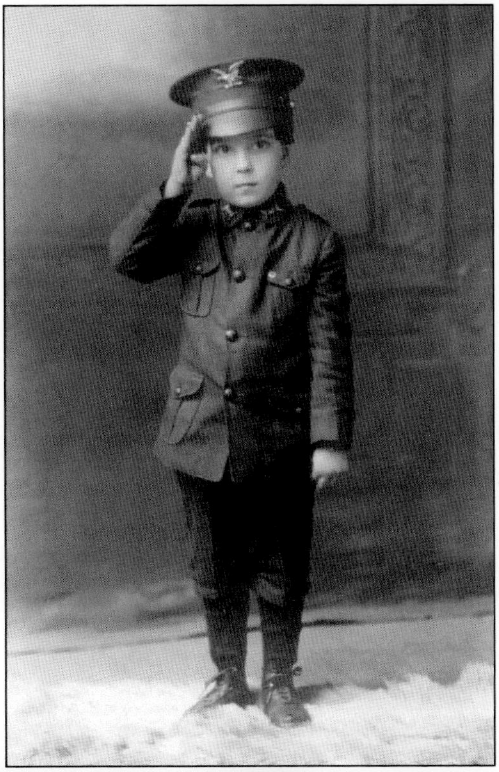

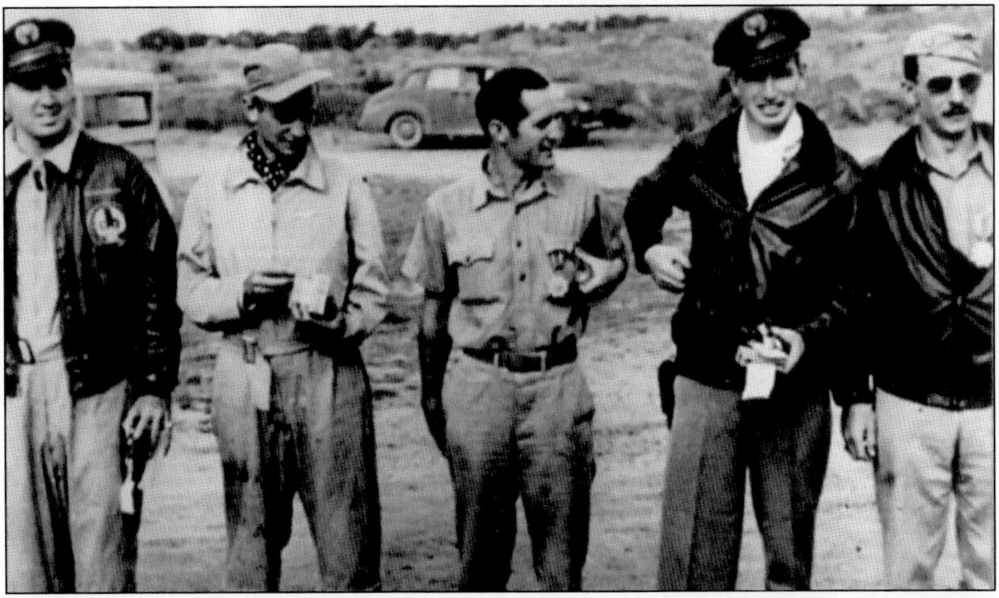

It could be argued that no World War II unit was held in higher esteem than the Flying Tigers. John Wayne starred in a film about their fearless exploits. Onetime Selinsgrove resident George Burgard (extreme left) flew in China and Burma with the American Volunteer Corps (AVC) before the United States officially entered the war. His name is mentioned with such legends as David "Tex" Hill and Greg "Pappy" Boyington. The daring pilot received one of only three double-ace awards ever given by a grateful Chinese government.

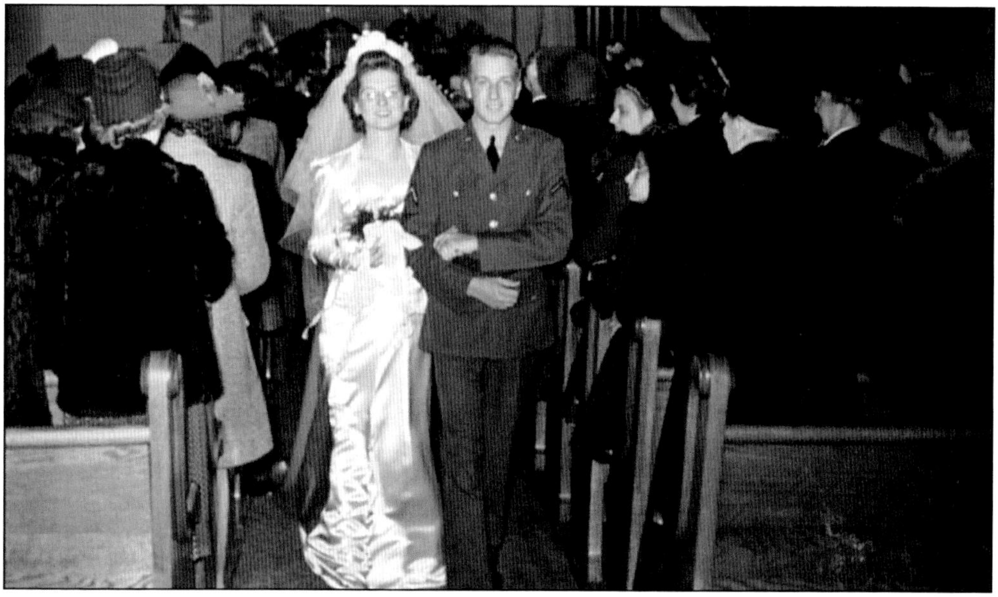

When Bill Marshall and Marion Renn were married, Marshall was already a private first class in the U.S. Army. The unsuspecting couple had no idea what the second day of their marriage would bring. They married at Selinsgrove's St. Paul's church on Saturday, December 6, 1941. The next day was "a date that will live in infamy," the day of the Japanese sneak attack on Pearl Harbor and the country's official entry into World War II. Happily, the young couple survived the rigors of war.

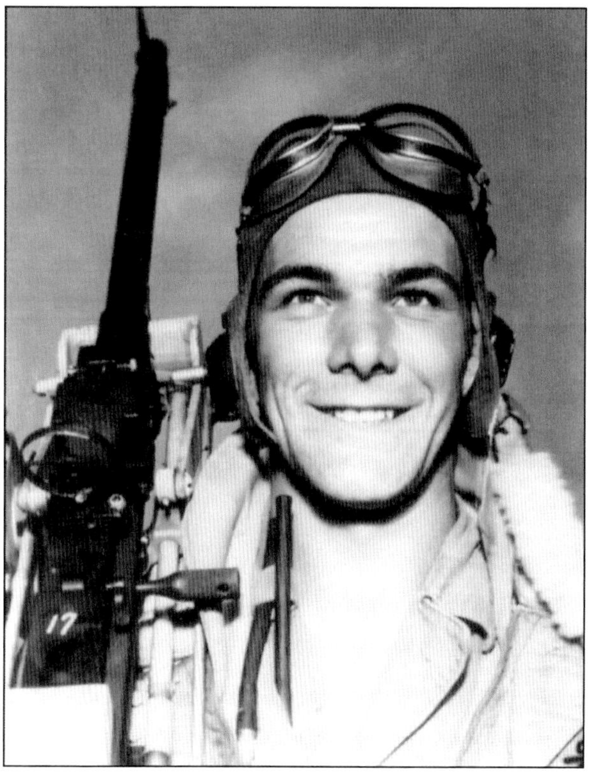

Tech. Sgt. Charles A. "Butch" Bolig was in the Army Air Corps a little over a year when on October 20, 1943, his B-17 Flying Fortress *Shatzi* was shot down over Holland. Bolig, a flight engineer and top-turret gunner, was among 6 of 10 crew members who parachuted to safety only to be captured by Germans. Initially, he was reported missing in action but was a prisoner of war in Stalag 17-B. On May 3, 1945, Bolig and others were liberated by Gen. George S. Patton's Third Army.

Dave Gross went from Susquehanna University to the Army Air Corps Aviation Cadet Program in February 1943. After a year of training and earning his wings, he was sent to the South Pacific, where he joined the Fifth Air Force's 345th Bomb Group, 498th Bomb Squadron in New Guinea. He flew 40 low-flying strafing missions over the Philippines, Marianas, and Solomons in a B-25 Mitchell. On one, a Japanese antiaircraft shell came within 10 feet of him; too close for comfort.

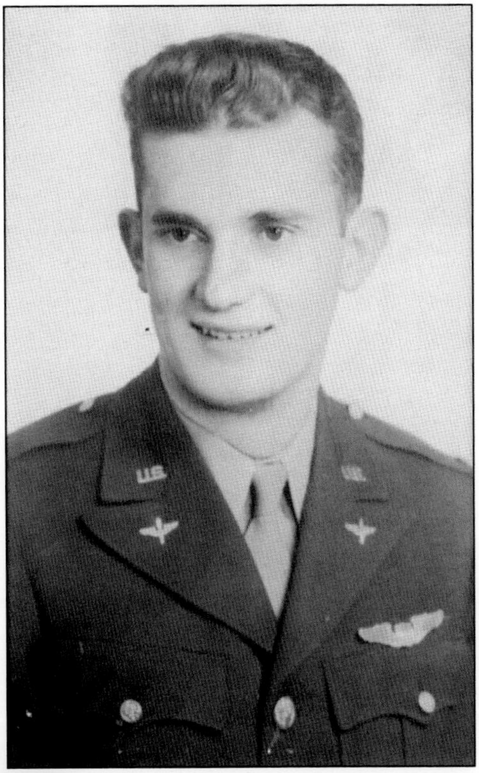

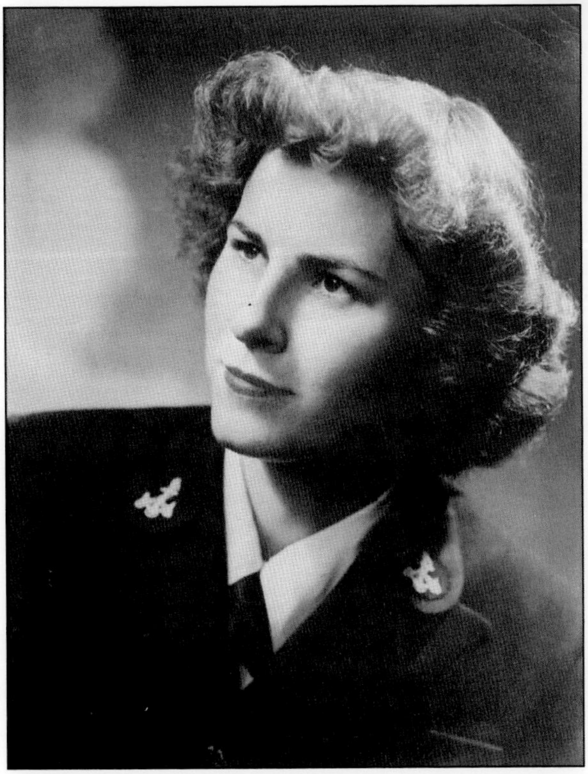

From 1943 to 1946, Jane Schnure served in the WAVES (Women Accepted for Volunteer Emergency Service). After boot camp at Hunter College in the Bronx, New York, she underwent further training at Stillwater, Oklahoma. As a second-class petty officer, she was assigned to recruiting duties in Pittsburgh. Her office produced and aired weekly entertainment and recruiting shows for radio. Later stationed in Philadelphia at the University of Pennsylvania, Schnure worked with Penn's Navy V-12 officer training program.

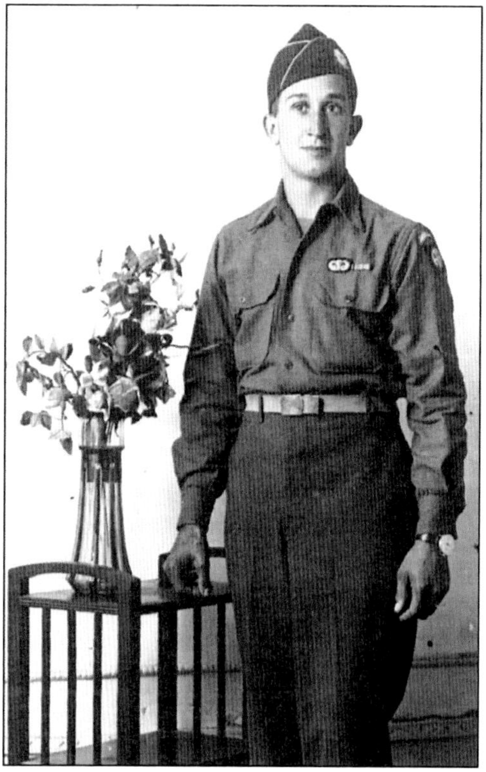

Like so many of the greatest generation, Marshall "Bud" Herman did not talk much about his World War II experiences; it was only in his later years that he mentioned anything. He was proud to have served under Gen. James Gavin with the celebrated 82nd Airborne. He took pride in "having jumped [in an exhibition] for the Big Three," his term for Pres. Franklin D. Roosevelt, Winston Churchill, and Joseph Stalin. This photograph was taken on the Isle of Capri while on R&R (rest and relaxation) in 1943.

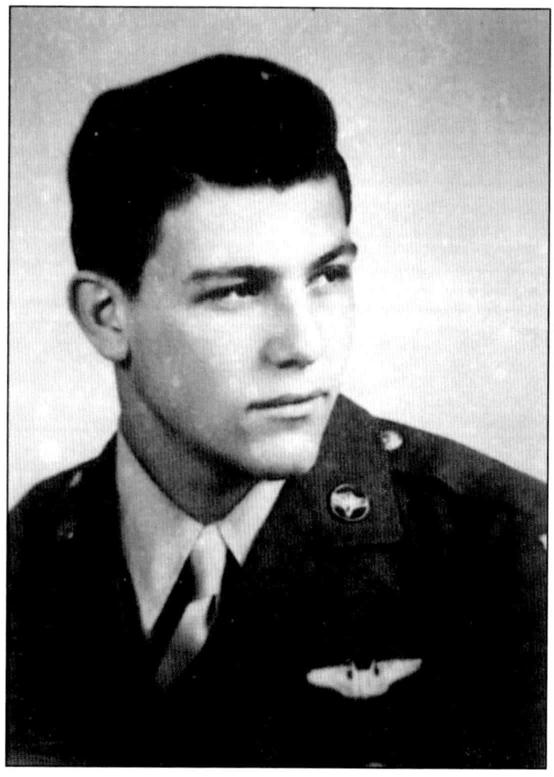

Cloyd Kunkel was a Selinsgrove airman who made the supreme sacrifice for his country. An avid model plane builder, he enlisted in the Army Air Corps after high school graduation. He became a tail gunner on a B-24 Liberator with the 404th Bomb Squadron based in Attu, Alaska, from where the B-24s bombed Japan's northern islands, which was 2,100 miles round trip. Kunkel's plane did not return from a January 23, 1945, mission over the Shimushu Straits. He was just 19 years old.

Cadet Chet Gaugler was stationed at Army Air Corps navigation school in Monroe, Louisiana, in 1944 when he got word from home that fellow townsman C. Warren "Froggy" Fritz was being treated at Foster General Hospital in Jackson, Mississippi. Fritz, along with others in his company, was poisoned by tainted water in Italy. Gaugler hitchhiked 150 miles to see his buddy. Later, while traveling by train cross country, Gaugler recalled "celebrating New Year's Eve in three different time zones."

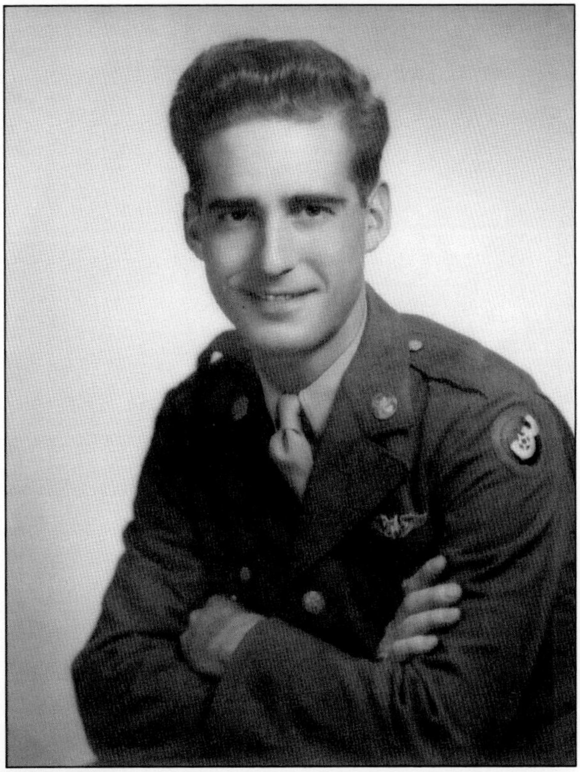

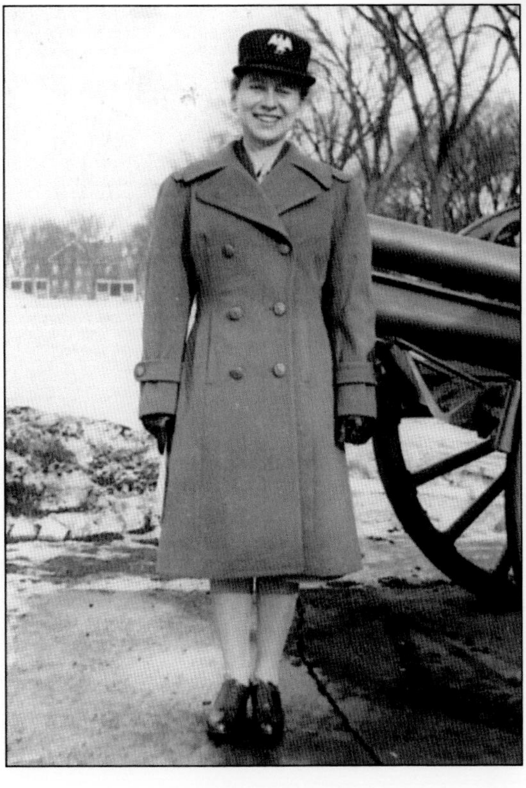

Martha Laudenslager Davis graduated from Susquehanna University and began teaching mathematics at Selinsgrove High School in 1931. When the United States entered World War II, she entered the WACs (Women's Army Auxiliary Corps) in 1942. Commissioned as a lieutenant, she served in various personnel positions. One duty post was Camp Phillips, Kansas, where she met her future husband, Lt. Col. Tom Davis. Discharged after hostilities, she returned to teaching.

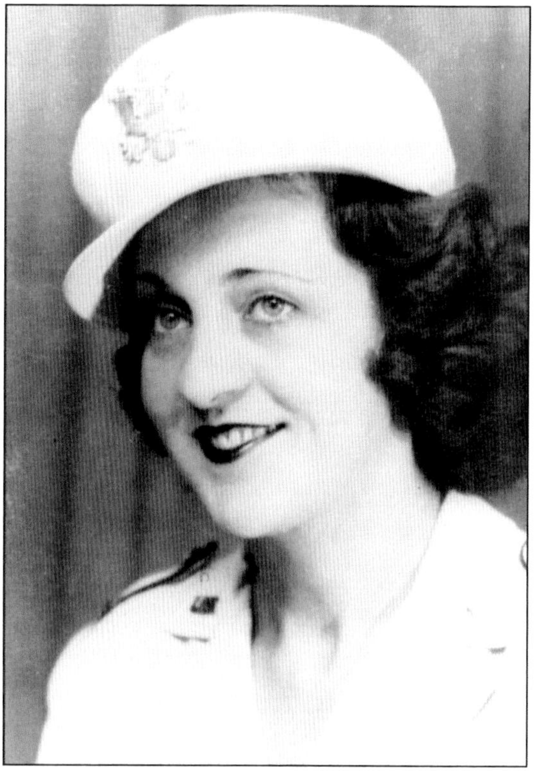

Mary E. Wochley Edlavitch, from Mount Pleasant Mills, did her nurse's training at the renowned Johns Hopkins Hospital in Baltimore. When World War II was in its opening days, she enlisted in the U.S. Army Nurse Corps and remained until 1967. Three times decorated, she served in the South Pacific in New Zealand and the Fiji Islands. She retired with the rank of major and spent her last years in Freeburg.

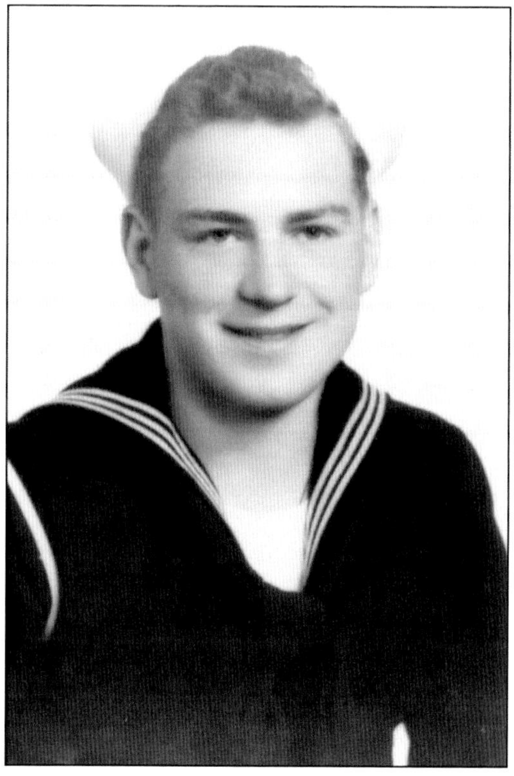

Allen Charles did not hit the beach with the first wave at Normandy's Omaha Beach on D-Day, June 6, 1944, but when he landed the day after, it was no cakewalk. A gunner's mate, Charles was part of the U.S. Navy Amphibious Repair Unit E-10. On the day after "the longest day," Charles and his mates cleared barbed wire, removed mines and tank traps, and defused unexploded ordnance. After that, his unit was involved in repairing and returning landing craft to service. His stay at Normandy lasted five months.

In late 1943, Dave Dagle was one of a group of students in good standing at Selinsgrove High School who was awarded a diploma in the spring of 1944 after joining the service. The others were Clark Arbogast, Sterling "Doc" Herrold, Doug Sanderson, and Harold Schuck. All joined the U.S. Navy. Mahlon Rathfon entered under similar conditions later on. Dagle was part of an LCT (landing craft, tanks) crew that trained on Tinian and Luzon for the invasion of the Japanese mainland that never came.

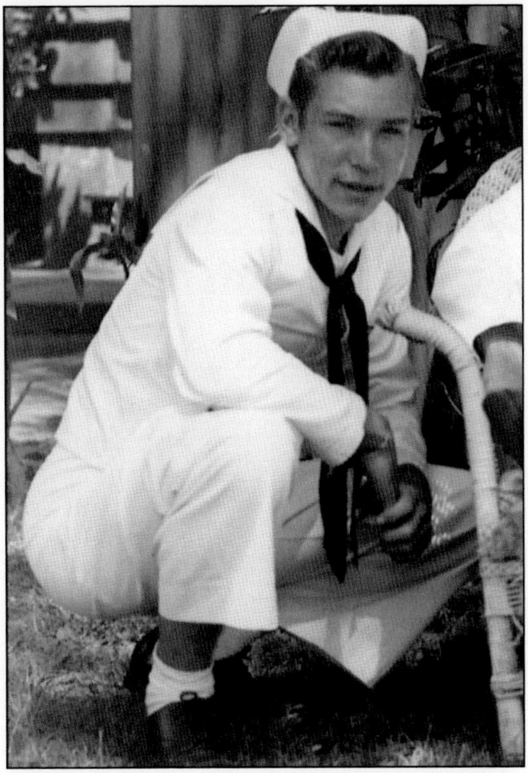

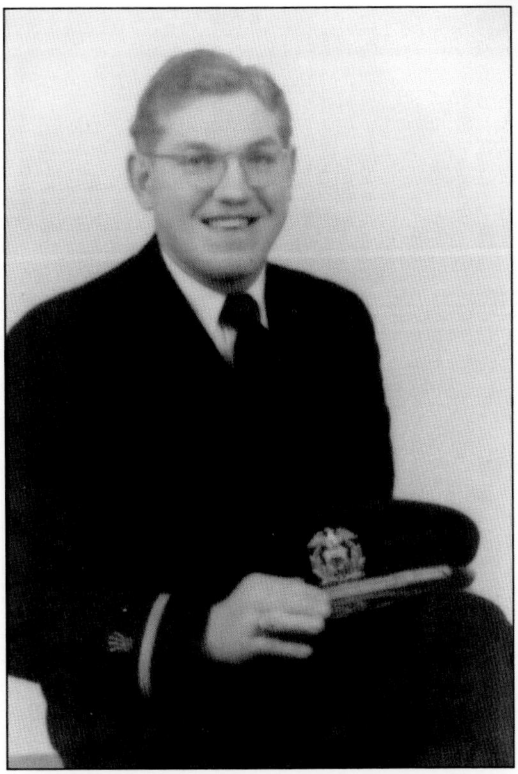

Rather than accept a deferment because he held an essential wartime job and was engaged in farming, Russ Hummel enlisted in the U.S. Merchant Marines. Trained as a radio officer, he crossed the U-boat infested Atlantic Ocean out of Baltimore, Philadelphia, and Hampton Roads, Virginia. He sailed mainly on cargo ships that took 15 to 20 days to cross. Hummel's ships delivered grain, coal, iron ore, ammunition, troops, and even horses. They sailed to England, Poland, Italy, and South Africa.

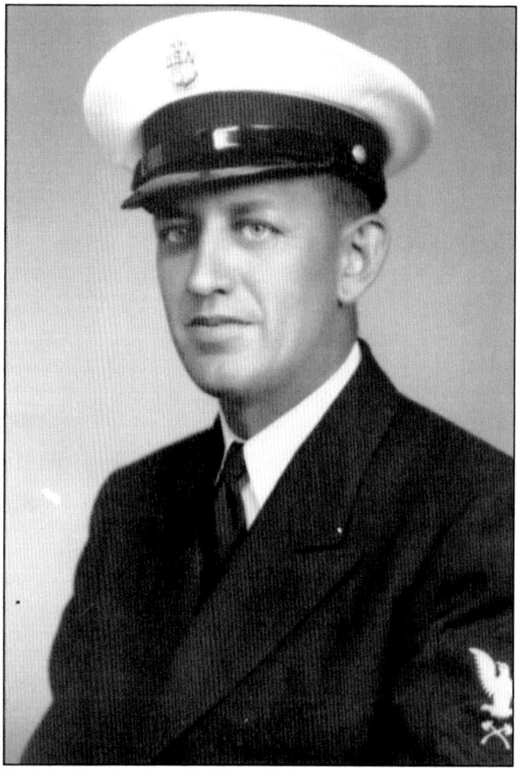

V. Mark "Mike" Bogar was a World War II service rarity. The military, specifically the U.S. Navy, took advantage of his civilian occupation and actually had him serve in a similar capacity. Bogar was engaged in the construction business with his father and brothers. A Pennsylvania National Guardsman from 1927 to 1929, he enlisted at age 36 in 1943 and earned the rank of chief carpenter's mate with the 129th Construction Battalion (Seabees) in the South Pacific.

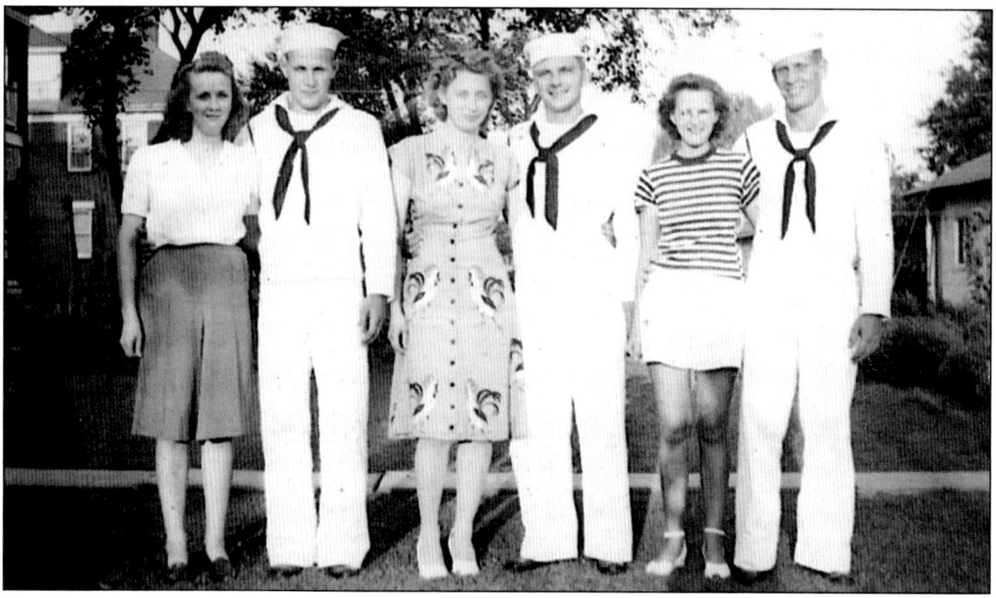

While home on leave, three Selinsgrove sailors and their wives posed happily for this photograph on July 6, 1944, not long after enlisting. From left to right, they are Ruth and Sam Orwan, Ruth and Paul Garrett, and Velma and Wendell Roush. The three amigos all served in the South Pacific: Orwan as a machinist's mate on the USS *Broadwater*; Garrett as a fire control man on LST (landing ship, tanks) 1126; and Roush was also a fire control man, on LSM (landing ship, medium) 299. All were discharged six months after Victory over Japan (V-J) Day.

Cal Witmer was a man ahead of his time. In 1943 and 1944, he was serving in Iran and Iraq. After training at Camp Chaffee in Arkansas, Camp Grant in Illinois, and Camp Atterbury near Indianapolis, he was shipped to the Middle East with the Third Platoon, 19th Field Hospital Company. After his discharge, he took part in the multigenerational operation of his family's all-purpose mill in the Clifford Mills area west of Selinsgrove.

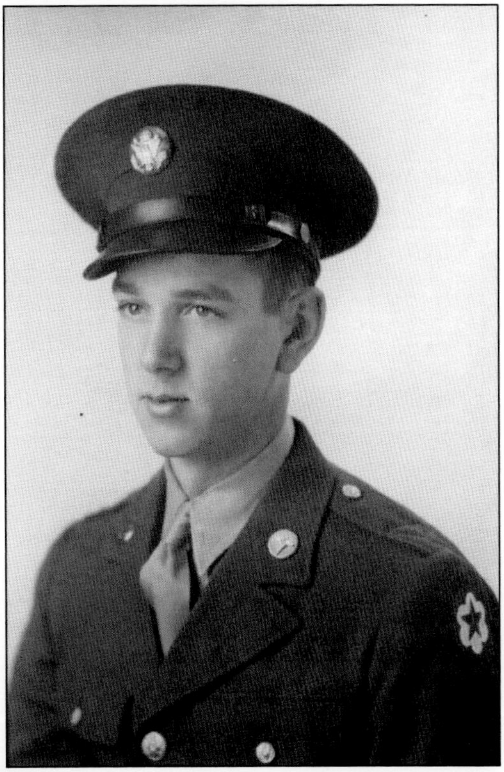

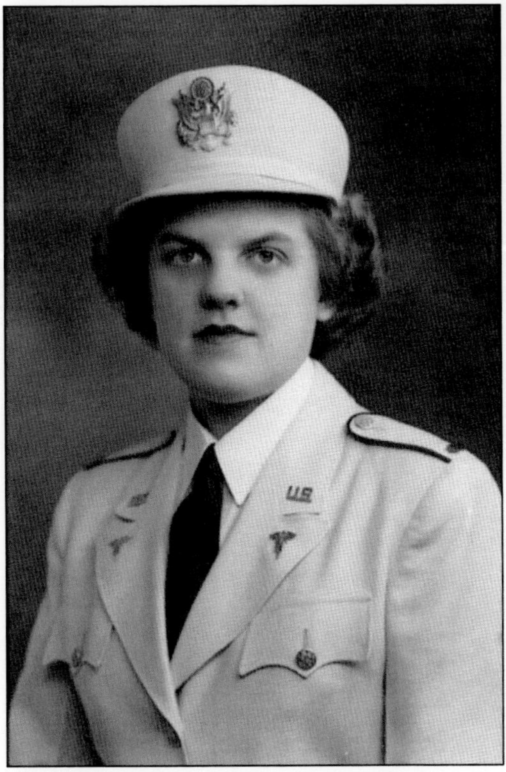

Jean Schrum Brandau Rathfon just followed a family tradition when she enlisted in the U.S. Army Nurse Corps in early 1944, shortly after graduation from St. Anthony's School of Nursing in Carroll, Iowa. Her father served in World War I, and two brothers enlisted early in World War II. Commissioned as a lieutenant, she was assigned to the 103rd General Hospital in Tidworth, England. While there, she met and married Henry Brandau, a U.S. Ordinance officer who later became a Lewisburg reserve officer.

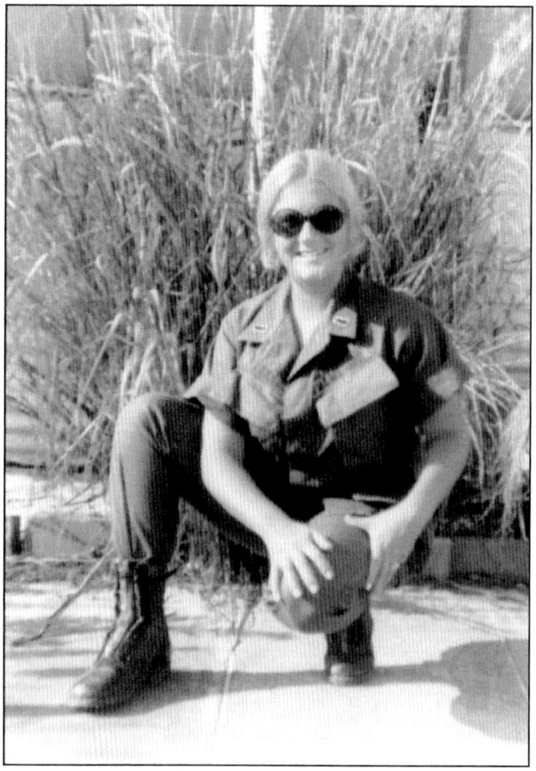

Carol Brandau Sundling, like her mother Jean Schrum Brandau Rathfon (seen on the previous page), followed family tradition by graduating from nursing school, Harrisburg Hospital School of Nursing, and serving in the U.S. Air Force. After flight training in aerospace medicine in 1970, she was "in country" in Vietnam for exactly one year—arriving and later departing on her birthday. She saw service from the demilitarized zone (DMZ) to Saigon with the 903rd Air Medivac Squadron. In the reserves after Vietnam, she concluded her 20-year career as a major and chief flight nurse.

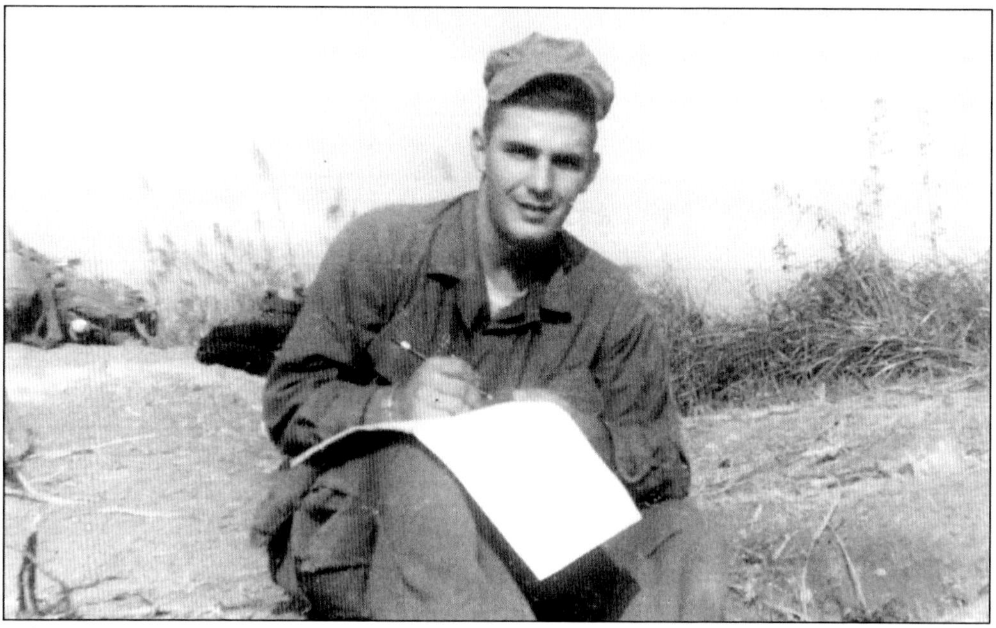

Bob Hunter became "one of the few; the proud" as a U.S. Marine Corps enlistee in 1965. Like thousands of others, he served a 13-month tour in Vietnam from late 1966 to early 1968. While stationed near Dung Ha in 1967, he caught an AK-47 slug in his shoulder. Awarded the Purple Heart, he returned to active duty shortly after being wounded. He was a machine gunner in Company L, 3rd Battalion, 3rd Marine Division. In civilian life, he is a skilled barber.

Four

Susquehanna University's Broad Campus

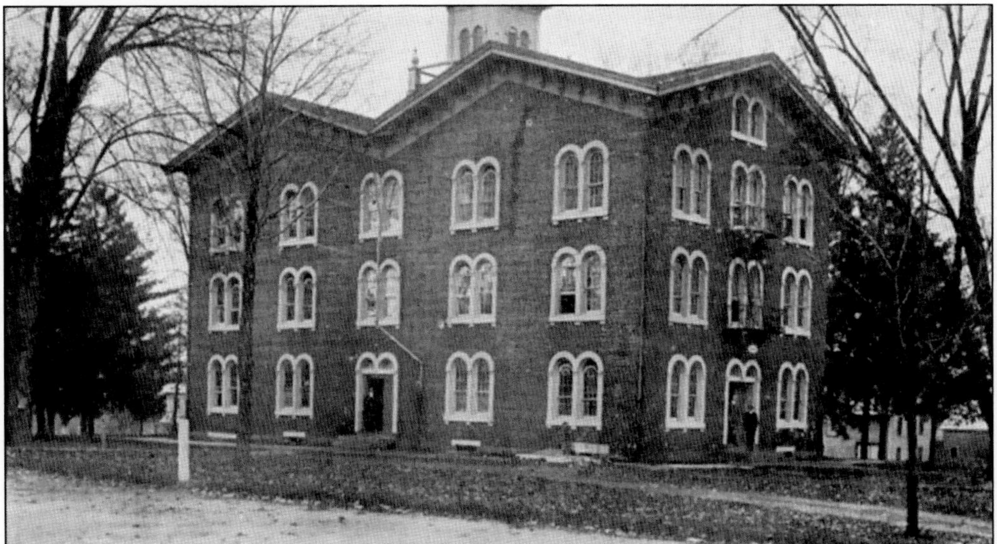

This real-photo postcard of Susquehanna University's Selinsgrove Hall is from the first decade of the 20th century. There is good reason why, in 1858, Baltimore's Lutherans chose Selinsgrove as the seat of the Missionary Institute (as Susquehanna University was first known) and why the first building on campus is named after the town. The citizens of the community pledged $22,500, a considerable sum 150 years ago, toward the college, whose stated goal was to prepare young men for the Lutheran ministry. Bricks from Jackson Gaugler's brickyard were use in the construction.

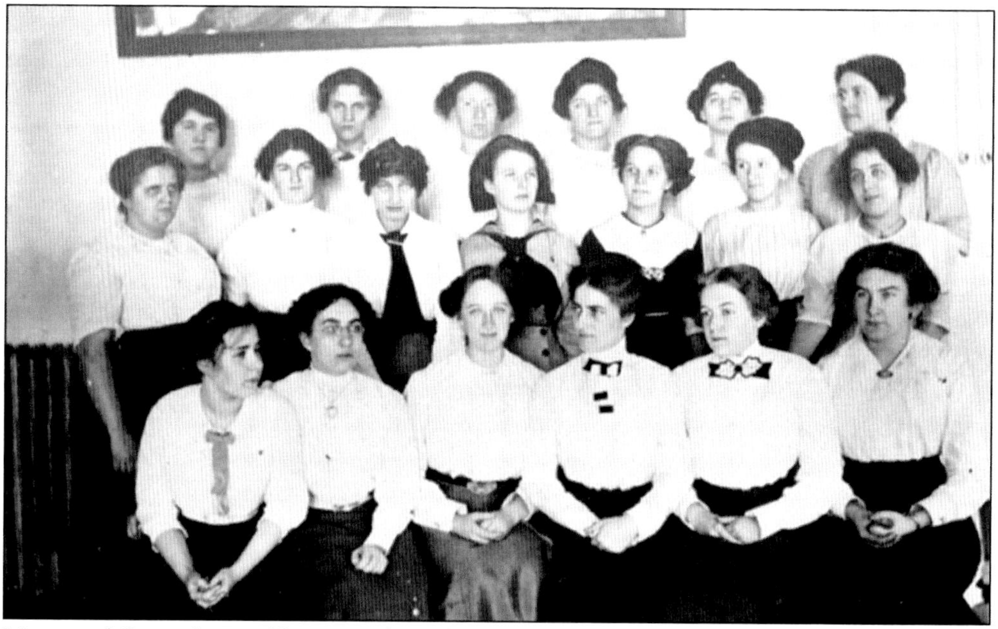

Music and Susquehanna University have been synonymous through the years. Although the conservatory disappeared in the 1950s and was replaced by a much more functional Heilman Hall, the old "Con" gave many a music teacher his or her career start. Professors such as Percy Linebaugh, Edwin Sheldon, Elrose Allison, Mary Potteiger, and Russell and Nancy Hatz were longtime fixtures on the music faculty. Pictured are members of the 1913 Girls' Glee Club, as stated on the print.

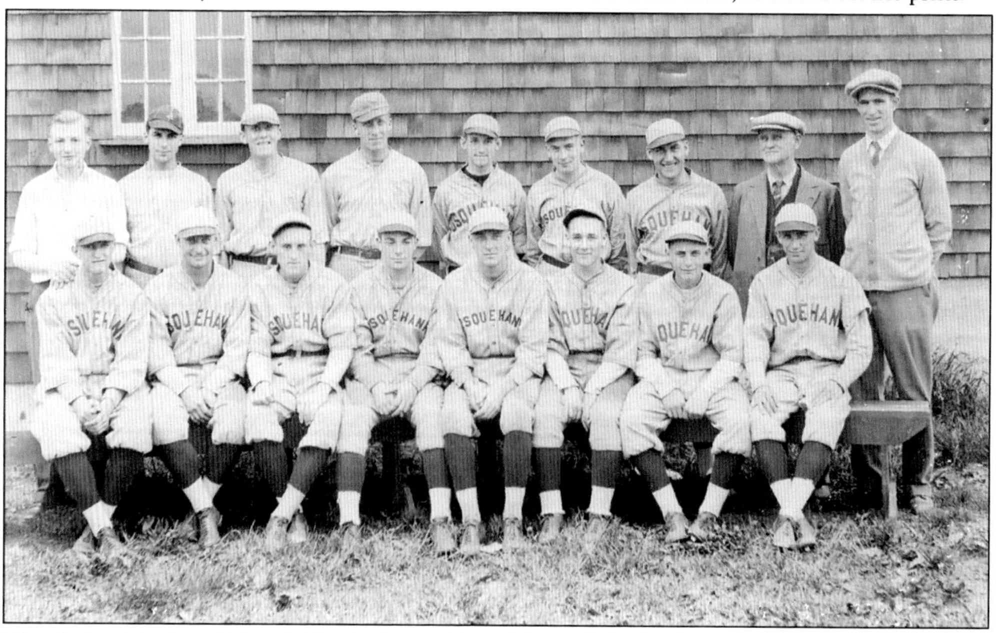

The shake shingles of the old football grandstand formed the background for the Susquehanna baseball team photograph of 1927. "Uncle Frank" Morgan served as coach. Willie Groce of Selinsgrove (first row, fourth from the left) was a mainstay and later an inductee in Susquehanna University's sports hall of fame, as was Sherman Good (first row, second from the right), a future West End educator.

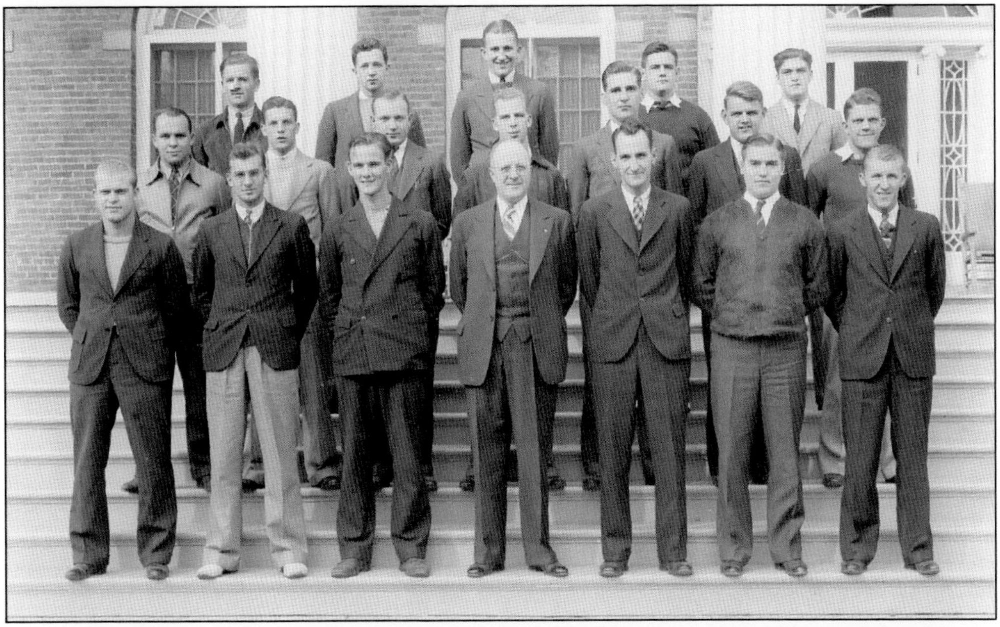

"The colony boys," a group of men, predominantly football players, were unique to Susquehanna. The Colony Organization, as it was more formally known, was founded in 1934. The men served mainly as night attendants at what is today the Selinsgrove Center. They attended classes by day, practiced their sport, studied, and slept whenever they could at night. Several men, including Ken Badger, Bob Keller, and Tom Valunas, made Selinsgrove their home after graduation.

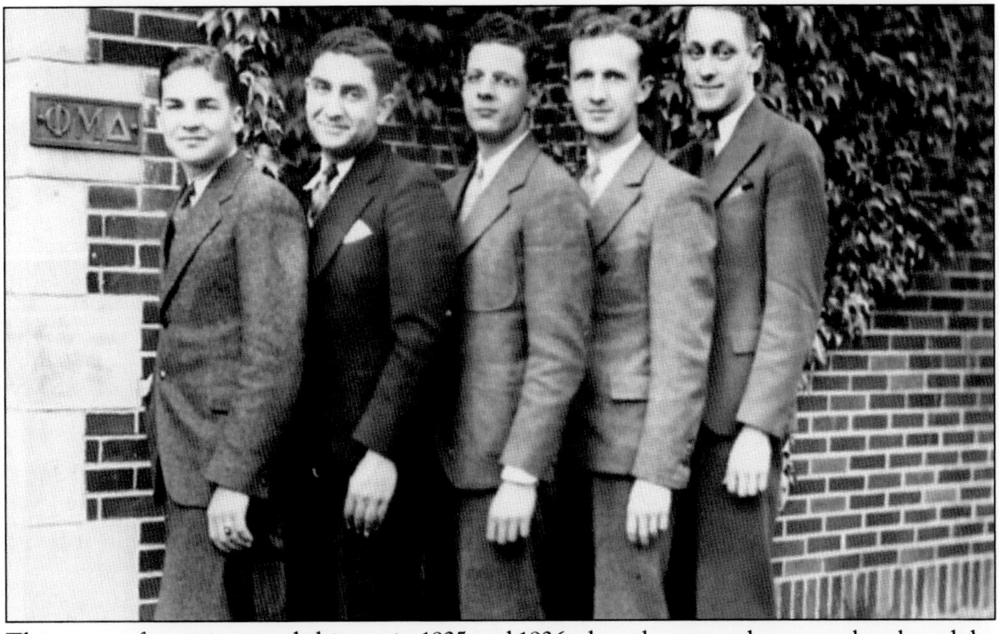

This group of musicians made history in 1935 and 1936 when they were chosen to play aboard the Cunnard White Star Line's *Aquatania* and *Sythia.* The combo was the first from a Pennsylvania school to make the transatlantic crossing as a shipboard band. Previous groups had all been from New England colleges. They played twice daily "over and back." From left to right are Pete Poyck '37, Frank Bennardi '35, Leonard "Jake" Newfield '35, leader Rudy Gelnett '37, and Al Eyer '36.

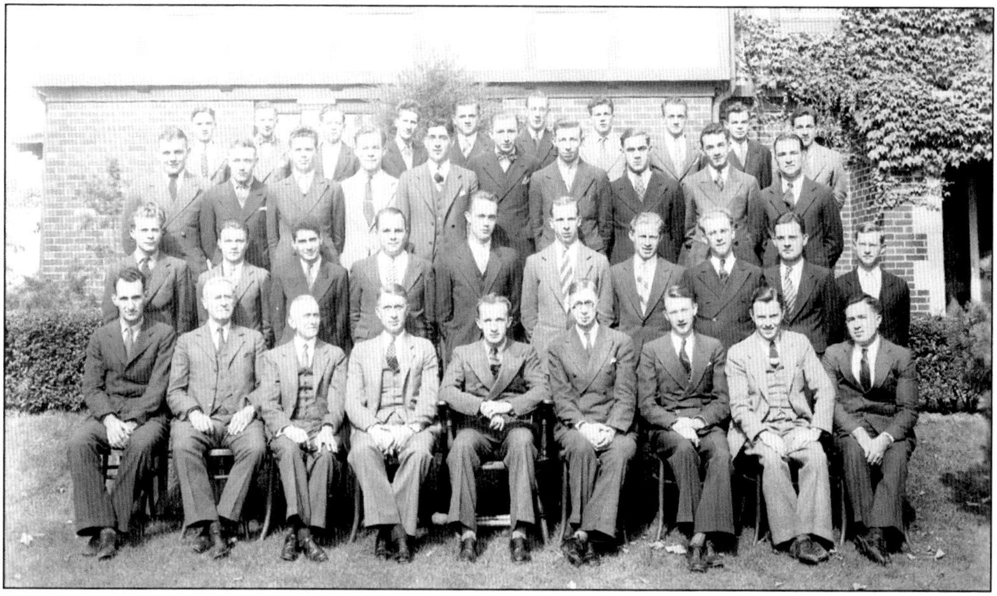

The classic Tudor architecture of the ivy-covered original Phi Mu Delta building fairly shouts "fraternity house." However, it fell into disrepair and no longer stands. Notables in this photograph from about 1937 are president Rudy Gelnett (first row, fifth from the left), Vernon Blough (first row, extreme right), Prof. Arthur Wilson (first row, third from right), Ray "Padre" Shaheen, a future campus icon (second row, third from the left), and Clyde Spitzner (second row, fourth from the left).

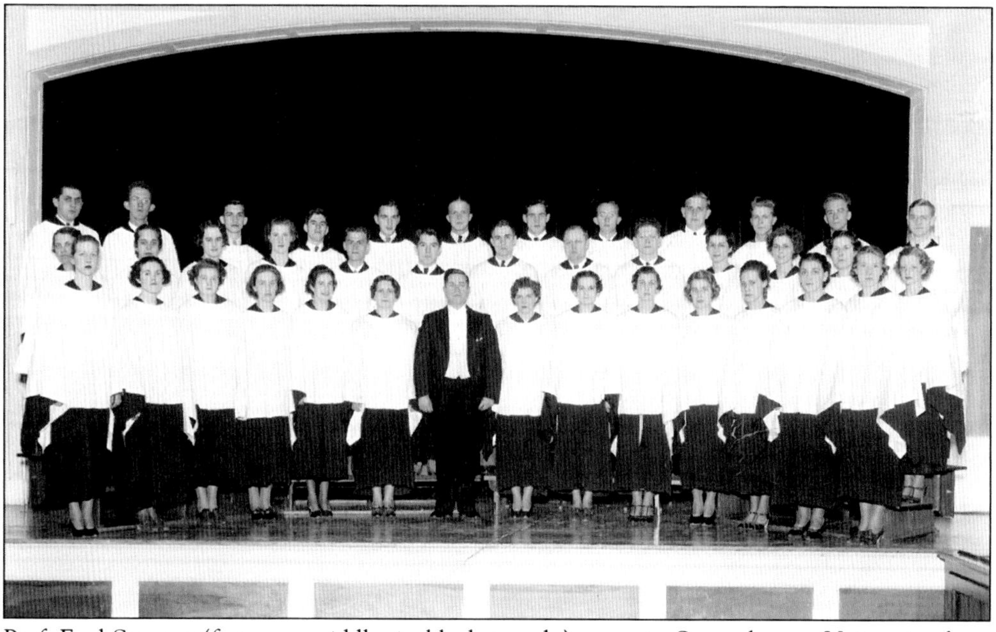

Prof. Fred Stevens (first row, middle, in black tuxedo) came to Susquehanna University from the University of Minnesota in the 1930s to direct the a cappella Motet Choir, first organized in 1933. The choir was so outstanding that they toured near and far. They even appeared on the nationally aired CBS radio network in 1936. This was as big a deal as there was in those pretelevision days. The choir disbanded in 1940, and Stevens became a sociology professor.

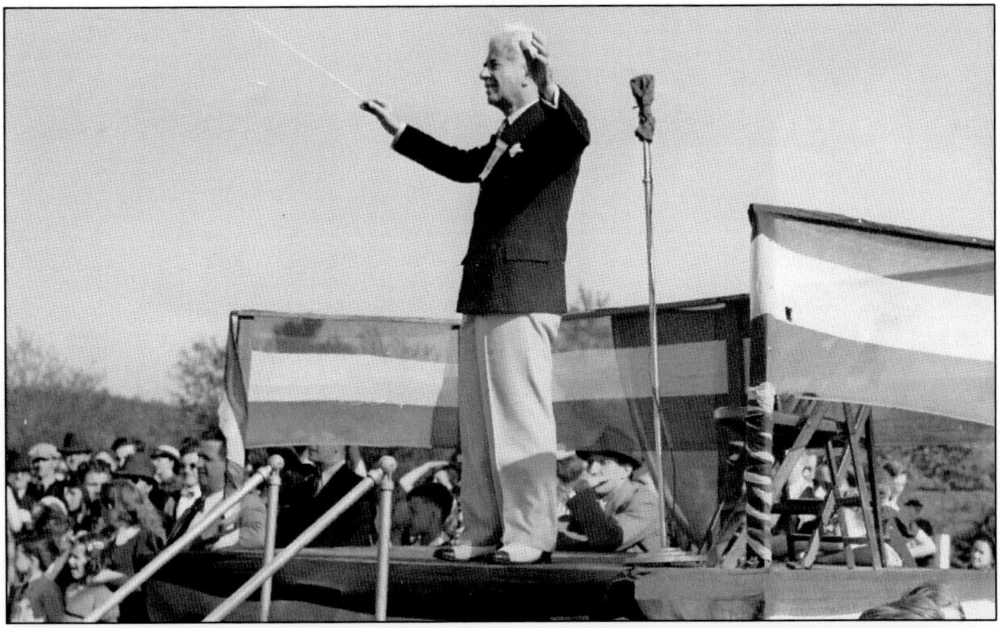

There was a time when the only conductor of band music in the nation bigger than Edwin Franco Goldman might have been John Phillip Sousa. In 1911, Goldman took over leadership of the New York Military Band. It soon became known simply as the Goldman Band. Shown here in 1940, Goldman is directing 500 high school musicians assembled on Susquehanna University's football field. The Goldman influence is still felt on band music today.

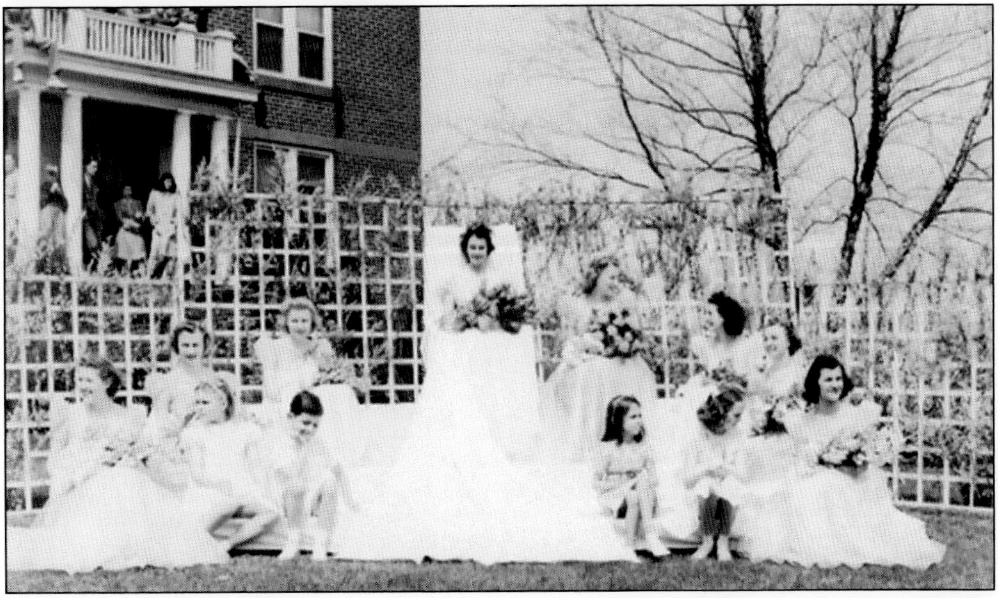

Although Susquehanna May Day celebrations have gone the way of black-and-white television and 34.9¢-per-gallon gasoline, there was a time when students and alumni mixed on campus for the long-standing spring ritual. Even townsfolk, mostly children, joined in. In addition to the queen and eight ladies-in-waiting, this 1940 photograph shows four youngsters in front. The dark-haired boy and girl are Arlan and Joyce Gilbert, son and daughter of Prof. Russell and Viola Gilbert.

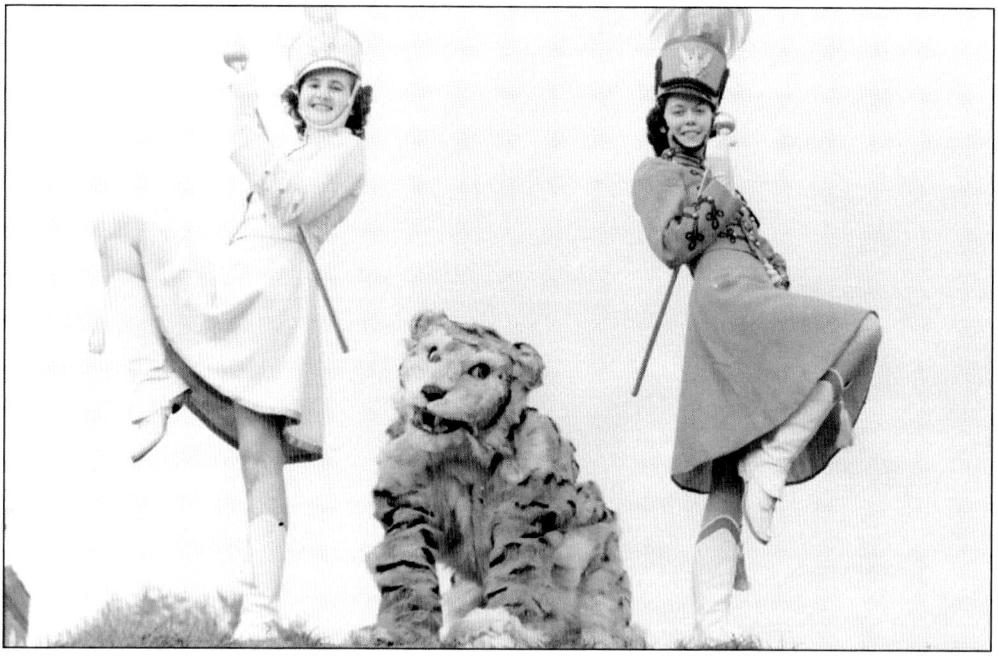

Big news in 1941 was Susquehanna University majorettes Dorothy Paulik (left) and June Hendricks making the national *Illustrated Football Annual* magazine. In barracks bull sessions, Susquehanna University and Selinsgrove servicemen bragged about and showed their hometown girl. June Hendricks spent a considerable amount on postage and stationery answering letters asking for verification that the letter writer and she were, indeed, acquainted. As the wife of Wilmer Hoke, June was a beloved local music teacher for years.

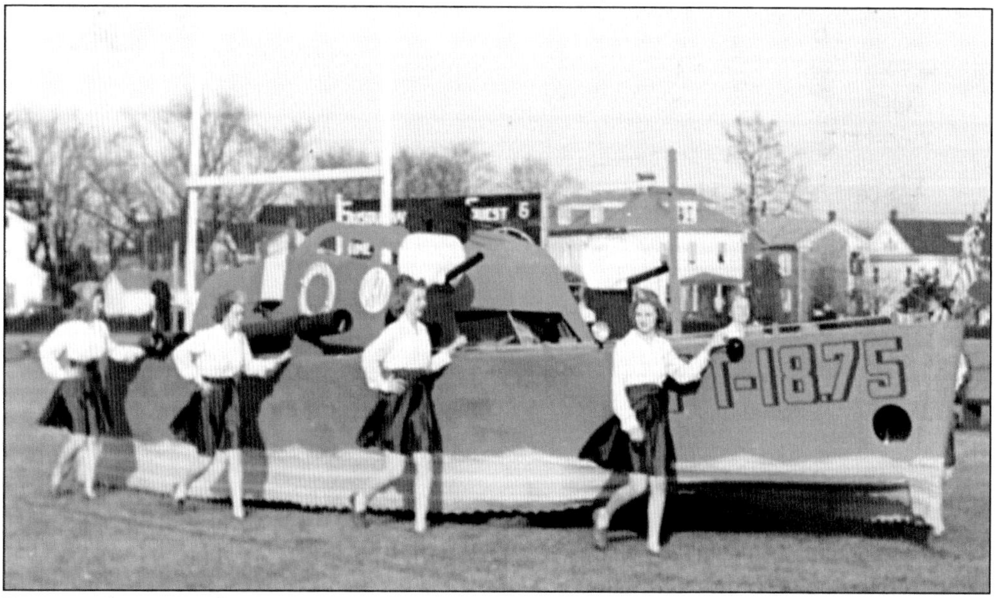

By November 1942, the nation was on a war footing. This was reflected in business and industry and in nearly every other aspect of daily living. Crusaders football games also featured a patriotic theme. Here Susquehanna coeds help propel a float in the form of a PT boat as part of the halftime show.

First, Ted "Dutch" Van Kirk (right) studied at Susquehanna University. During World War II, he became an Army Air Corps navigator and became famous as a crew member of the *Enola Gay* B-29 piloted by Col. Paul Tibbets that dropped the first atomic bomb (code named "Little Boy") on Hiroshima, Japan. This was after Van Kirk completed 58 missions in the European theater. He completed his education on the GI Bill at Bucknell University and chose a career in chemical engineering. He is the last survivor of the *Enola Gay*'s crew.

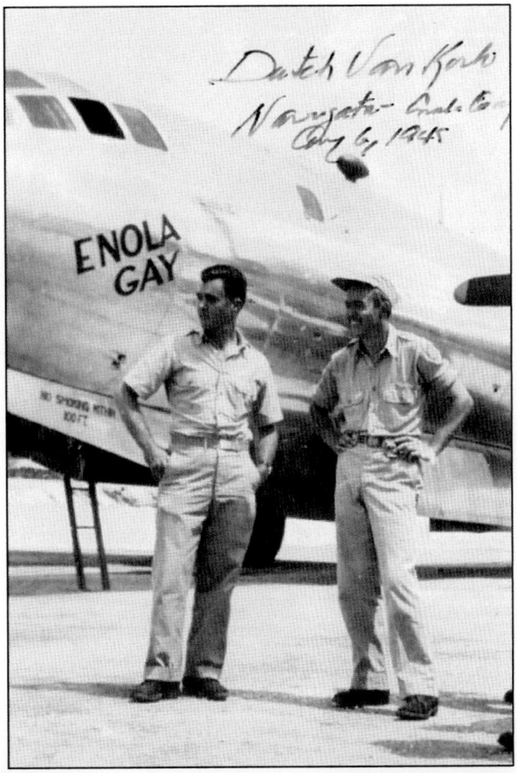

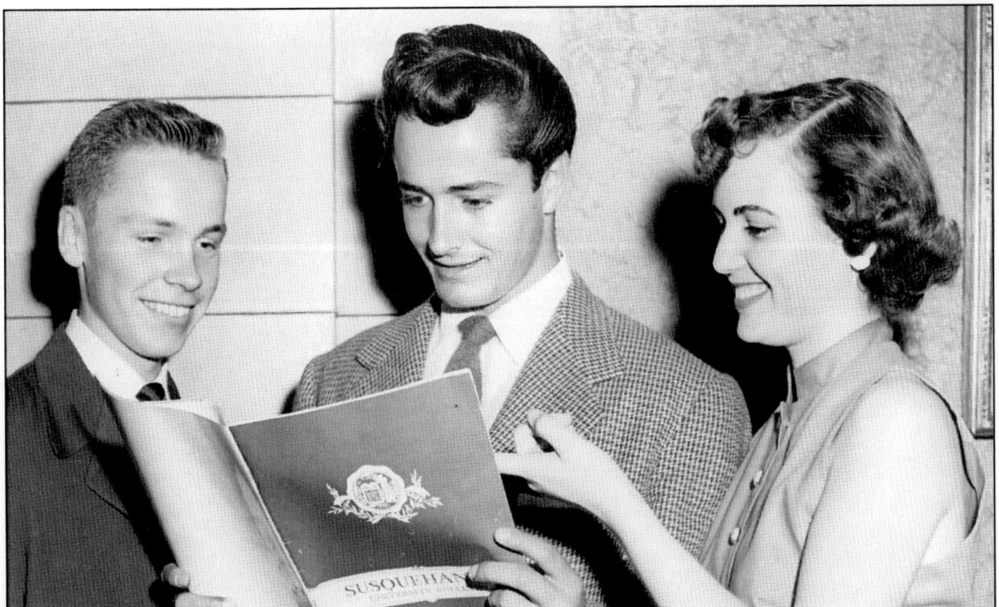

One of his wives became 10-times as famous, but when John Derek visited Susquehanna University's broad campus in 1952 for the dedication of the Benjamin Apple Little Theatre, he was a true Hollywood heartthrob. His movie credits include *All the King's Men*, *Saturday's Hero*, and *The Ten Commandments*. Derek (middle) is pictured with sophomore student thespians Herb Craft and Jayne Daily. Bo Derek was the actor-director's slightly more famous wife.

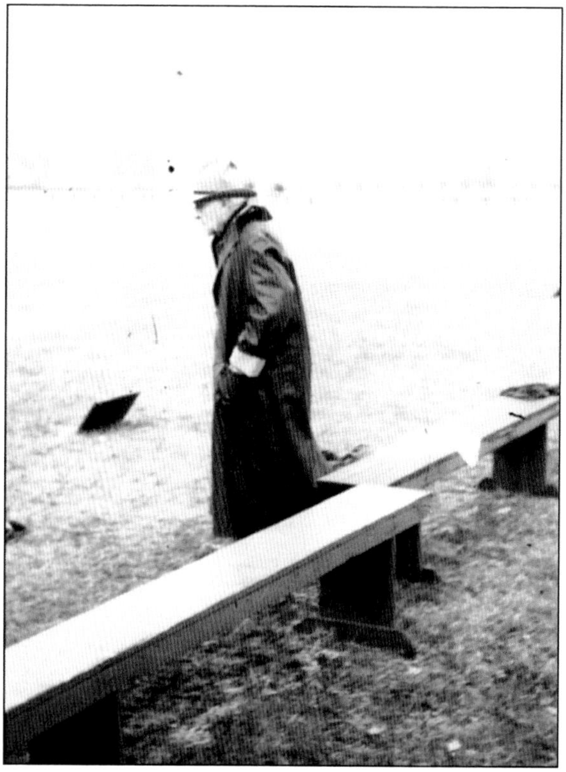

Legend is a word thrown around quite loosely, especially in sports. But nothing better describes "the Grand Old Man of Football," Amos Alonzo Stagg Sr. He co-coached at Susquehanna University with his son Amos Alonzo Jr. from 1947 to 1952. Together, they produced the Crusaders' first unbeaten, untied team in 1951. This poignant snapshot was taken as the elder (90 year old) Stagg left the field, which was later named in his and his son's honor, for the last time on November 15, 1952. Susquehanna University defeated Haverford College 47-14 that day.

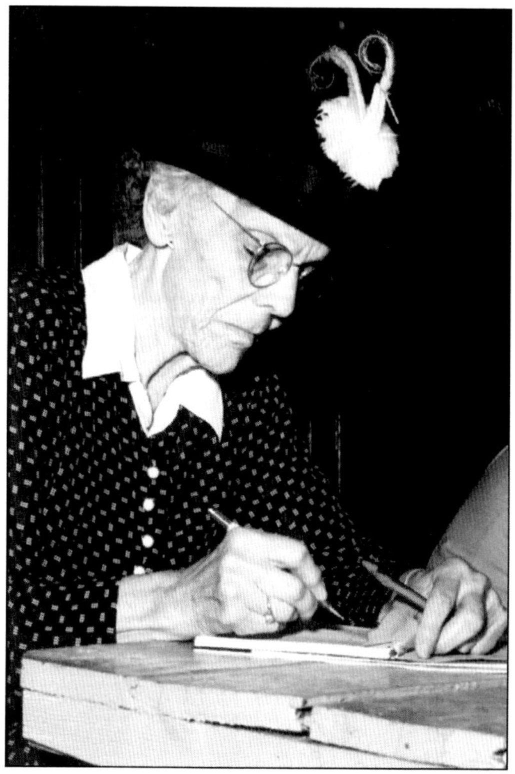

For years, football and other sports' press boxes were off limits to women. An exception was made for Stella Stagg, the wife of immortal coach Amos Alonzo Stagg Sr. He called his wife "the best scout I ever had." Bob Yerger, who later played football at Susquehanna University, recalls seeing the grand old man on Saturday mornings walking his wife to the Greyhound bus stop for her to go scout a future opponent. More than once, her scouting reports produced victory for Susquehanna University.

There's an old song from around the 1930s that advises, "you gotta be a football hero, if you wanna get along with the girls." That apparently was still good advice in 1953. Here Susquehanna University football heroes Jim "Dinger" Dell (90) and Sam Ross (70) provide a platform for head majorette Rose Marie Sharretts, who was also homecoming queen that year. Campus photographer Gene Kolva produced the photograph.

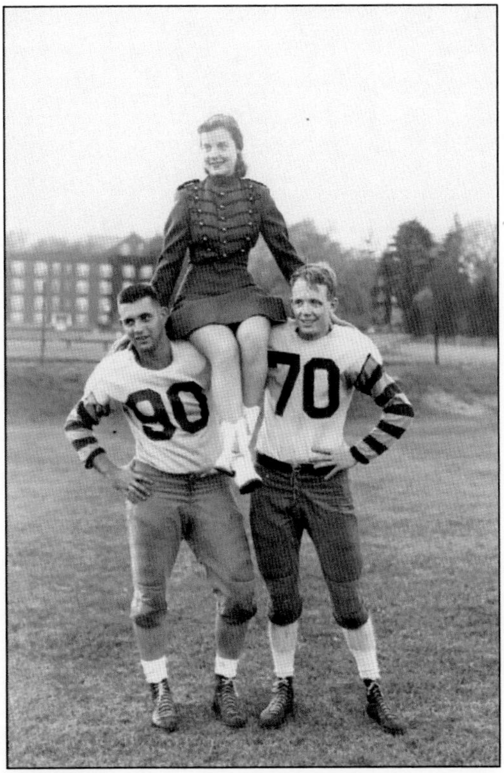

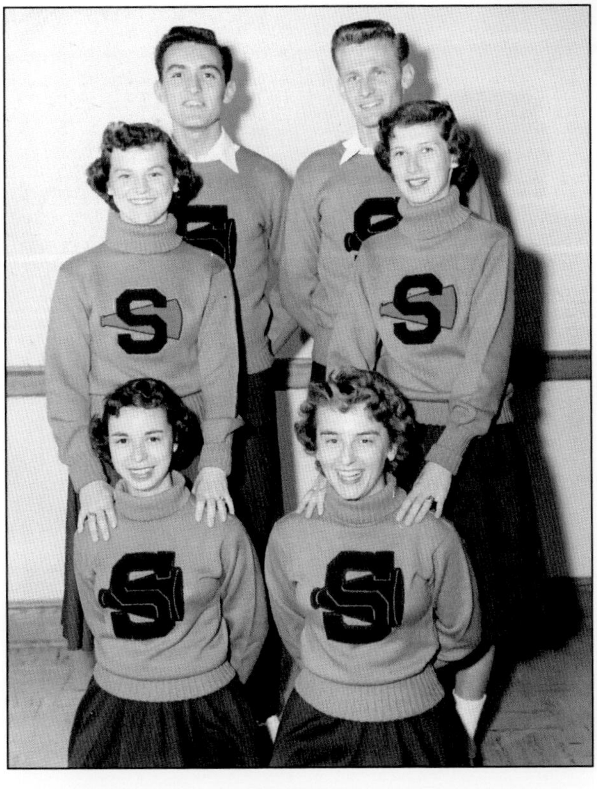

"Back in the day," as is now said, cheerleaders led cheers. Fans knew the cheers and joined the boisterous support of their team. Today the old-fashion cheerleaders have been replaced by what could be called a gymnastics team. In 1955, this group cheered on the Susquehanna University teams. From left to right are (first row) Pat Hess and Janet Laue; (second row) Margie Lamon (a former Selinsgrove High School cheerleader) and Nancy "Toots" Richards; (third row) Walt Albert and Dwight Keener.

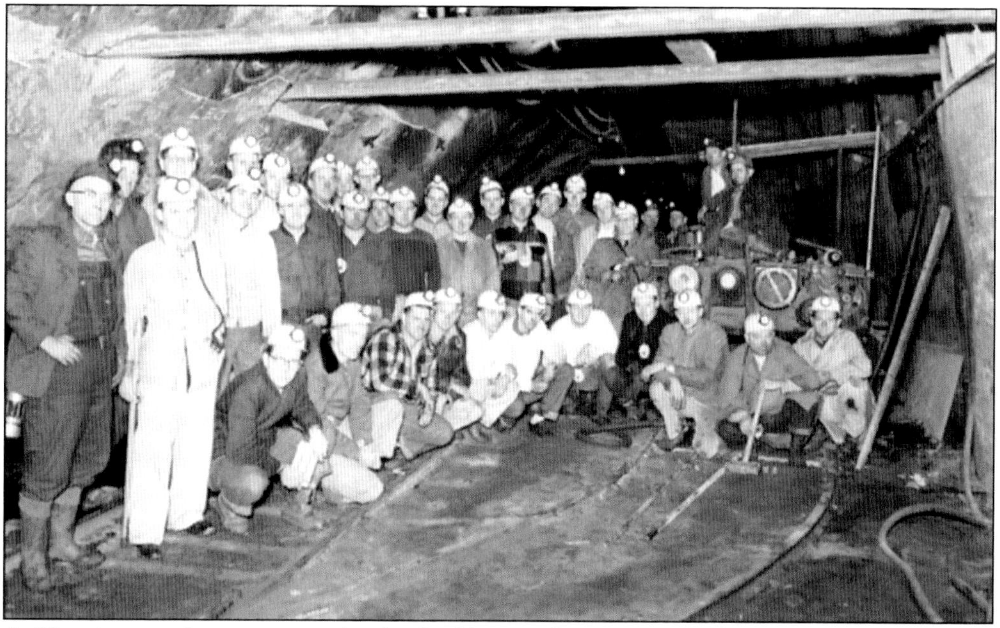

A liberal arts education is truly the backbone of America's higher-education system. At Susquehanna University, it was not all book learning and classroom recitation. On April 7, 1953, a sociology class visited the Locust Gap Colliery near Ashland. Students and miners are shown 520-feet deep in the Anthracite mine. It is said that no student wanted to trade places with the miners.

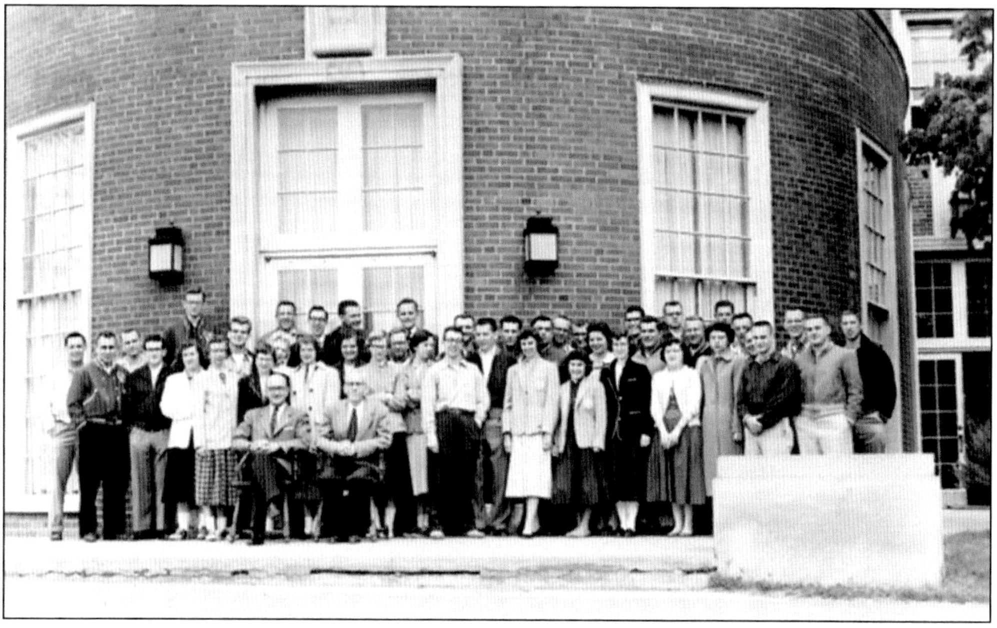

Here is another great example of town and gown relations. On May 4, 1957, history professor Dr. William Russ invited former Selinsgrove burgess and then-state assemblyman Harvey P. Murray Sr. to address a class on local and state government. After class, Murray (seated left) and Russ (seated right) posed with class members outside of Susquehanna University's Benjamin Apple Little Theatre.

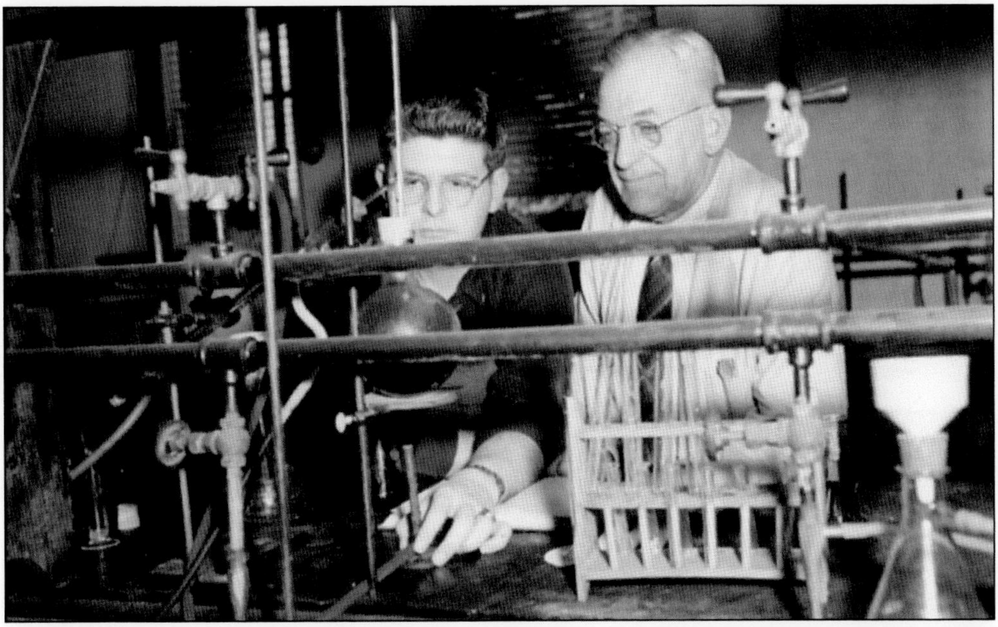

The rich teaching tradition at Susquehanna University is highlighted by professors who come to campus and stay for decades. One such instructor was Dr. John J. Houtz Jr. (right), who taught chemistry in a hands-on manner for years. He was the son of revered professor Dr. John J. "Pappy" Houtz Sr. and a contemporary of such faculty stalwarts as professors Russell Gilbert, William Russ, William Ahl, Arthur Wilson, George Fisher, and others.

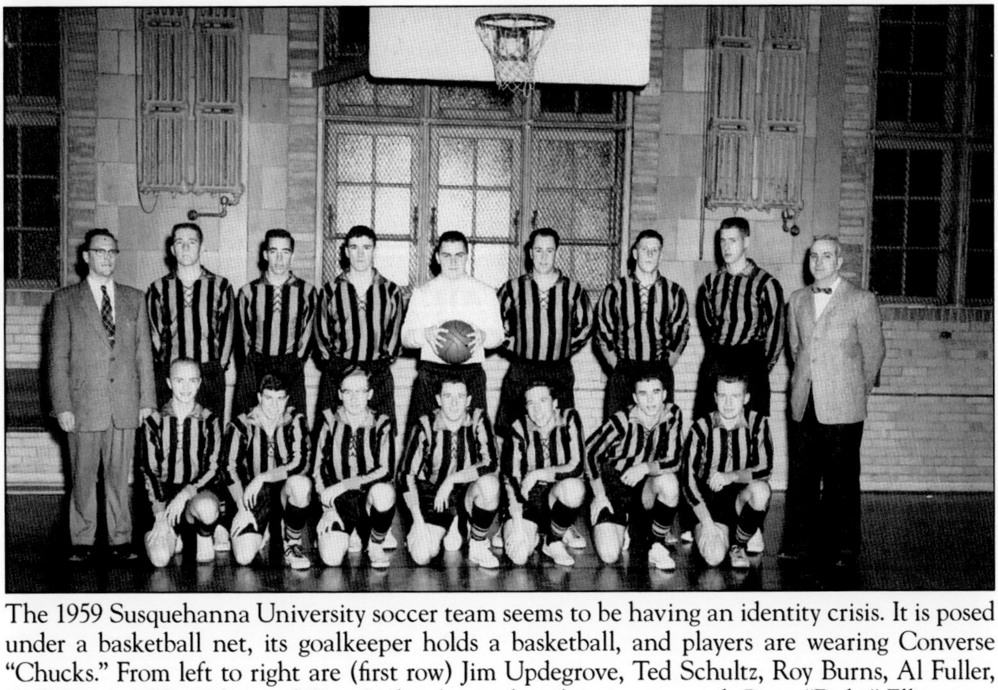

The 1959 Susquehanna University soccer team seems to be having an identity crisis. It is posed under a basketball net, its goalkeeper holds a basketball, and players are wearing Converse "Chucks." From left to right are (first row) Jim Updegrove, Ted Schultz, Roy Burns, Al Fuller, Dick Rowe, Mike Yohe, and Tom Leiby; (second row) assistant coach Peter "Duke" Elkington, Bob Williams, Dan Snyder, Alan Kiel, Frank Yaggi, Lenny Purcell, Bob McKee, Wes Hunt, and head coach Bill Heim.

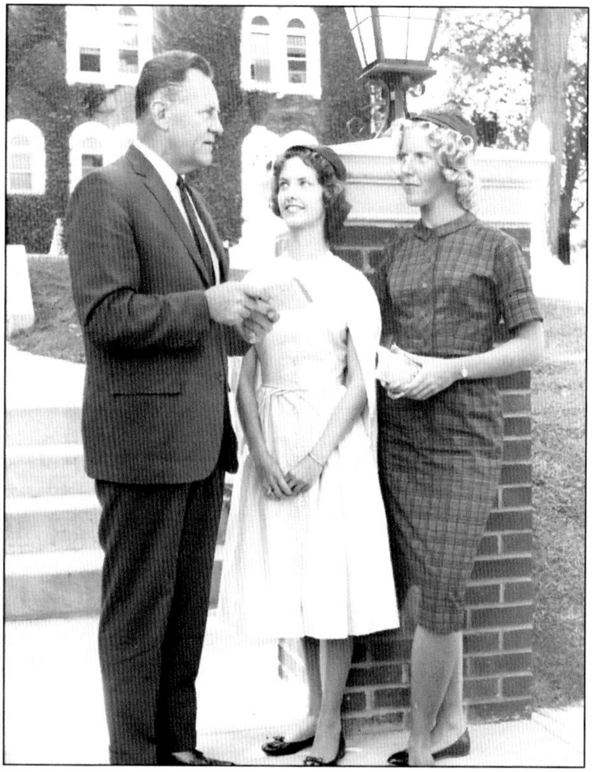

Many Susquehanna University alumni, the author included, feel that if Dr. Gustave W. Weber had not come to campus when he did, there would be no Susquehanna University today. When Weber arrived in January 1959, he brought a vision and expansionist ideas and quickly implemented them. Here he is shown with beanie wearing, handbook toting first-year students Cindy Peterson (left) and Judy Rothermel during orientation week, 1960.

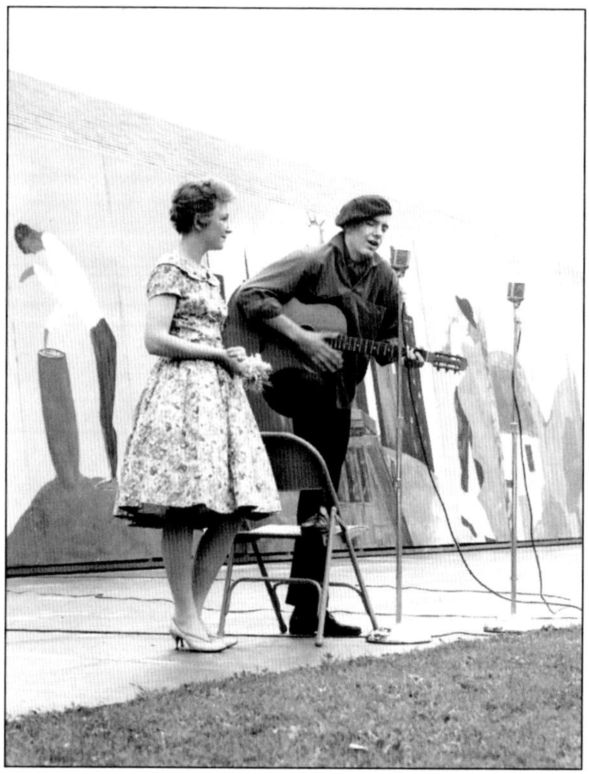

May Day is no longer celebrated at Susquehanna University, but it was still a pretty big deal in 1960. The coronation of the May queen was the highlight, and this year it was Millie Barabas, but entertainment was also a feature. Here students Francois Engel (right), a native of France, and multilingual Lynn Vekassy provide an international flair to the musical events of the day.

Shown in a snappy 1960 Chevrolet convertible is Susquehanna University's sophomore homecoming representative, Jane Beers. The little girls riding with her are the daughters of Bob and Peggy McFall of Selinsgrove, Pat (left) and Pam (right). The popular Jane Beers won about every campus election possible—homecoming representative, homecoming queen, class officer, May court representative, May queen, student council member, and business society officer.

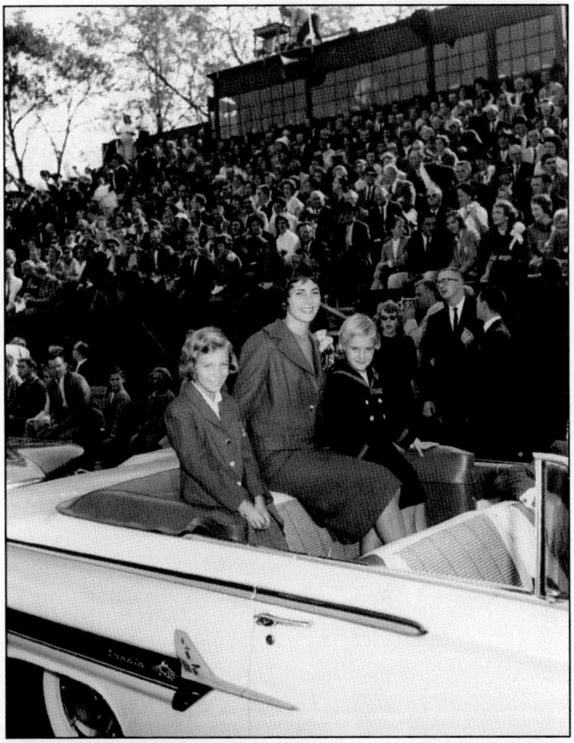

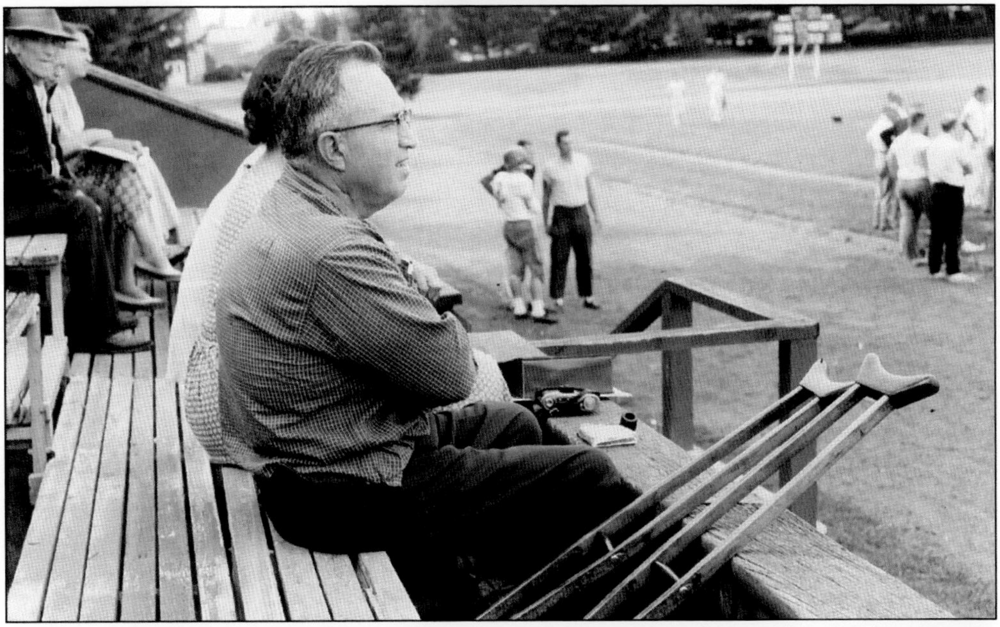

H. Vernon Blough '31 used crutches to get around longer than he could remember. But get around he did. He once looked at them and told a campus visitor, "Yep, my buddies here [as he patted them affectionately] and I didn't miss much." Very active as a student at Susquehanna University, he remained on campus after graduation and filled what today is known as the public relations and sports information director's positions. Here, he and his wife, Marie (obscured), watch a 1960 football practice.

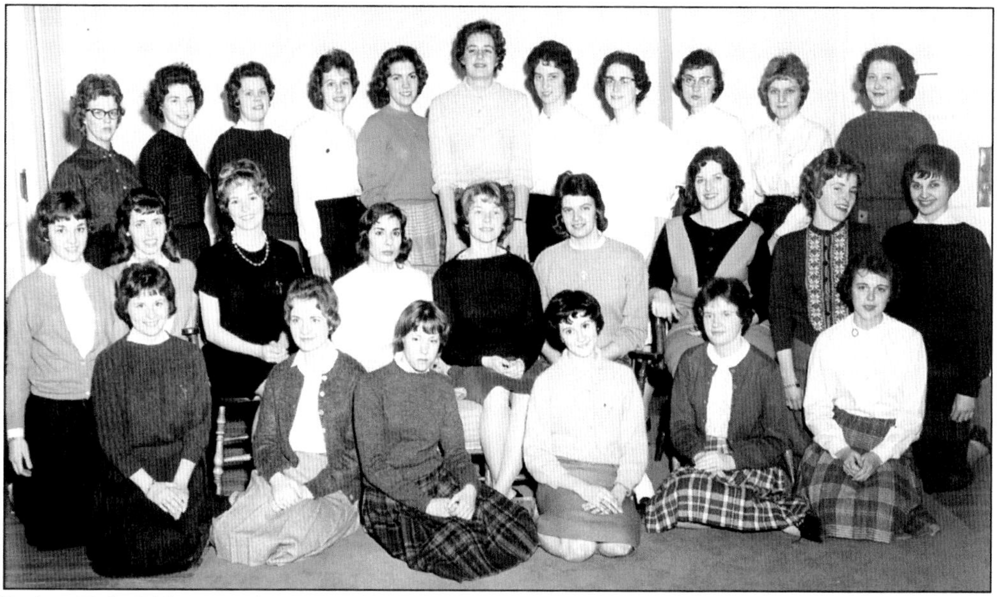

Before Title IX became law in 1972, opportunities for women were limited to field hockey and basketball. Pictured is the 1961 Women's Athletic Association at Susquehanna University. From left to right are (first row) J. Weathered, P. Stamps, M. Brown, S. Myers, S. Martin, and D. Pederson; (second row) J. Brndjar, B. Jordan, A. Hewes, P. Goetz, E. Turner, J. Lawley, N. Davis, J. Behrens, and J. Haefle; (third row) A. Ostheim, G. Kratz, M. Wernikowski, T. Brodisch, A. Riessmeyer, J. Ewald, J. Kump, P. Terry, A. Ferrence, L. Traub, and P. Sewell.

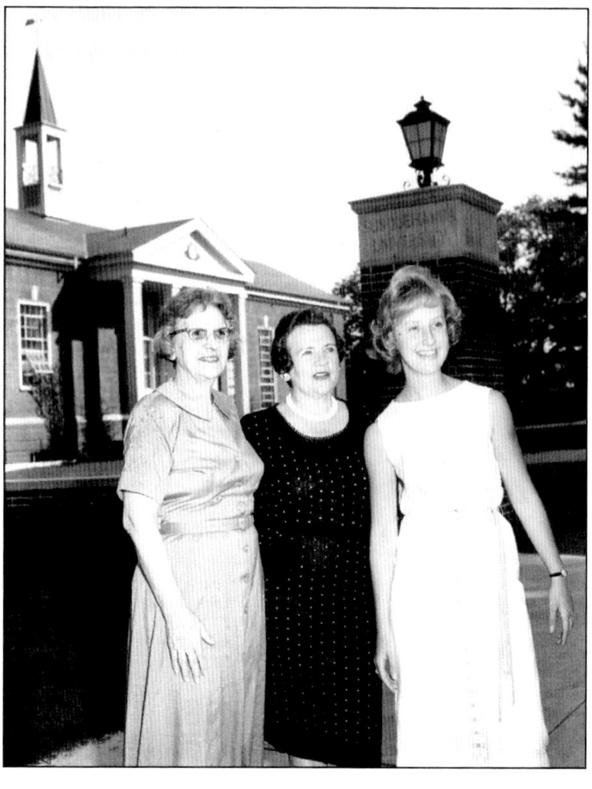

Attending Susquehanna University is a generational thing. Students arrive on campus, following in the footsteps of parents, grandparents, and, perhaps, great-grandparents. Three generations of the Phillips family of Selinsgrove are represented here. From left to right are Aberdeen Phillips '15, Marjorie Phillips Mitchell '33, and Barbara Adams '65. The photograph was taken in 1961, Adams's first year on campus. Through the years, dozens of Phillipses have become Susquehanna University alumni.

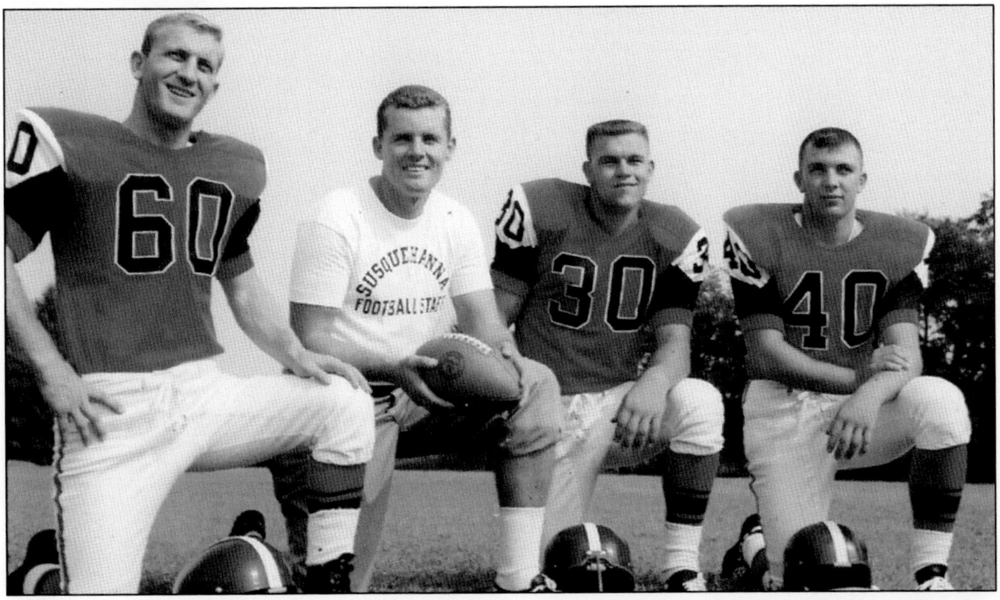

Henry "Whitey" Keil returned winning football to Susquehanna University in the 1950s, but in the 1960s Jim Garrett put the Crusaders in the top echelon of small-college football, as Division III was then known. From left to right, three stalwarts of the 1960s teams are Ben DiFrancesco (60), pound-for-pound Susquehanna University's best-ever lineman; Garrett; Larry Kerstetter (30), a powerhouse fullback; and Terry Kissinger, a versatile halfback. All are hall of famers. Kerstetter and Kissinger played at Selinsgrove High School.

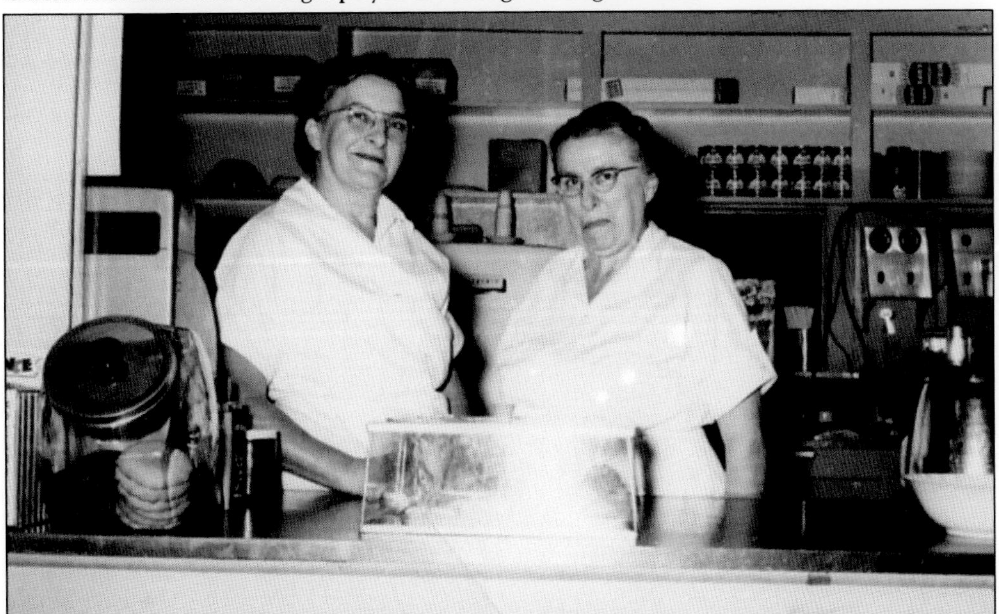

Long before the Degenstein Campus Center was a reality, the gathering place for Susquehanna University students was the snack bar in Gustavus Adolphus Hall (GA). One of those staffing the student union was Selinsgrove resident Mildred Gemberling (left). Her coworker is unidentified. Even before GA burned in November 1964, a series of vending machines replaced the human touch.

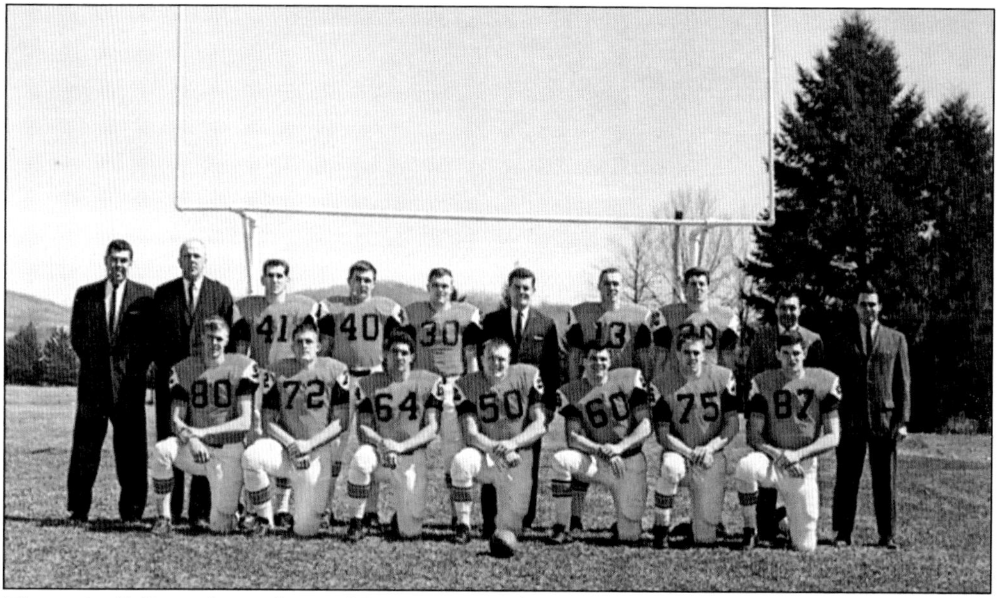

The early 1960s at Susquehanna University was the golden era. Under coach Jim Garrett, the Crusaders compiled a 39-4-1 record. Arguably the most important victory was a road win over Temple University on November 16, 1963. Larry Erdman's late 77-yard dash sealed the 22-18 verdict. From left to right, the 1963 first stringers are (first row) J. Gibney, B. Muir, R. Caruso, J. Rowlands, J. Garrett, D. Revak, and M. Rupprecht; (second row) B. Windish, D. Sekanovich, L. Erdman, T. Kissinger, L. Kerstetter, J. Garrett, D. Green, J. Vignone, B. Pittello, and J. Gannon.

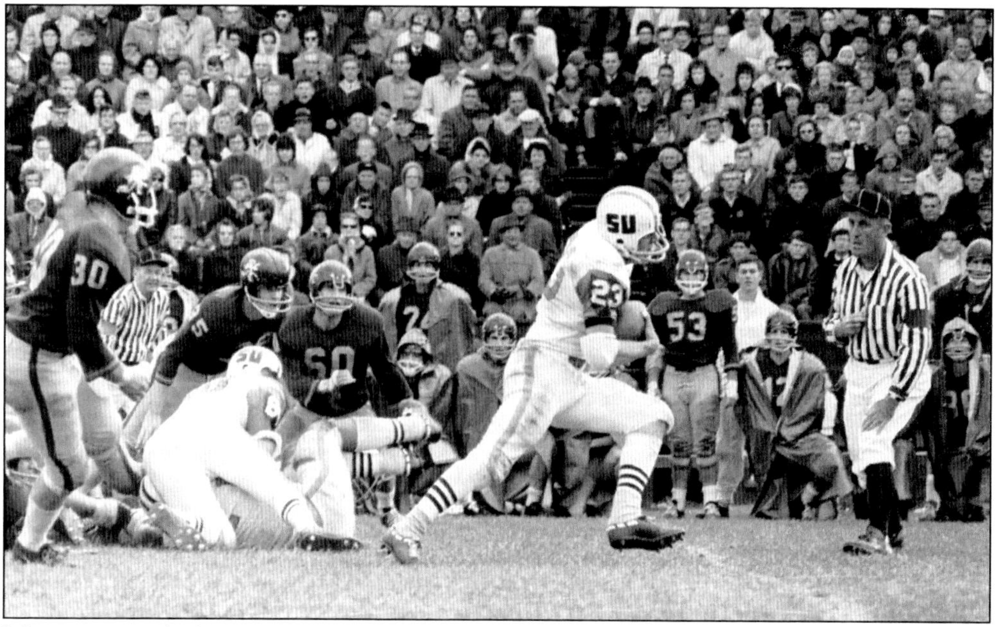

John Vignone (23) is a member of Susquehanna University's sports hall of fame. He played professional football and baseball and was good enough to be a Crusaders basketball cocaptain. As a two-way halfback, he piled up yardage on offense and intercepted enough passes on defense to hold the career record for decades. His pickoff of a Temple University pass preserved the historic 22-18 victory for Susquehanna University. This free-range run is from the 1964 season.

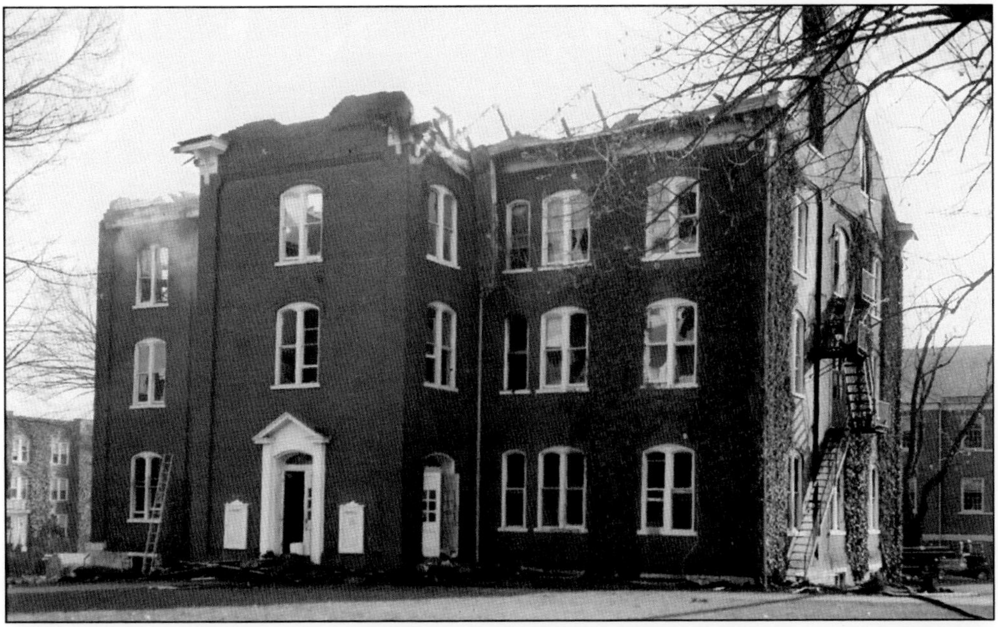

GA was built in 1895, the year Susquehanna University became coed—one of a relatively few such colleges in the nation at the time. It remained an important building until a crisp November night in 1964 when it was destroyed by fire. A multipurpose building, to use a present-day term, it housed two floors of dormitories, the mail room, a lounge, a snack bar, a day-students' room, and the bookstore. It was never rebuilt.

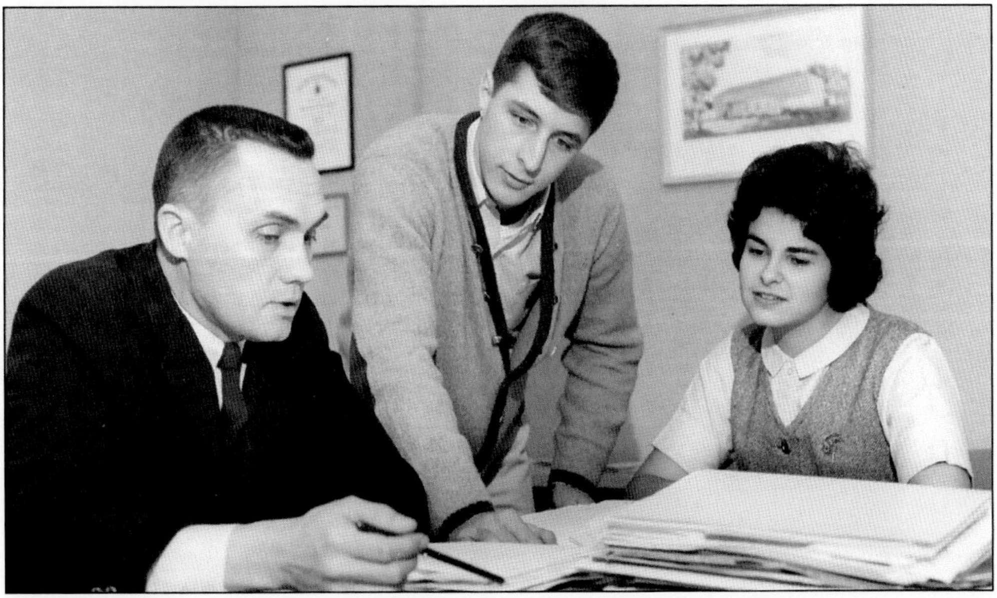

Like many Susquehanna University staffers of president Gustave (Gus) Weber's administration (1959–1977), George R. F. Tamke (left) came early and stayed late. He left the university in the late 1980s. Tom Dodge, Charles "Buss" Carr, and Dottie Anderson are others who come to mind. Tamke held the title of assistant to the president, but public relations was his forte. His efforts to publicize and promote Susquehanna University were cutting edge. He is shown in 1964 with students Art Bowen and Janet Clark.

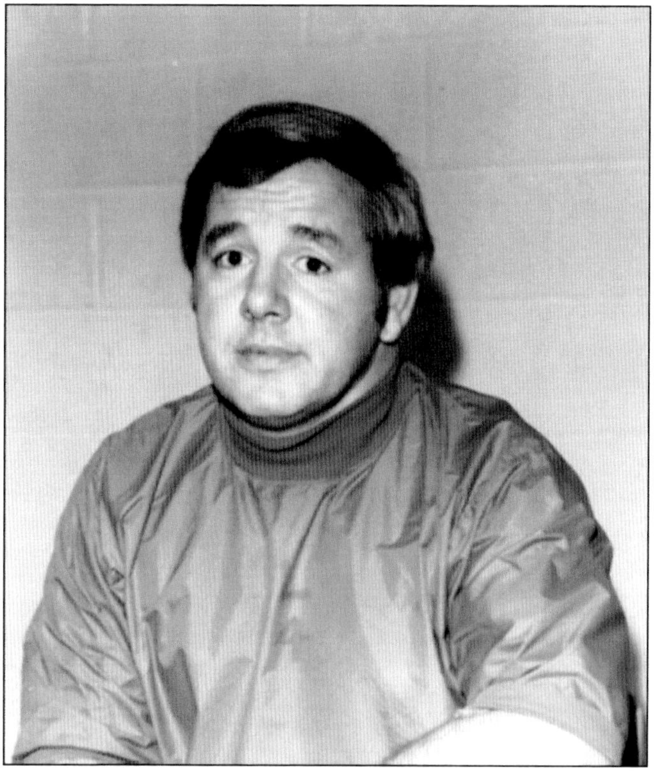

Selinsgrove residents, who doubled as coaches at Susquehanna University, helped to cement town and gown relations—as the symbiotic cooperation between the community and campus is sometimes called. Bill Boynton was an executive for Allied Marine Products, better known locally as AMP. His other role was assisting Charlie Kunes with Crusaders wrestling. Boynton brought dedication, skill, and leadership to the position in the late 1960s and early 1970s.

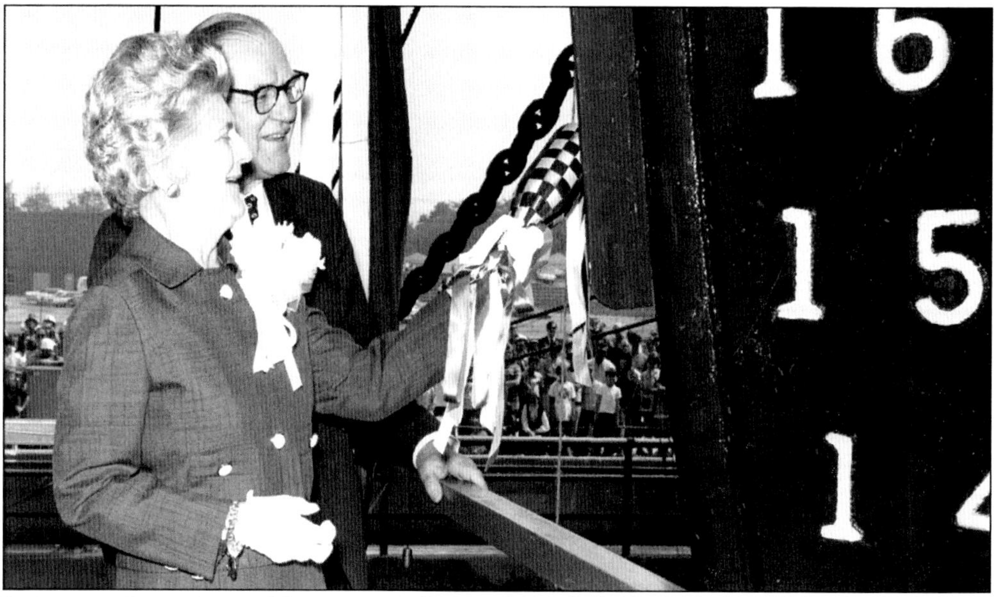

Perhaps no Susquehanna University graduate achieved a higher standing in the business world than Roger M. Blough '25. He rose to be U.S. Steel's chairman of the board and gained national attention in 1962 when he defied Pres. John F. Kennedy over steel prices. Blough looks on as his wife, Helen, christens a U.S. Steel Great Lakes 858-foot ore boat, the *Roger M. Blough*, at Cleveland on June 15, 1972. Blough was further honored when his alma mater named the campus library for him.

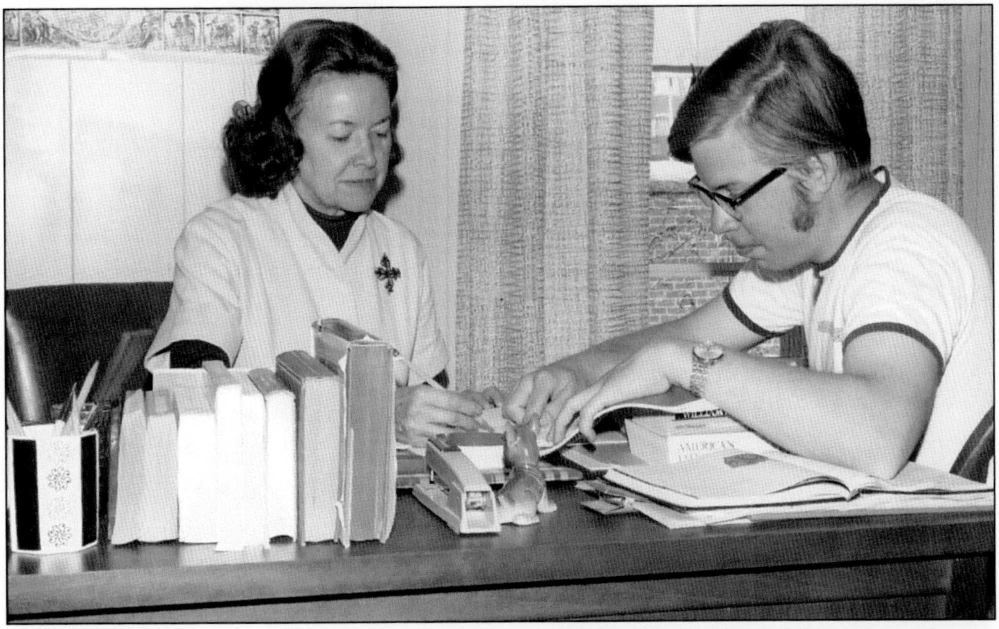

Saturday, May 22, 1943, was a big day for Marjorie Wolfe. She graduated from Susquehanna University and got married later that day to the Reverend John McCune '37. She subsequently earned advanced degrees and returned to her alma mater as a knowledgeable and interesting literature professor. She is pictured counseling a student in American literature during the 1977–1978 academic year.

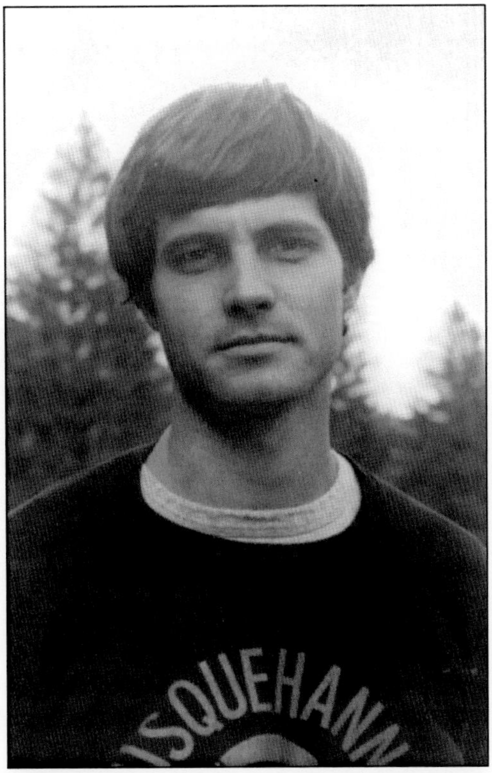

Jim Aurand of Middleburg was the head soccer coach at Susquehanna University from 1980 to 1982. He brought Steve Steffen (shown) to campus as an assistant. Steffen eventually left the university to inaugurate the soccer program at Selinsgrove High School and make it a perennial power. However, Steffen died much too young. The high school coaching torch has been successfully passed to Chris Lupolt, a Susquehanna University player and graduate.

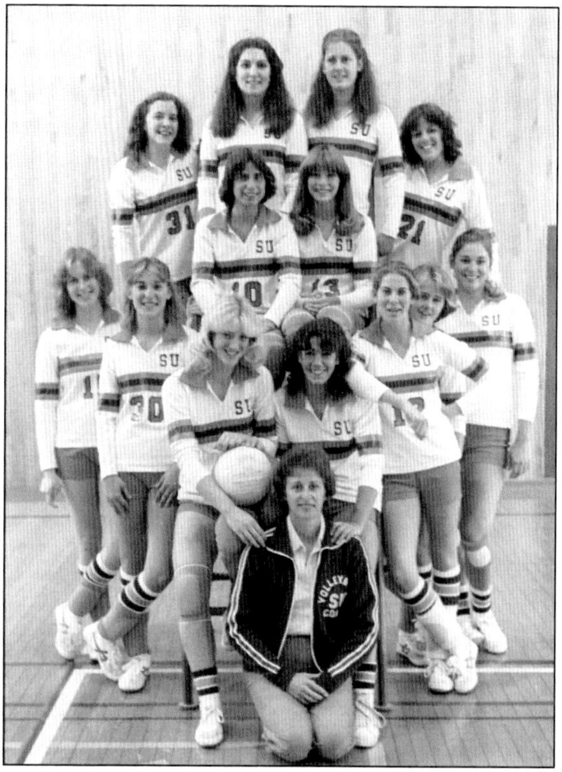

With the coming of Title IX in 1972, Susquehanna University's women's athletics program moved well beyond field hockey and basketball. One of the dozen or so women's sports added to the menu was volleyball. Pat Rieland (kneeling), now the wife of Dick Hess, is shown with her spikers and setters during the 1980 season. Both Pat and Dick are competitive racewalkers.

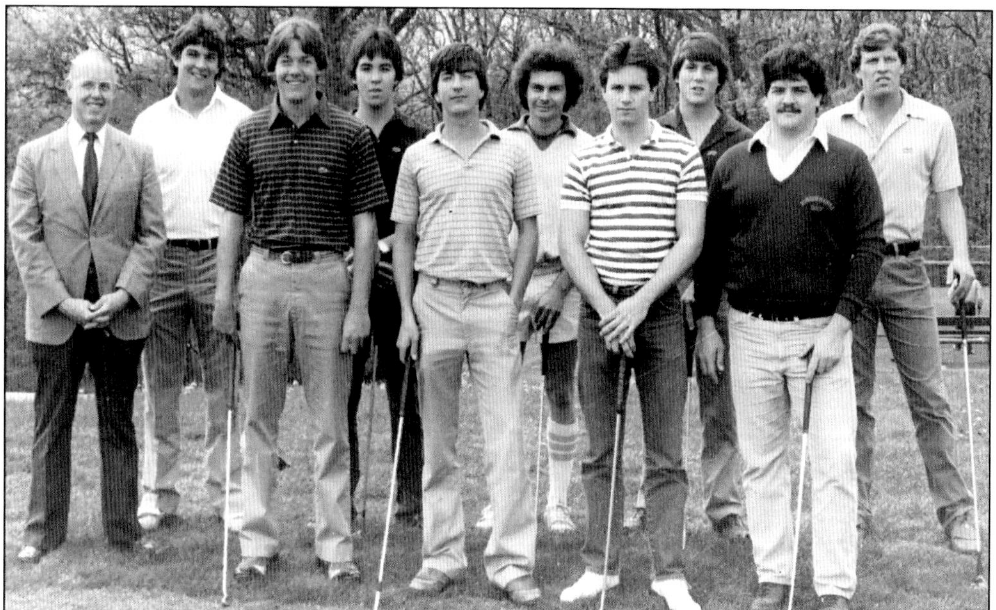

Charles "Buss" Carr (extreme left) is a unique figure in Susquehanna University's storied past. A rarity as a music major who earned letters in football, he served two decades as director of alumni relations. He also coached the Crusaders' men's golf team. A Mid-Atlantic Conference title under Carr's tutelage was not an extraordinary event. His teams earned many. One of his golfers on the 1983 squad is Bob Bertram (third from the left), a Selinsgrove High School product.

Five

THE SUBURBS

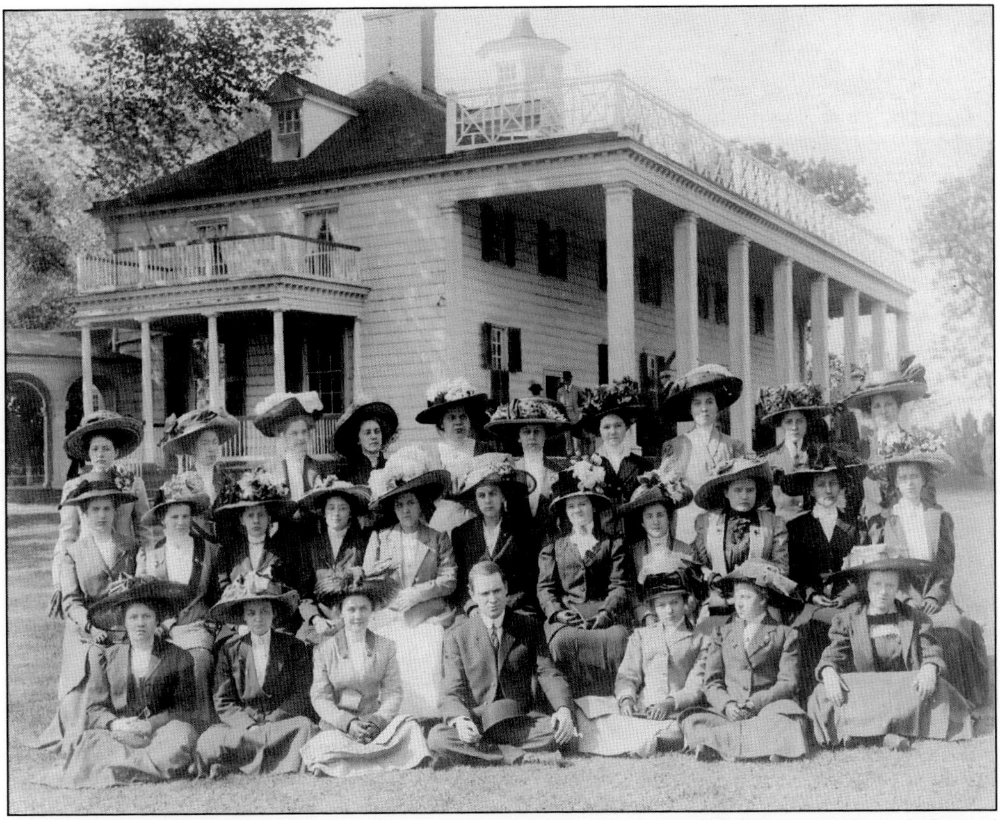

In 1910, not many men went to college, and even fewer women did. However, these behatted young ladies made the trip on Friday, May 6, to Mount Vernon from the Mechanicsburg campus of Irving College. Named after author Washington Irving, the all-girls school existed from 1858 to 1929 and was the first Lutheran college to grant degrees to women. Ella Rine, (second row, second from the left) of a prominent McKees Half Falls family, is shown with her fellow students.

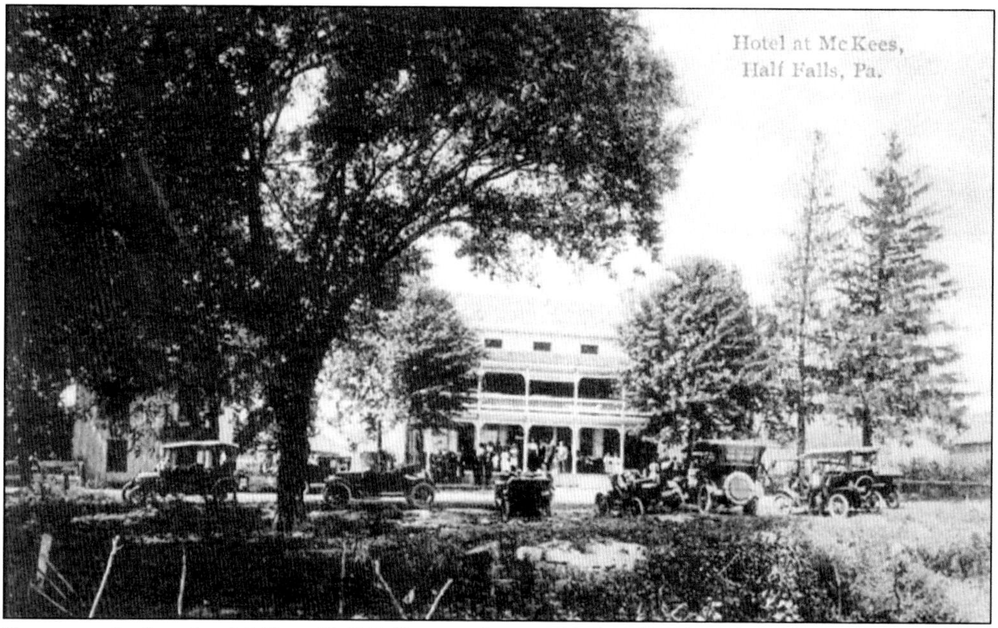

For years, the hotel at McKees Half Falls was a hospitable landmark. While this postcard plainly notes the location, no hint is given to the event that is taking place there. Judging from the people on the veranda and automobiles, it must have been a gala—perhaps a summer wedding. The many automobiles appear to be models from the post–World War I era. Later the building became a residence, occupied by Bill Rine, proprietor of the Hoffer store.

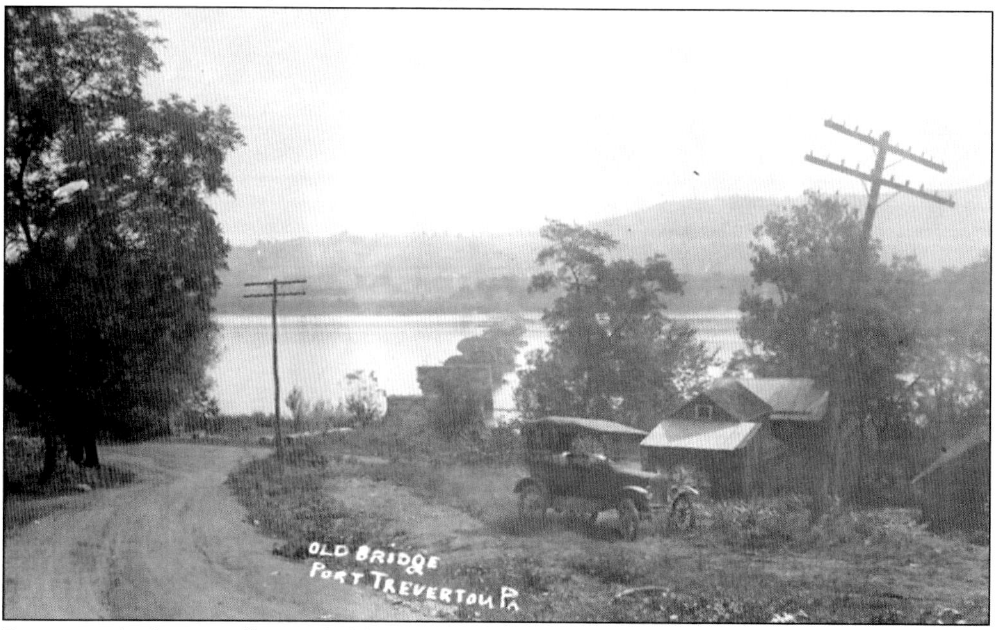

For years, the historically minded have searched for a picture of the bridge that allowed coal trains to bring black gold from the Anthracite region across the Susquehanna River to be shipped on from Port Trevorton. A spark from a locomotive is thought to have caused the fire that destroyed the covered span, which was only in use a short time, between 1890 and 1895. This real-photo postcard shows only the sturdy stone piers; they are still there today.

The jointure agreement that made Selinsgrove an area school district instead of a local one took effect in 1953. That summer, Charlie Fasold took photographs of all 25 rural one-room schools that were no longer needed. Shown is the Port Trevorton school—a rarity in that it is a two-story building, which was located right in town on Main Street close to where the Port Trevorton Volunteer Fire Company now stands.

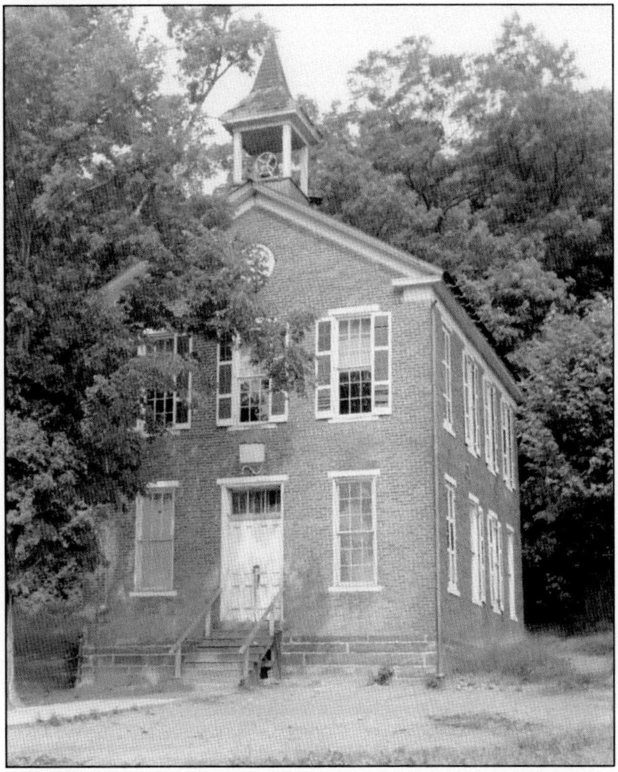

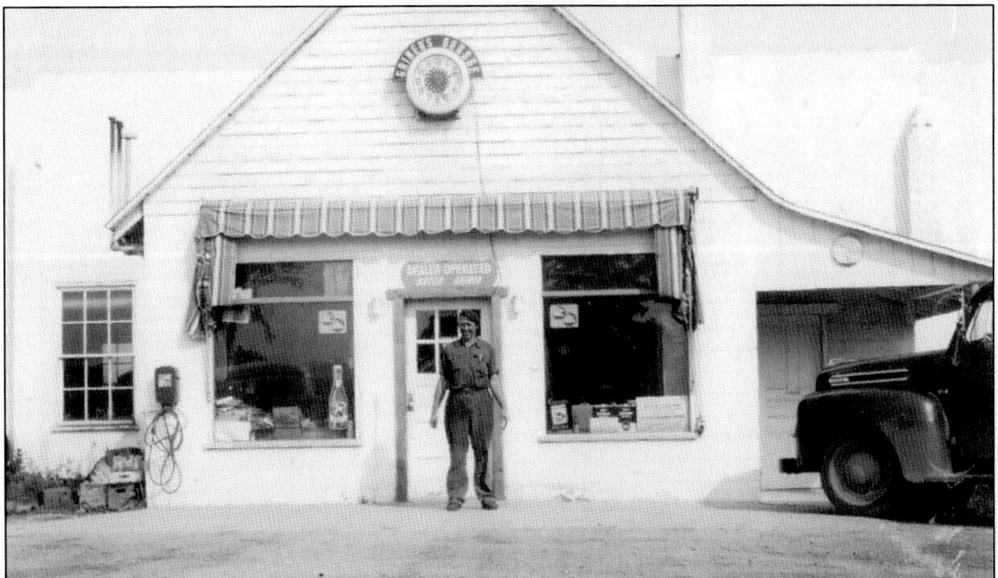

At one time, there were many service stations that were owned and operated by men who grew up under Fords, Chevrolets, Plymouths, and the many other short-lived makes of automobiles. One of these men was "Dutch" Griner. Griner, standing proudly in the doorway of his dealer-operated Gulf station around 1960, which was located on Routes 11 and 15 between Sheetz's and Wal-Mart, was one of those "who could fix anything on wheels."

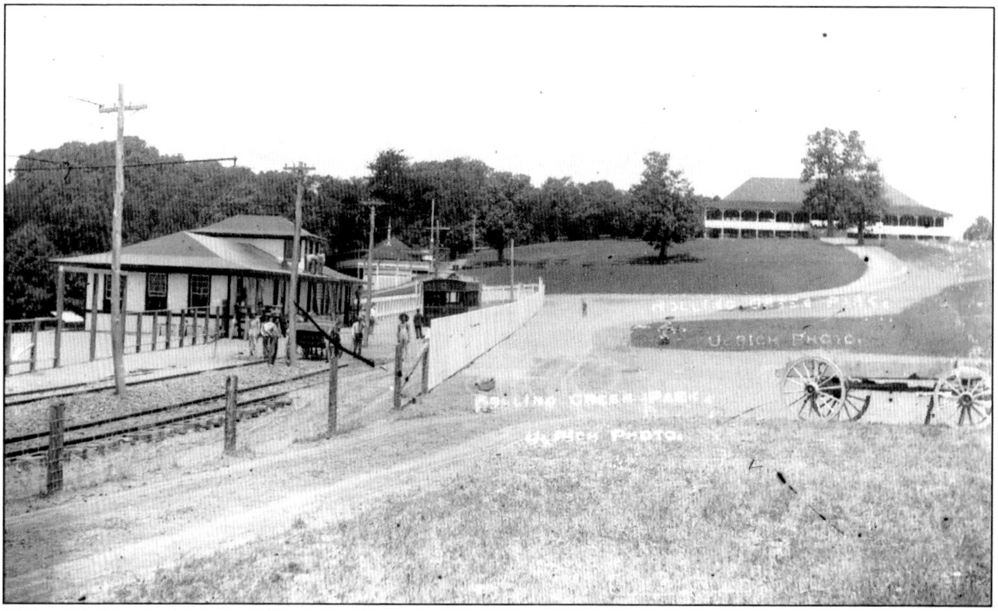

When Rolling Green Park opened on Saturday, August 25, 1908, on acreage purchased from Phillip Teats for $49,841.66, it was done to promote travel on the S&S trolley line. The thinking was that the amusement park at the halfway point, Hummels Wharf, would be a drawing card. The thinking was right on target. This R. L. Ulrich photograph was taken in the park's earliest years.

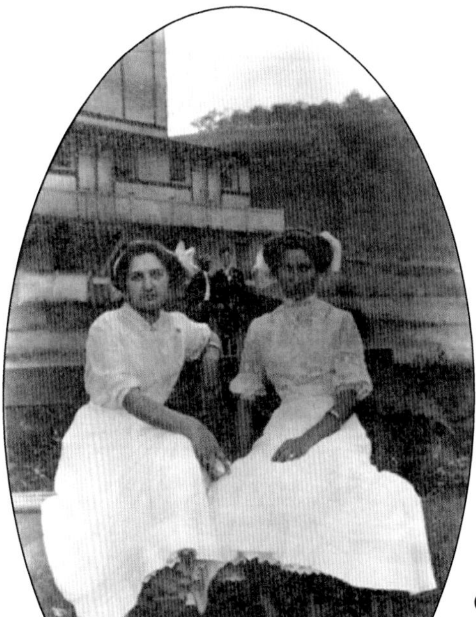

After this 1911 real-photo postcard of two comely lassies posing in front of the theater at Rolling Green in the early days of the park was published, Ray Conrad informed the author that they were his grandmother and great-aunt. They are Claire Shamory (left) and her sister Hazel Shamory. Their parents were Adam and Amanda Shamory. Adam was Snyder County commissioner when the Camelback bridge was built over Penn's Creek near Selinsgrove in 1919.

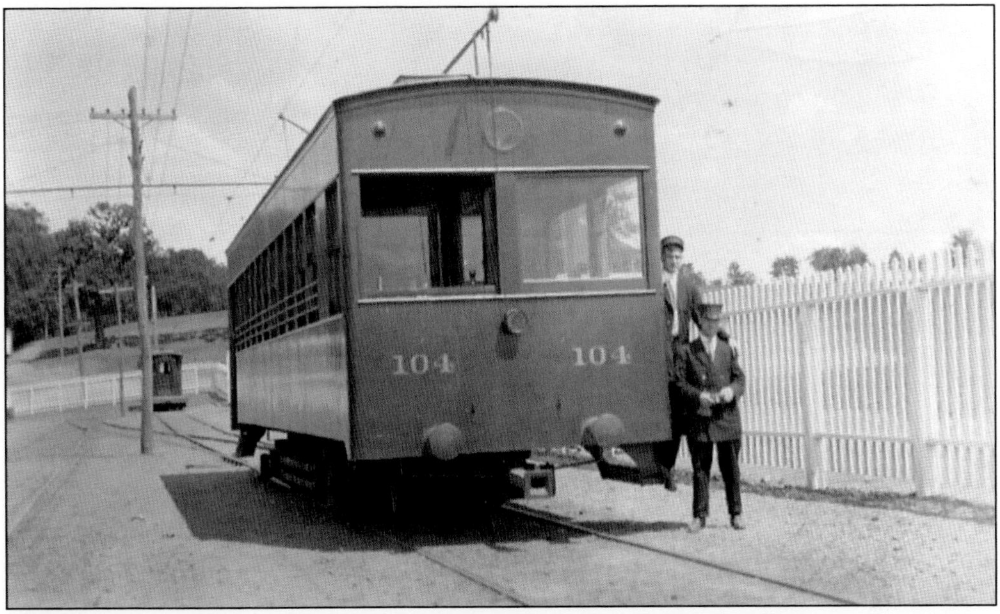

In the early days of Rolling Green Park, "the Peoples' Playground" and trolleys were synonymous. This real-photo postcard depicts the second iteration of trolley cars. The first cars of the S&S trolley line were open, purchased from the Baltimore United Railway and Electric Company. The pictured car, put in service about 1920, was manufactured by the Cincinnati Car Company.

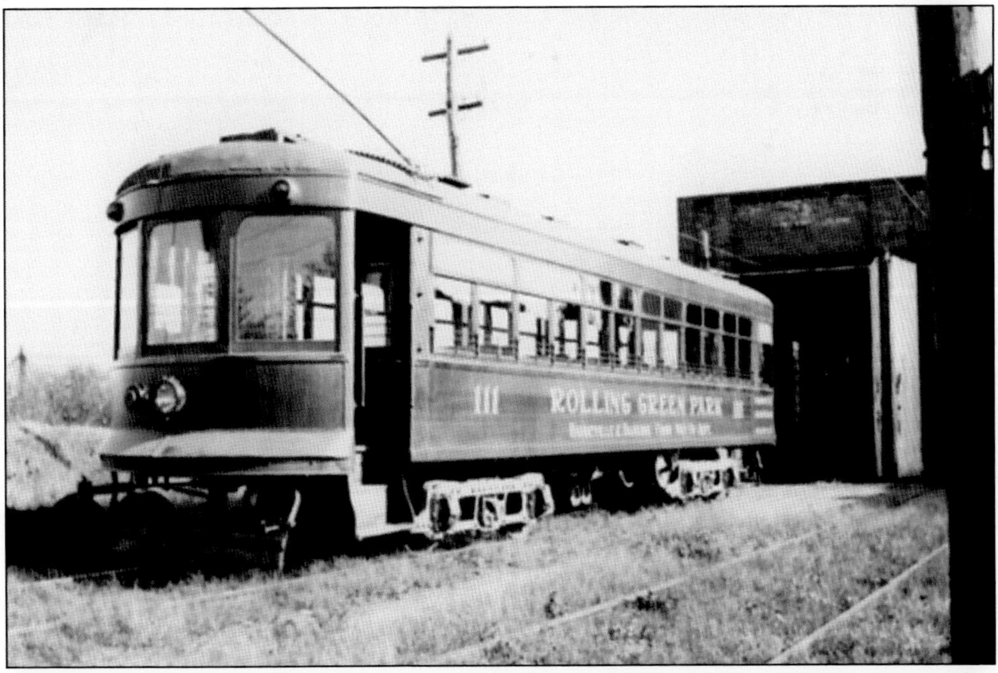

When business on the S&S trolley line needed a shot in the arm back in 1908, the powers that be came up with the idea of Rolling Green Park. It proved to be a wise move over the years. Paying passengers rode the line, especially on weekends. Car No. 111 (shown) and two others like it—No. 112 and No. 113—were in operation by 1922. Emblazoned on the side was "Rolling Green Park—vaudeville and dancing from May to September."

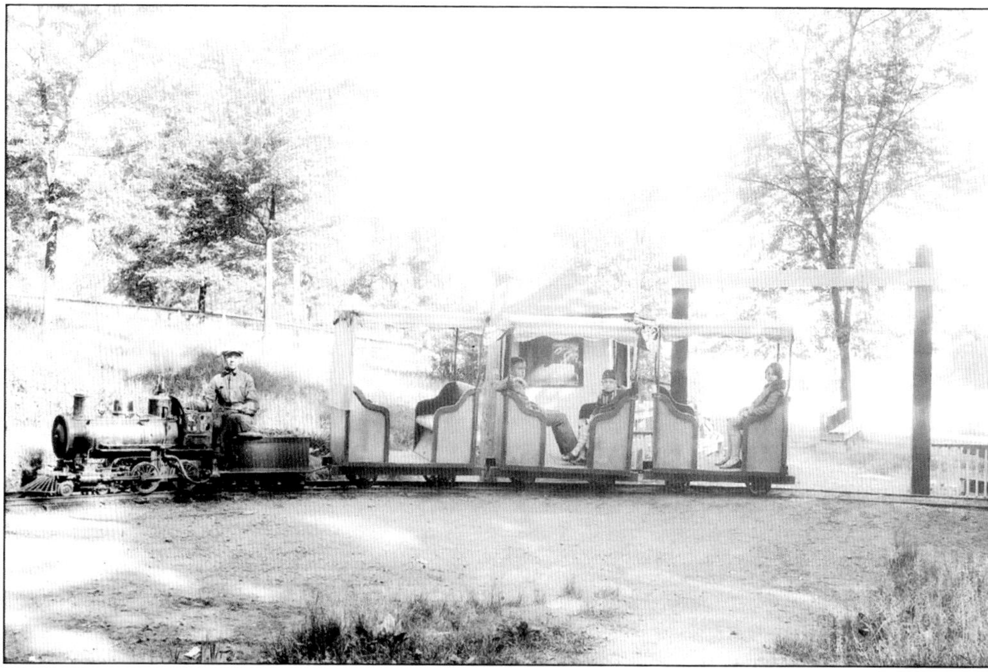

What is an amusement park without a miniature railroad? Still an amusement park; however, one that is somewhat lacking. Sensing this, management at Rolling Green Park made sure a miniature railroad ran through the park's terrain. This photograph dates to 1925, but what appears to be a scale-model engine and tender debuted in 1923. From that date to the closing of the park in 1972, train rides were available to all.

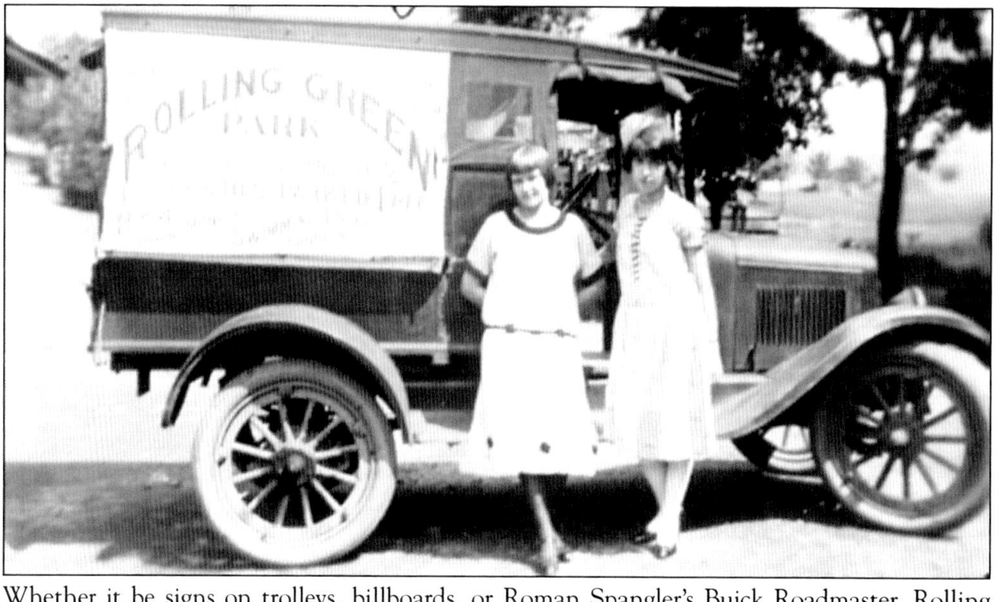

Whether it be signs on trolleys, billboards, or Roman Spangler's Buick Roadmaster, Rolling Green Park and its 35, later 50 "ways of amusement" were heavily advertised. This 1920s Overland truck, still in use in 1925, boasts of "room for 20,000 autos parked free, and four rides." The Giant Twister (roller coaster) and Tilt-A-Whirl were not added until the 1930s and 1940s. The stylish young ladies are unidentified.

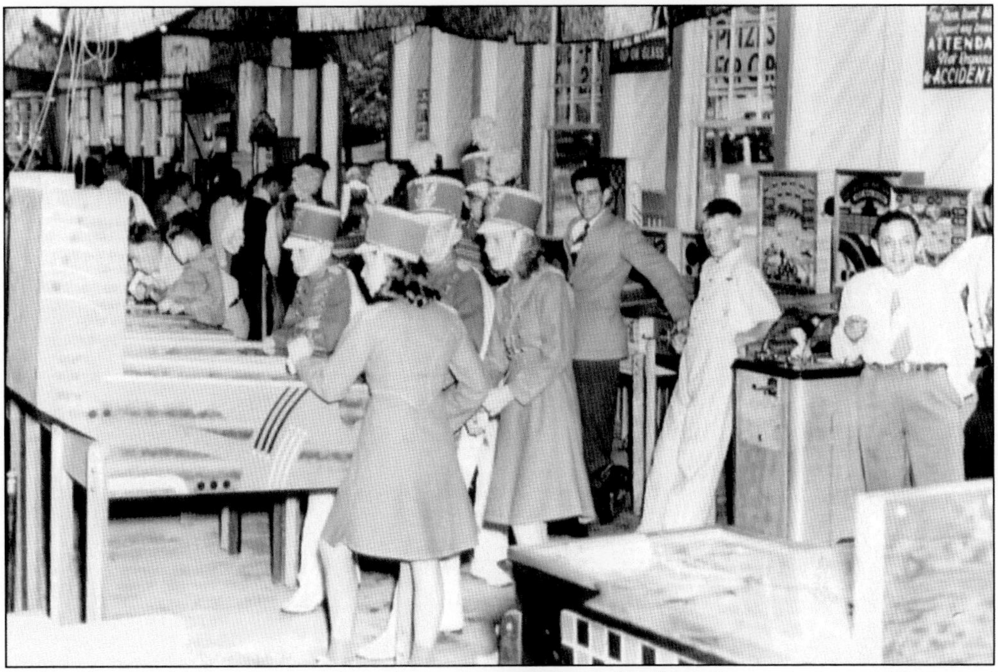

Right after World War II, Spangler, who took ownership of Rolling Green Park in 1935, invited high school bands to perform on Sundays. When not playing, band members were free to sample the park's amusements. Here musicians and color guard members seem as fascinated with the penny arcade's pinball machines as the laid-back youngster at the right is with them. The band is unidentified, but the date is 1950.

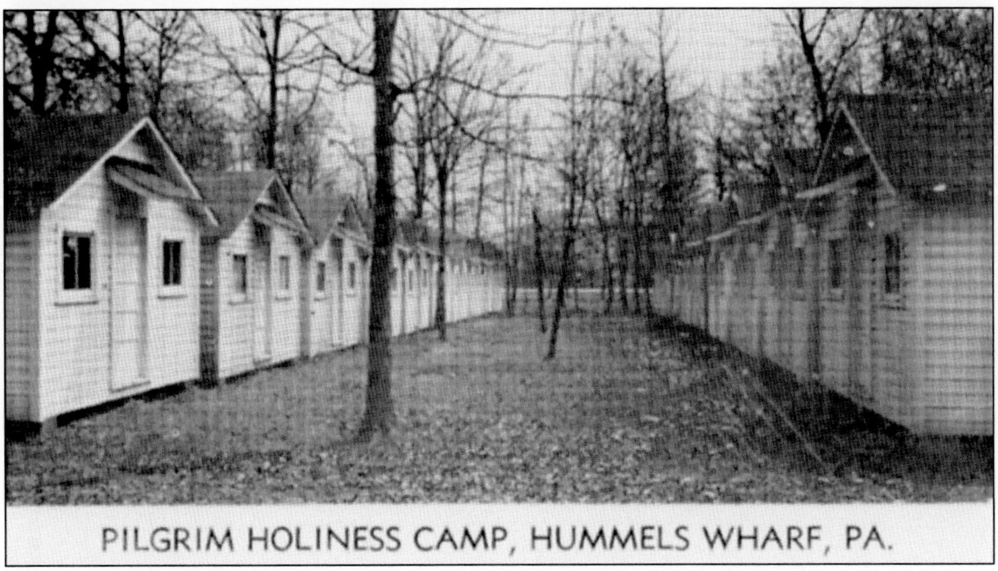

The Pilgrim Holiness Grove, as seen in this postcard, was a landmark, first along the S&S trolley line and after the trolleys stopped running along what are now Routes 11 and 15 in Hummels Wharf. Camp meetings were held during various weeks each summer for decades. The Pilgrim Holiness Grove is one of the properties that made way for Monroe Marketplace shopping center.

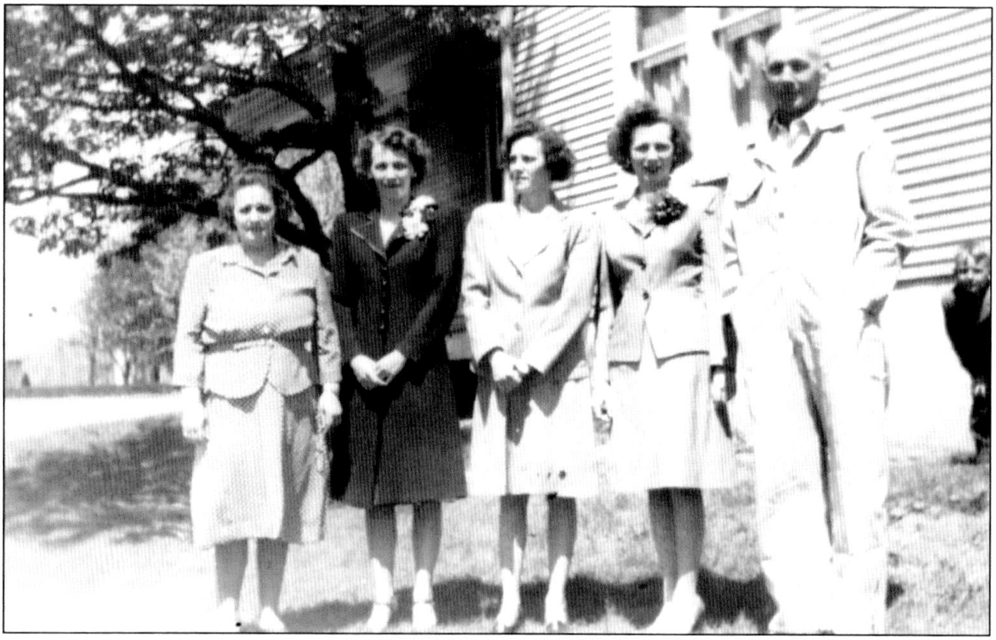

Easter and new outfits have gone together like ham and eggs or tea and crumpets for years. Songs and movies, such as *Easter Parade*, popularized the theme. In 1943, despite wartime restrictions, the women of the M. L. Bailey family of Hummels Wharf posed in their Easter finery. The only thing missing was Easter bonnets. From left to right, they are mother, Carrie, and daughters Grace, Mary, and Ruth. M. L. stands to the right.

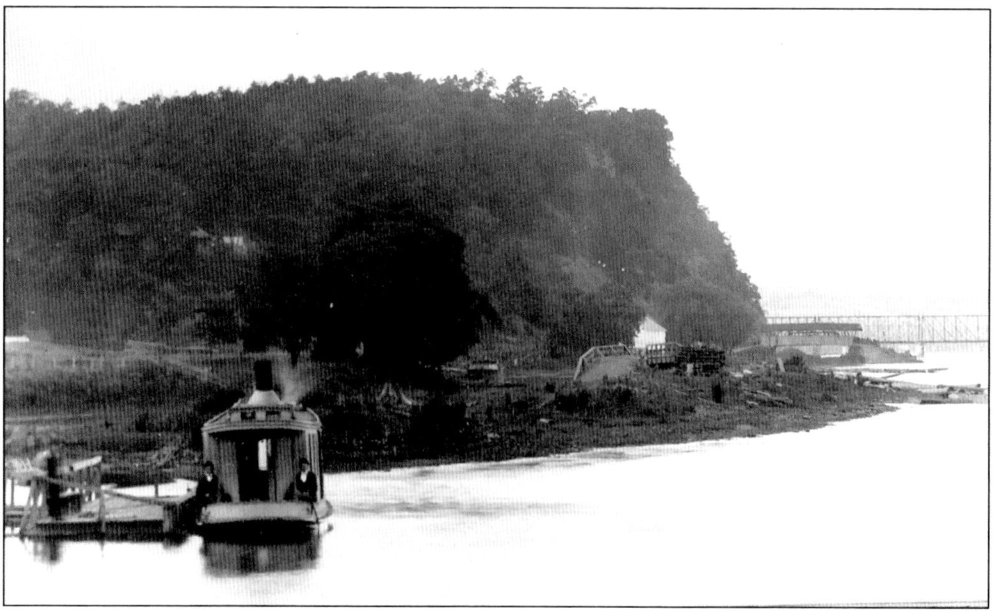

Shamokin Dam was once known as Clements Ferry. The ferry, building up steam, is seen at the left. Blue Hill provides the backdrop, as does the railroad bridge across the Susquehanna River and a wooden bridge over the Pennsylvania Canal. Once the Bainbridge Street bridge linked Shamokin Dam to Sunbury in 1906, the ferry (shown at around 1900) became obsolete. The ferry operated from the Snyder County side at about where the Northumberland Boat Club is now.

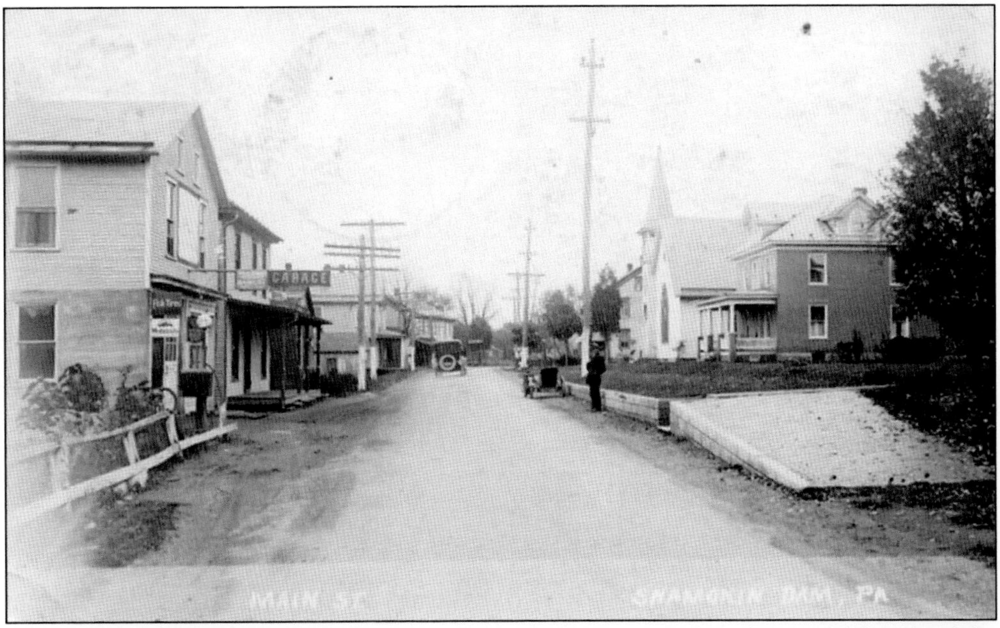

Main Street in Shamokin Dam, shown in this real-photo postcard in the second decade of the 20th century, was unpaved. Today Main Street is better known as the Old Trail. The card depicts the northern part of the borough. A garage, offering Fisk tires and Mobilube lubricants, stands to the left. The Shamokin Dam Methodist Church is seen on the right. The larger building, in the center where the road curves, is what was for years called the Old Trail Inn.

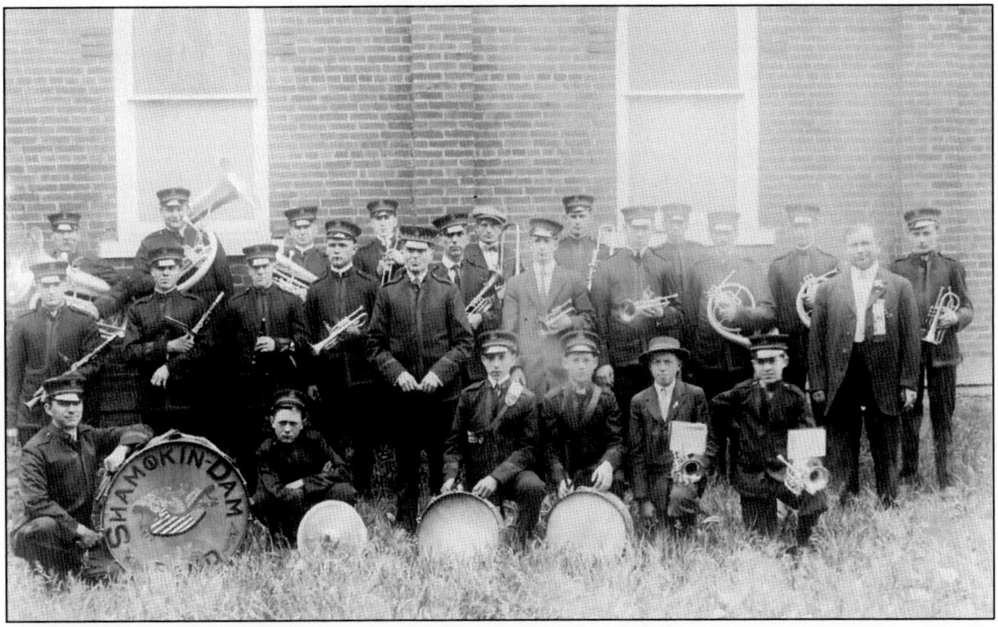

Before iPods, MTV, television, or even radio, people provided their own entertainment. Nearly every community of any size had a brass band or, in some cases, a silver cornet band. Shamokin Dam in the early decades of the 1900s was no exception. Posing in front of a Shamokin Dam landmark—St. Matthew's Lutheran Church—is the Shamokin Dam community band. Note the hand-painted eagle on the drum.

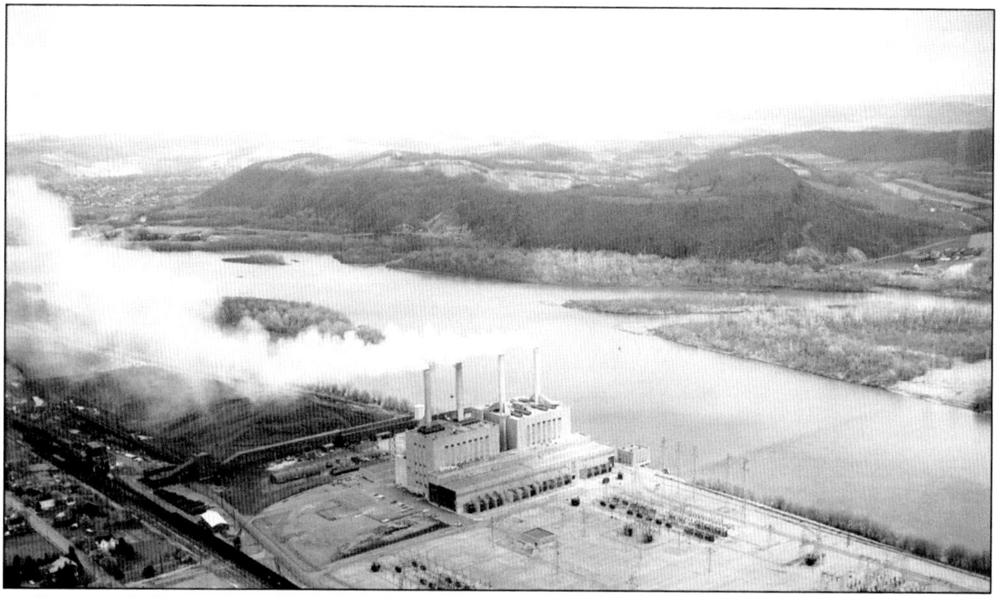

A fine aerial shot not only shows the Pennsylvania Power and Light power plant—still the largest Anthracite burning, steam-generation plant in the world—but also the surrounding hills and valleys. Known as the Sunbury Generation Plant, a label that never sat well with those on the west shore of the Susquehanna River, the plant was sold not long ago. Taken on an unclouded day with a stiff easterly breeze, the photograph shows the plant not long after it went on line on August 17, 1949.

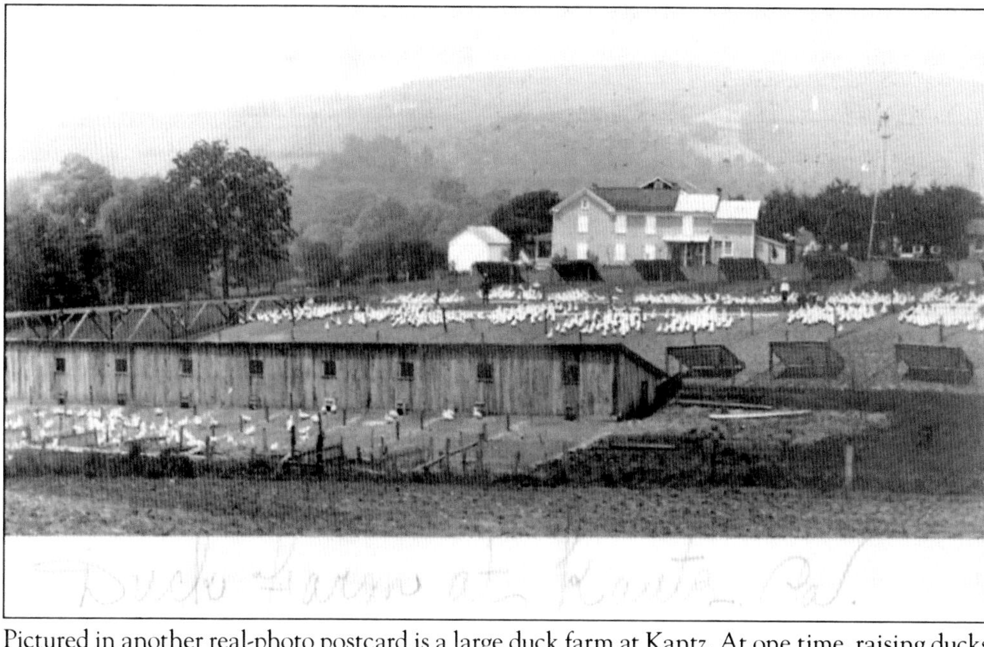

Pictured in another real-photo postcard is a large duck farm at Kantz. At one time, raising ducks was a booming business in the area. This card is from before 1907, the year the U.S. Postal Service first allowed correspondence other than the address on the reverse side. Older cards often had writing on the front, some of which interfered with what was pictured. This card, probably from close to 1907, allows for a message on the plain strip at the bottom.

The spire of St. Peter's Church towers over all of Freeburg. It has been that way since shortly after the cornerstone laying on August 2, 1868, and it is likely to remain so. Approaching Freeburg, the first thing to catch one's eye is the steeple of the house of worship. This real-photo postcard is postmarked 1909. In the Lutheran/Reformed tradition, the church still holds two separate and distinctly different services (Lutheran and until recently, United Church of Christ) each Sunday.

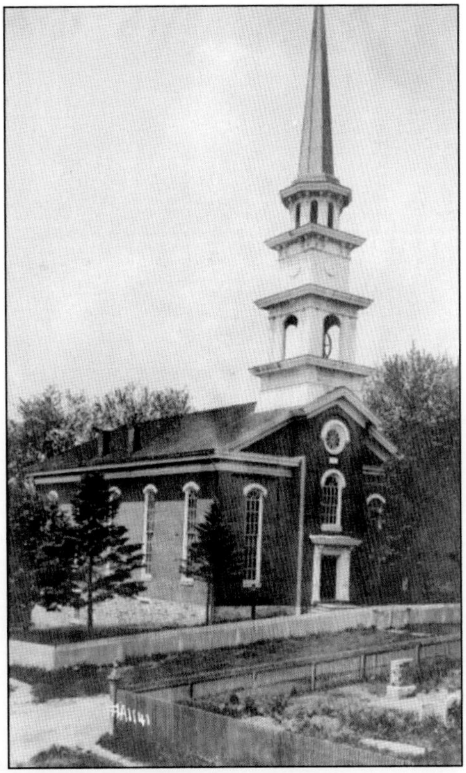

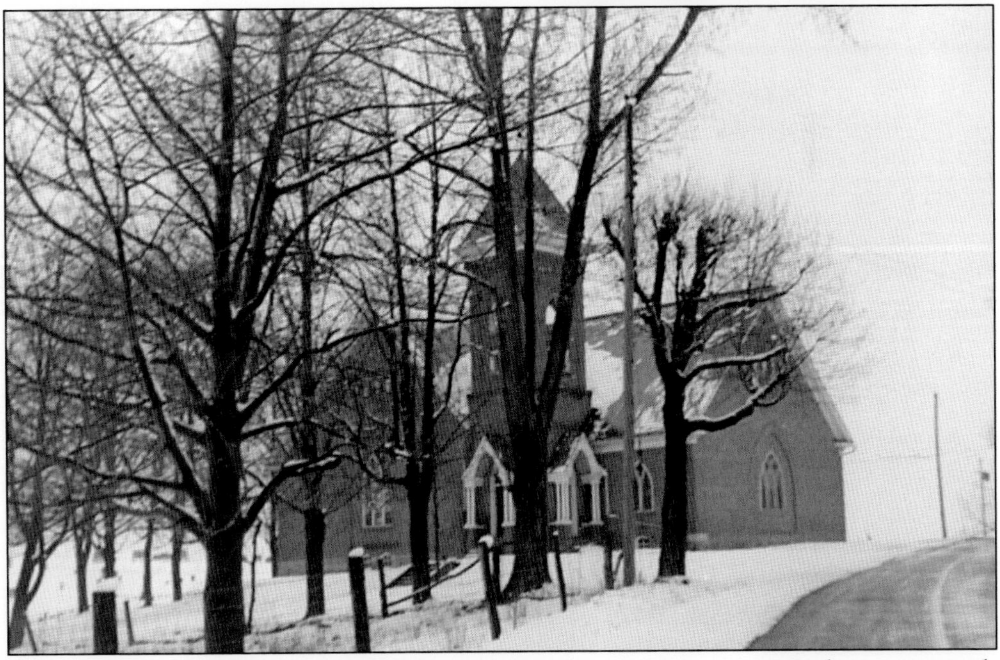

Before the Salem Lutheran Church existed, as viewed here in February 1942, there was a much older building known as Row's Church. It was in close proximity of the Salem School. The present building's cornerstone was laid on Sunday, May 30, 1897. As is often the case, the recently fallen snow simply adds to the serenity of the scene.

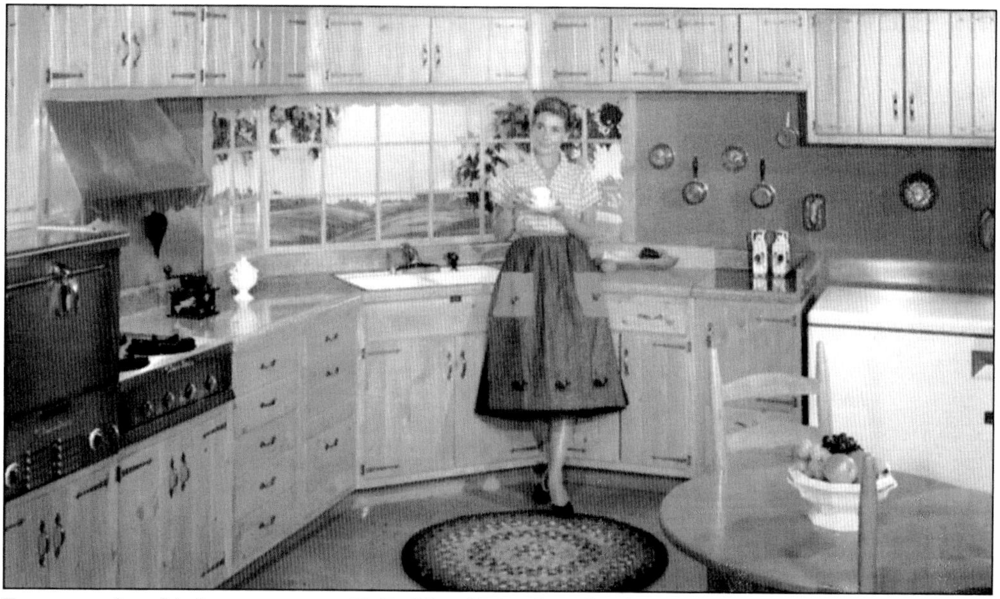

From very humble beginnings in 1942, Wood-Metal evolved into a worldwide leader in custom cabinetry. Now known as Wood-Mode, the Kreamer industry is Snyder County's single-largest employer, with approximately 2,000 men and women. Shown in this 1950s advertising mail-back postcard is the latest modern kitchen, the colonial knotty pine. The kitchen leader was still known as Wood-Metal at that time. Inquiries were to be mailed back to the M. E. Steffen Company at 320 West Pine Street in Selinsgrove.

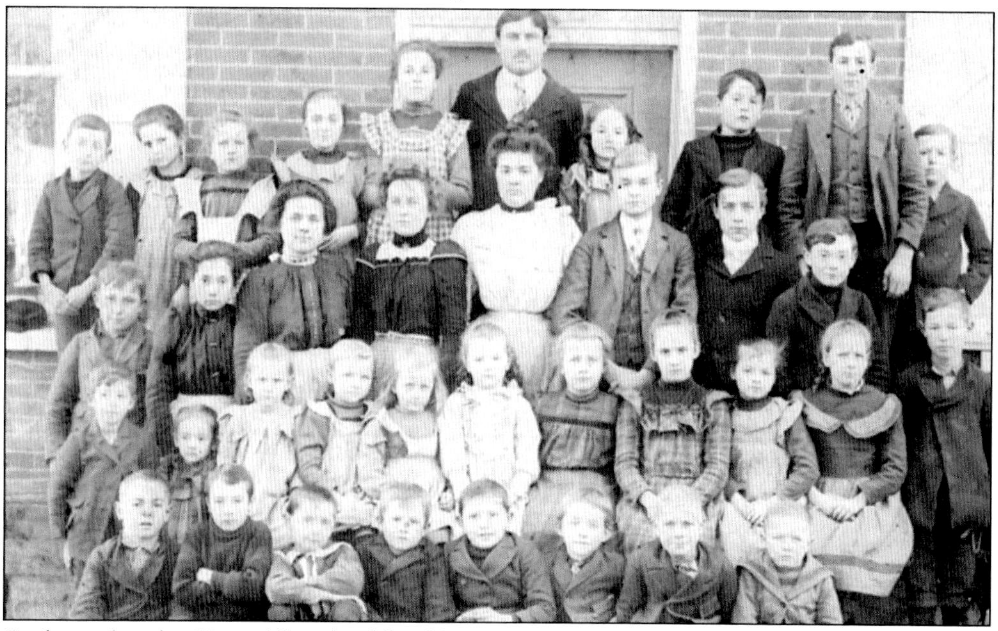

Students of teacher Hayes Albert (middle of the fourth row) pose outside of the one-room Kratzerville School around 1899. Both Eva and Phoebe Herman are among the pupils. Phoebe is in the second row, third from the right, and Eva is in the fourth row, fourth from the left. Others identified include Bright Naugle (first row, fourth from the left) and Carrie Leitzel (second row, fourth from the left). The school still stands in a grove of trees but has not been a classroom for over a half century.

Six

Business and Industry

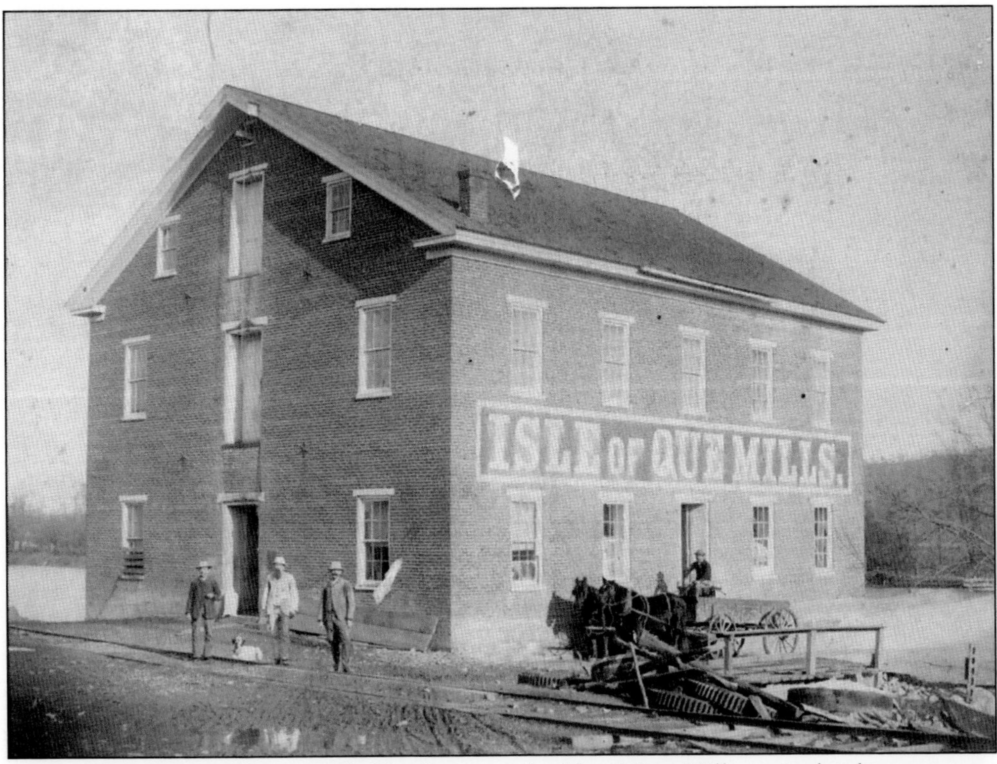

Because Howard D. Schnure called his business the Isle of Que Mills, as is plainly seen, many thought the gristmill operated on the island. Not so. The mill's auxiliary buildings still stand at the terminus of East Mill Street in Selinsgrove. It is what gave the street its name. From left to right, the men in the 1890s photograph are Schnure, William Roush, Abe Long, and teamster Howard Klingler.

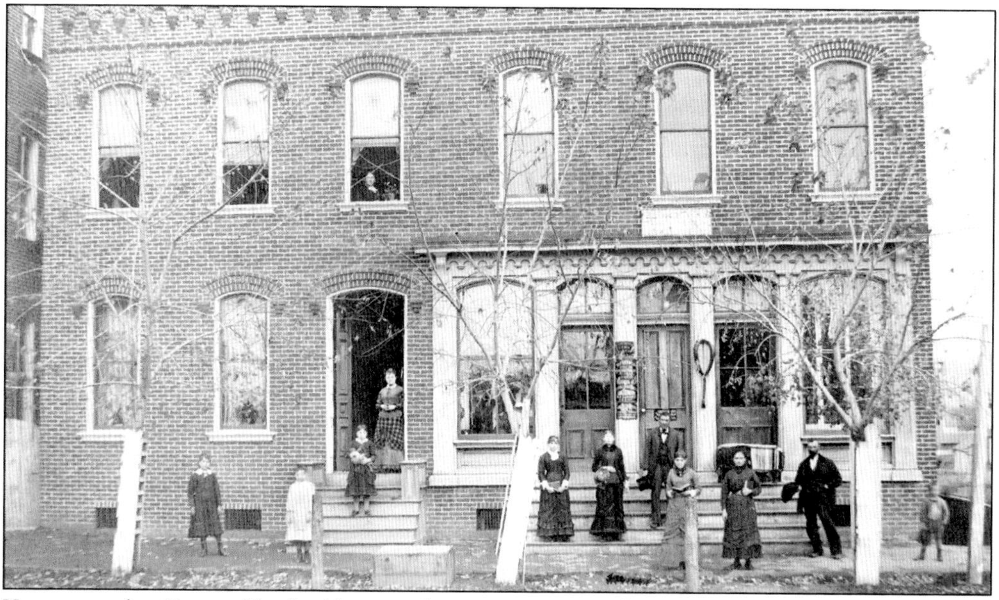

Known as the George Eby building at this time in 1881, this structure still stands just south of B J's, a Place for Ribs on North Market Street in Selinsgrove. The sign between the doors identifies various insurance agencies and mutual-aid societies. Ironically, the mutual-aid societies were outlawed the next year in 1882. This section of Market Street was destroyed by the 1874 fire, but the Eby building was quickly erected. Note the vacant lot to the right. Eventually buildings occupied that space—one is Miller's Insurance.

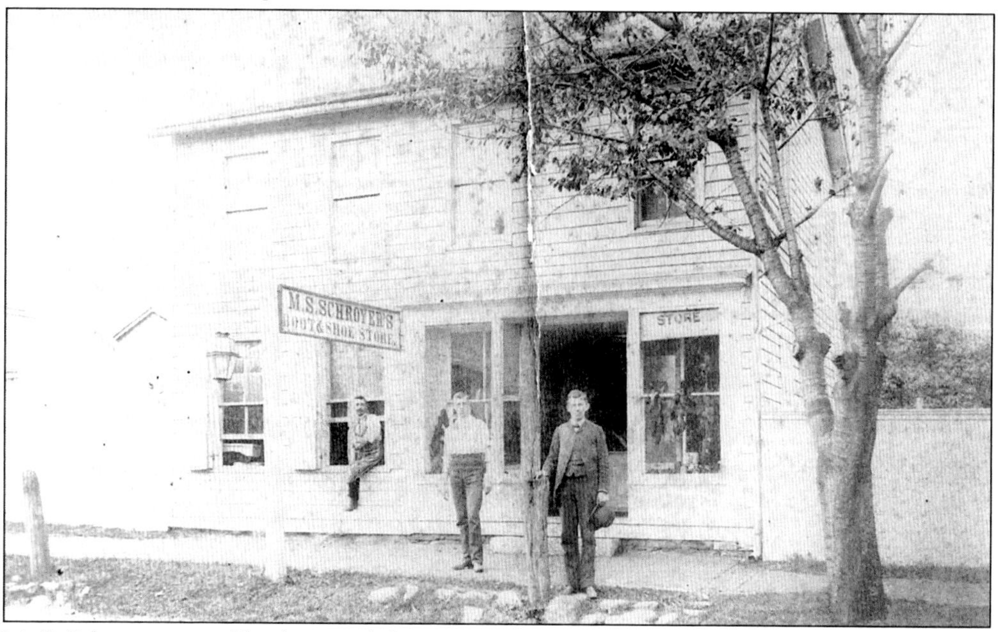

M. S. Schroyer opened his boot and shoe store in August 1872, so it was a going concern when photographed on July 16, 1889. Schroyer was a Civil War veteran, one of "Our Boys" from Company G, 147th Pennsylvania Volunteer Infantry. The building stood for years on the south side of West Chestnut Street between Union Alley and High Street. Undoubtedly, shoes and boots sold by Schroyer's were manufactured in several of the town's shoe factories.

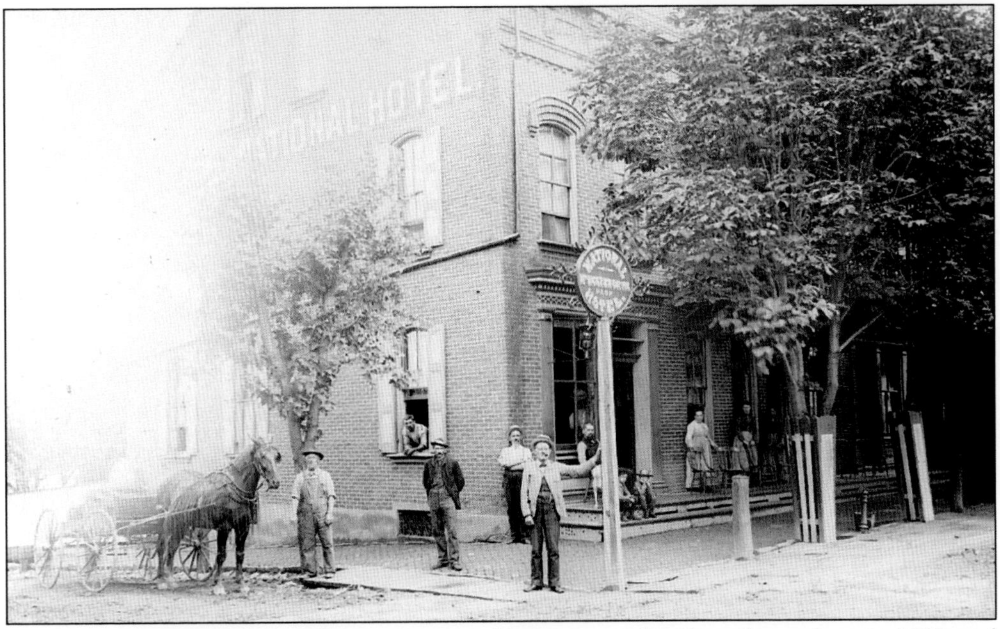

For years, the National was a fixture in town. First, it was a hotel, as shown here in 1885, and later, it was a restaurant run by the Bob Mease family. The structure, later known as the Legion building when it housed the American Legion Victory Post 25, had a third story added. Located at the southeast corner of Market and Chestnut Streets, it burned in 1991. As shown, the proprietor was William Holtzworth. Perhaps it is he who is holding up the business's sign.

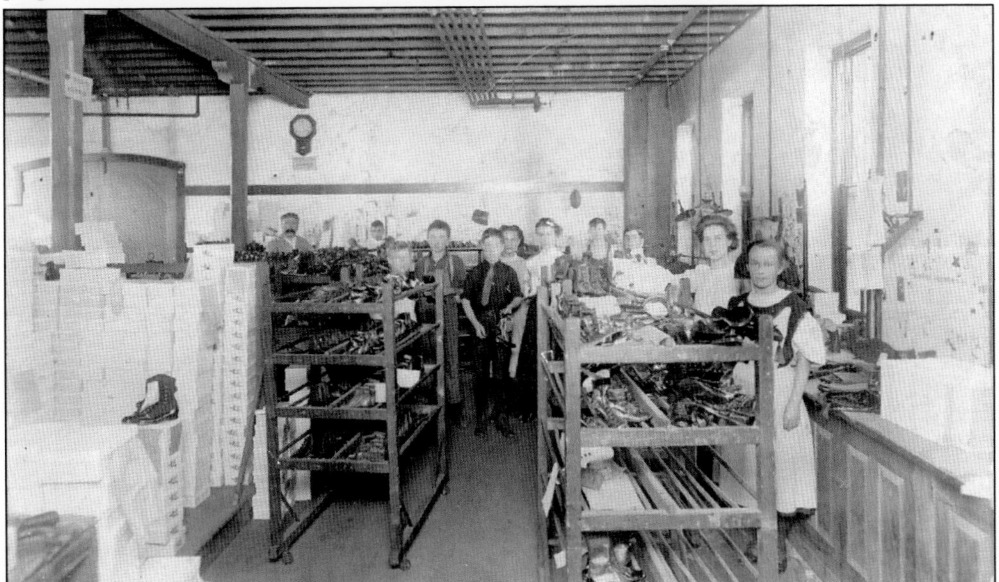

Shoes were manufactured in Selinsgrove factories by the thousands, at one time. One facility was that of T. H. Eisenhuth, located near the railroad station at the corner of High and Snyder Streets. Shown are about a dozen workers—many of them relatively young—amid the racks of high-button shoes they have turned out. The photograph dates from 1906. The factory ran from 1898 to 1910 when it moved operations to Williamsport. The R. E. Yeager Shoe Company replaced it.

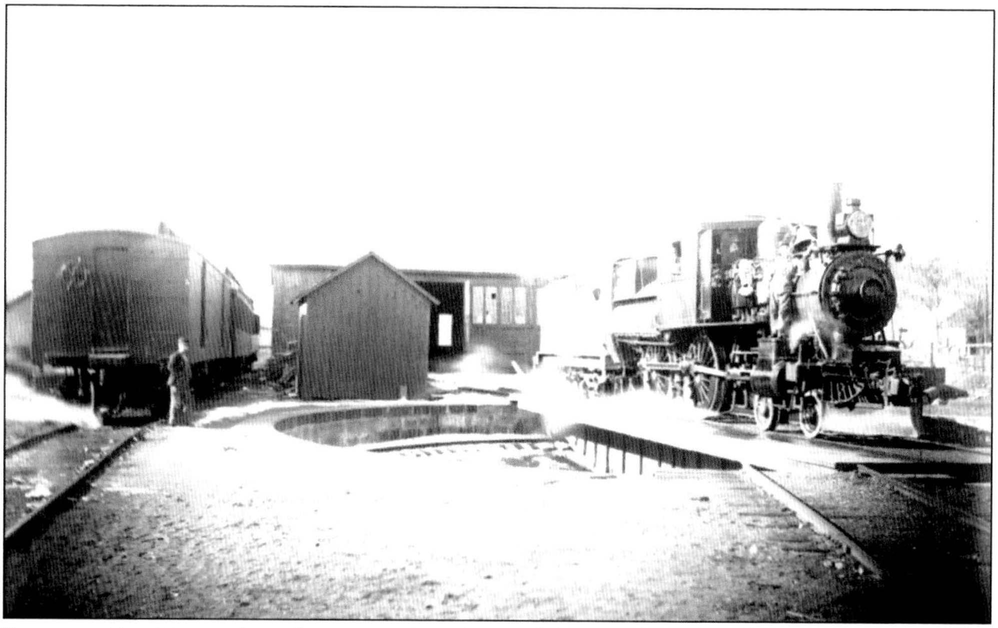

For a considerable number of years, a railroad turntable existed on the Isle of Que. It was located near the tracks between the Penn's Creek railroad bridge and the Susquehanna River and allowed trains to change direction. When the turntable no longer existed, milk trains had to back up all the way from McClure. The Pennsylvania Railroad owned the device, which is shown at the dawn of the 20th century.

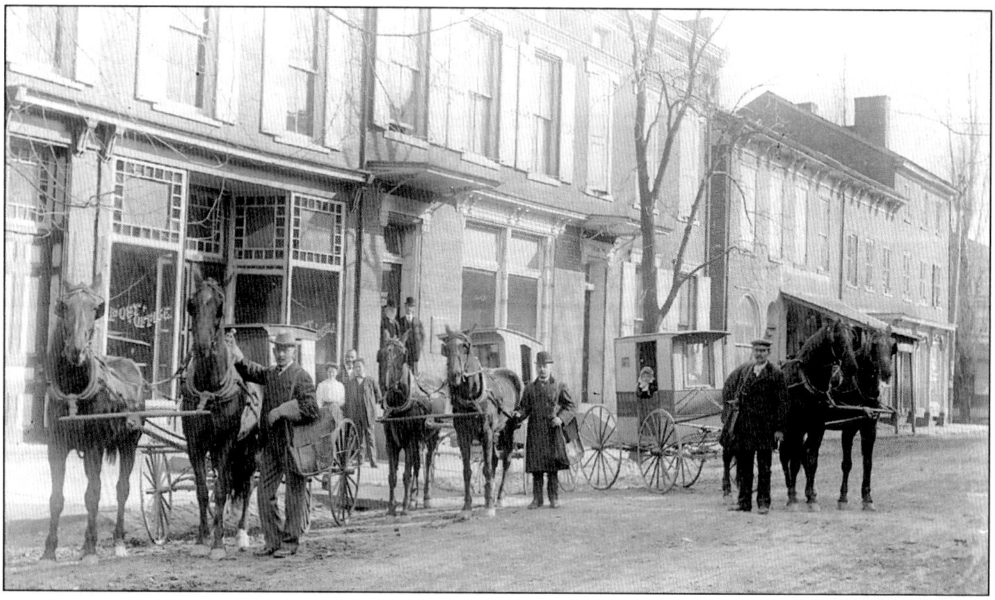

R. L. Ulrich took this photograph in March 1909. It shows several buildings on the west side of the first block of North Market Street, but it primarily features the Selinsgrove Post Office (first building from the left) and the mail wagons of the carriers, who are, from left to right, Art Carey, Billie Loose, and John Wagenseller. Standing in the door of the First National Bank of Selins Grove (next building) are father and son Calvin and Roscoe North. Note the young girl in Wagenseller's wagon.

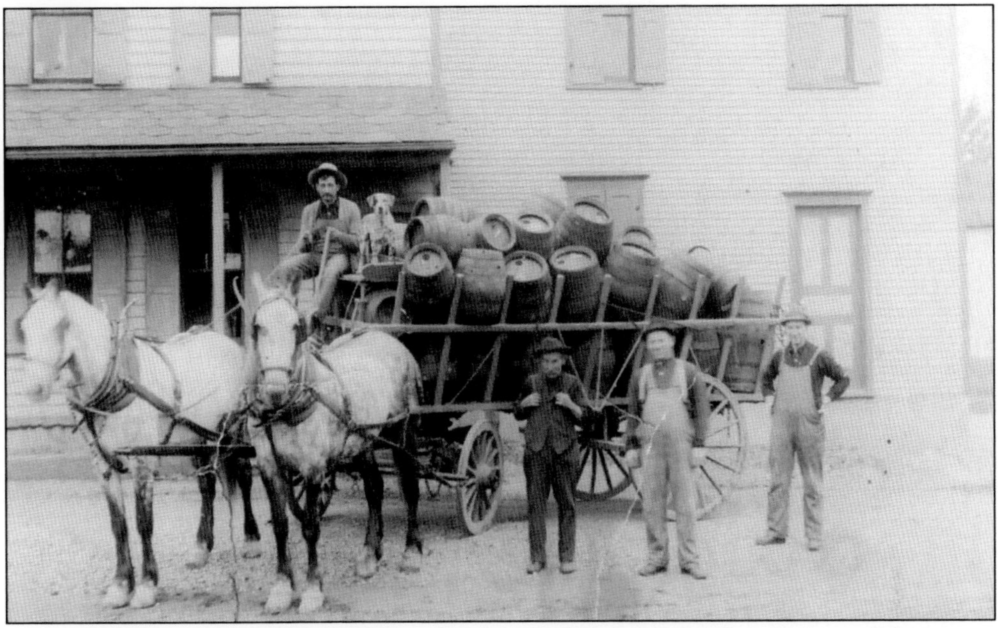

A. H. Whitmer produced soft drinks at a bottling works on North Water Street in Selinsgrove. The teamster, pictured with a faithful dalmatian, is Brig Wolf. This photographic evidence disproves a claim that Wolf's sister Liz made: "He never worked a day in his life, and never will." The other three men in the 1910 photograph are identified as Eddie Charles and John M. and Charles L. Whitmer.

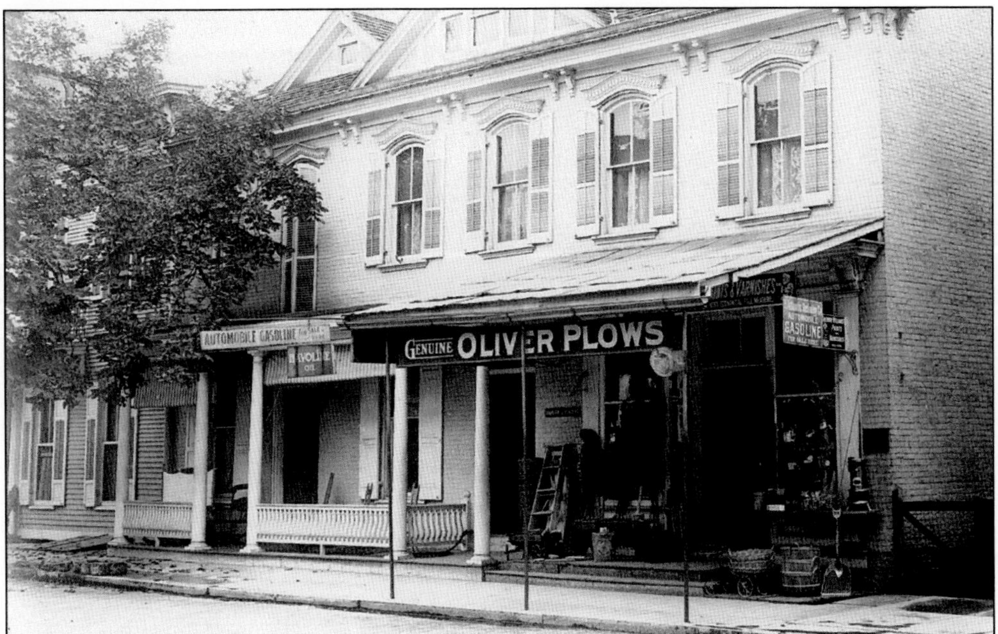

The George Hendricks home and hardware store was located in the middle of the first block of South Market Street in town. While Oliver plows cannot be bought today, one would not have to go far to find Havoline oil, another product advertised, along with Atlantic Refining automobile gasoline. Sarah-Kate Interiors occupies the sturdy brick building today.

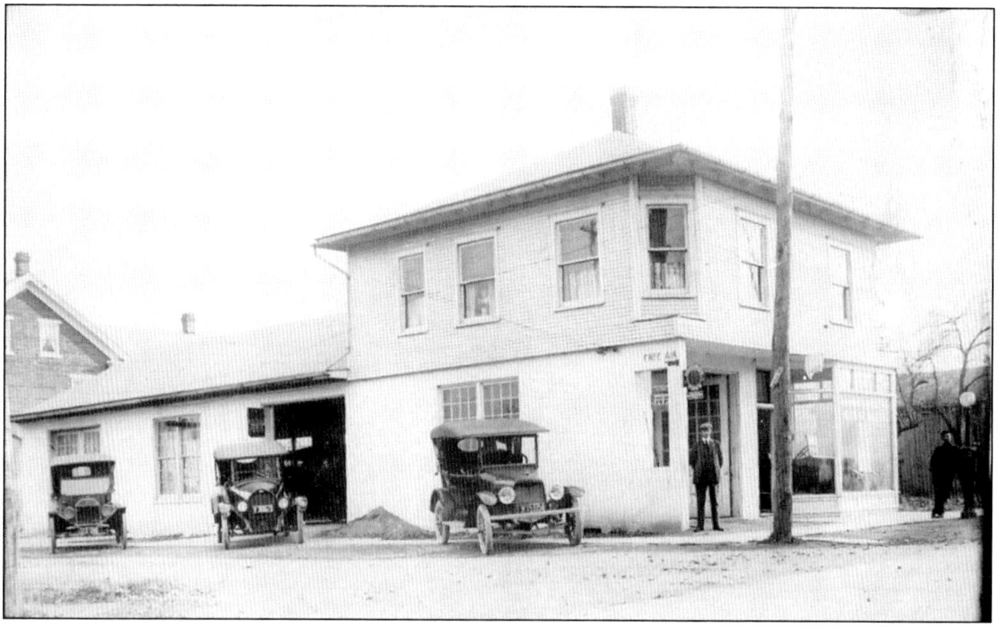

In the early days, M. C. Bonawitz and Sons was a Ford automobile agency, seen here recently expanded in 1918. Later it became an International Harvester dealership. The business was located at the corner of Market and Mill Streets, the present-day location of Dominoes Pizza. Roy Bonawitz is in the doorway; Guy Bonawitz is at the extreme right. Discernable signs advertise Goodrich tires and free air.

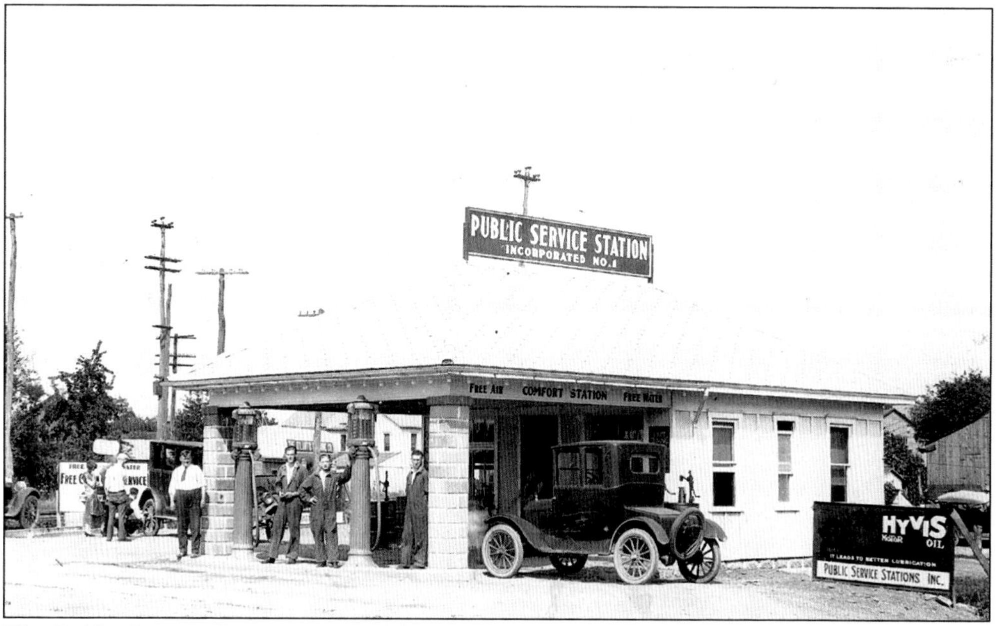

The Public Service Station operated by George Heidig in 1924 at the corner of Market and Spruce Streets could have boasted, but probably did not, that "service is our middle name." In addition to pumping gas, which probably cost 19.9¢ a gallon, they provided free air, free water, and a "comfort station." Later an Esso station run by Freddie Ferguson and his wife occupied the locale. It is now a soft serve ice-cream shop called What's Shakin'.

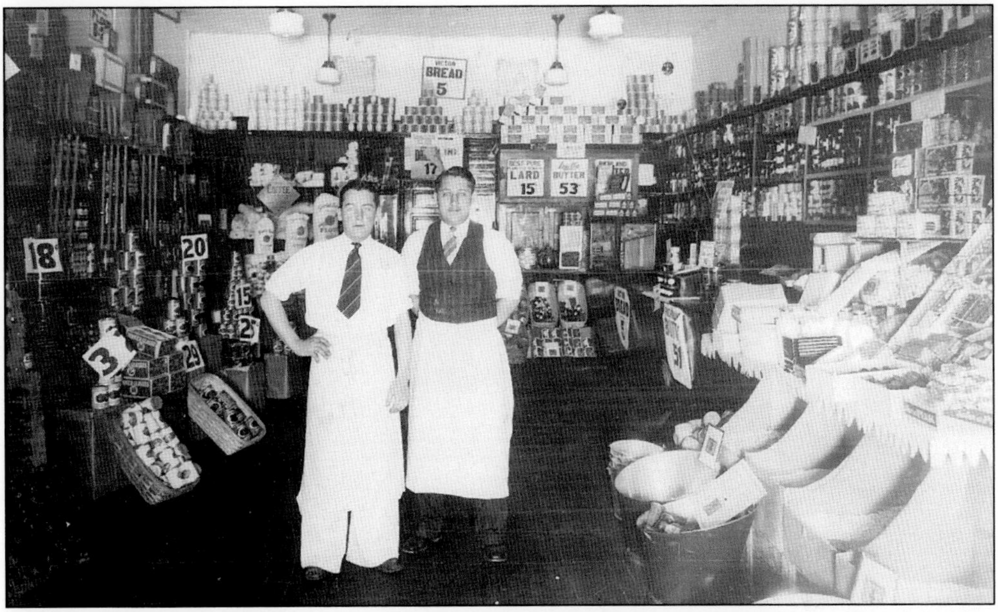

Here is another store interior from 1934 of the American Store on the west side of South Market Street, now the location of the Mustard Seed. Manager Bob Wendt (right) and clerk Lansford (Lance) Bowen stand before an array of merchandise, the price of which one can only now fantasize about, including bread for 5¢ a loaf and butter for 53¢ a pound. In 1935, Wendt operated his own store on East Pine Street.

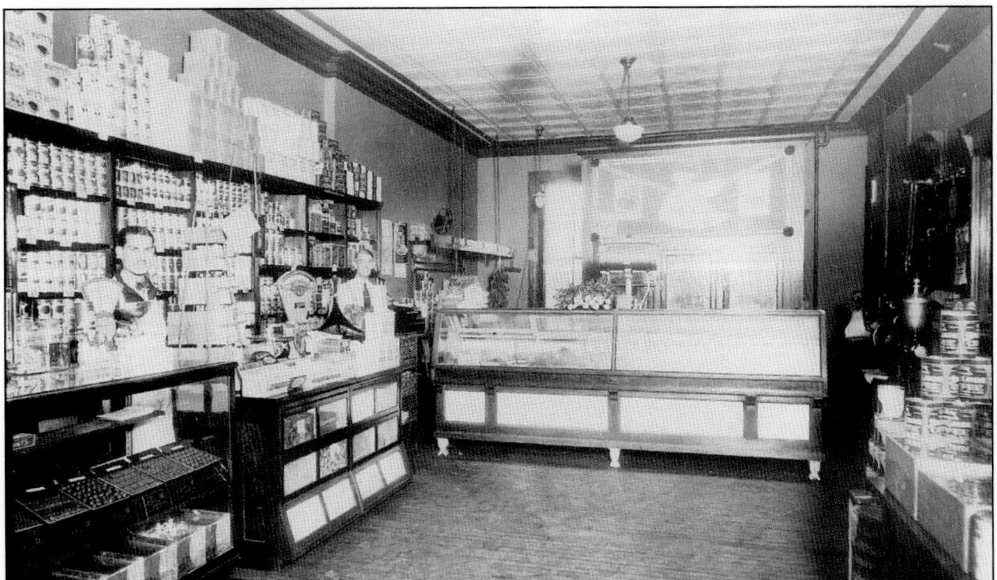

The Charles Keller family figured prominently in the commerce of Selinsgrove. The senior Keller was a longtime operator of a vital icehouse, and later a beverage distributorship was added. Eventually his son Charlie ran the business. Another son, John (left), owned and operated several stores in town. Here the always-dapper John stands behind neatly stocked showcases and before equally neatly stocked shelves. Note the ornamental tin ceiling in this photograph from the 1930s.

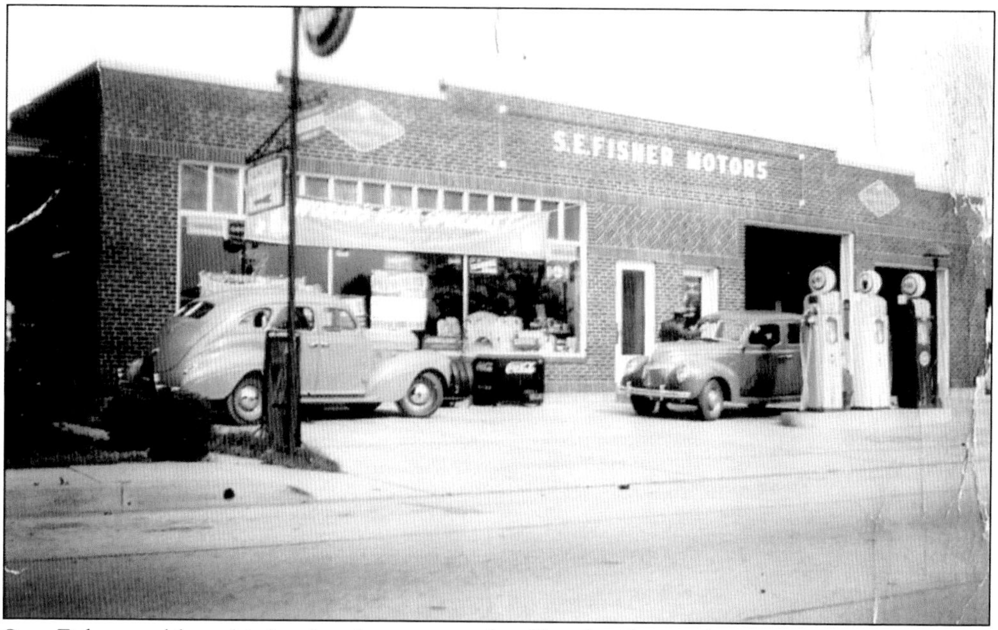

Sam Fisher, and later his brother Lee, operated a Chrysler-Plymouth agency on North Market Street in Selinsgrove for decades. An attendant provides full service to a Pure gas customer. Off to the left is a 1939 Plymouth four door, which is probably the object of the banner proclaiming "World's Fair Specials." At present, a NAPA Auto Parts store occupies the building, not significantly changed from 1939.

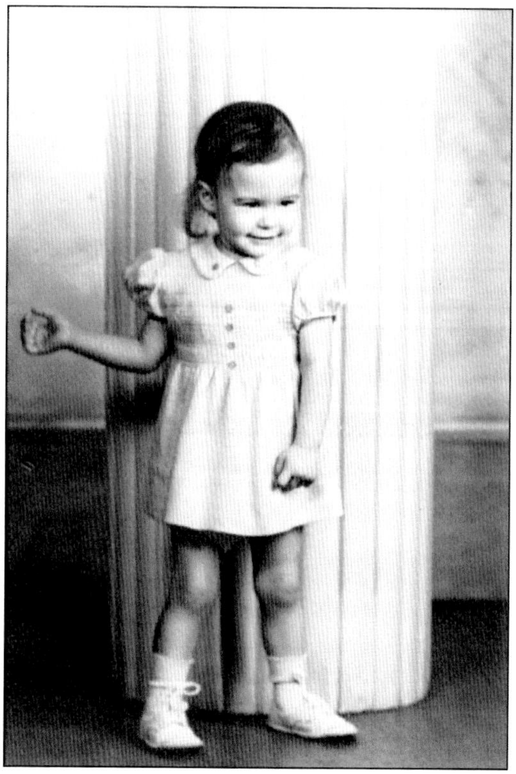

This tot is Vivian Gemberling, and she was the 1940 cover girl for her family dairy operation's calendar. She bears a striking resemblance to her and Terry Beaver's daughter, Jennifer Bernstein, or maybe it is the other way around.

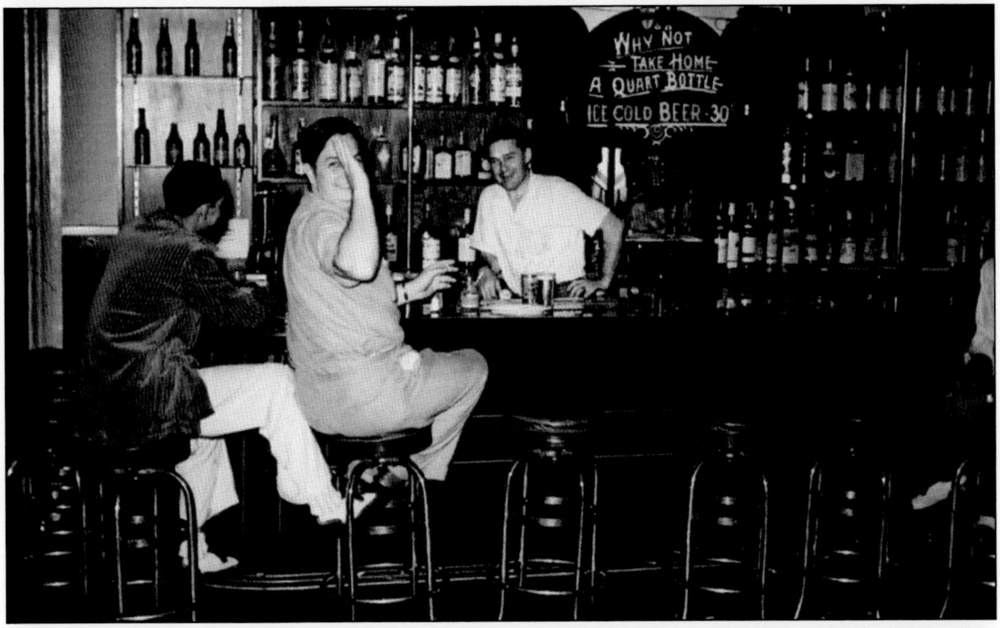

Regardless of the name—the Keystone, Sterner's, or Hotel Governor Snyder—the building that is now B J's, a Place for Ribs has always been a center of hospitality. Longtime proprietor Walter Pinand, and later Bob McFall, provided a convivial atmosphere for many faithful patrons. In this 1942 photograph, Pinand smiles in front of a well-stocked back bar, while Fred Machmer Jr. waves to the camera.

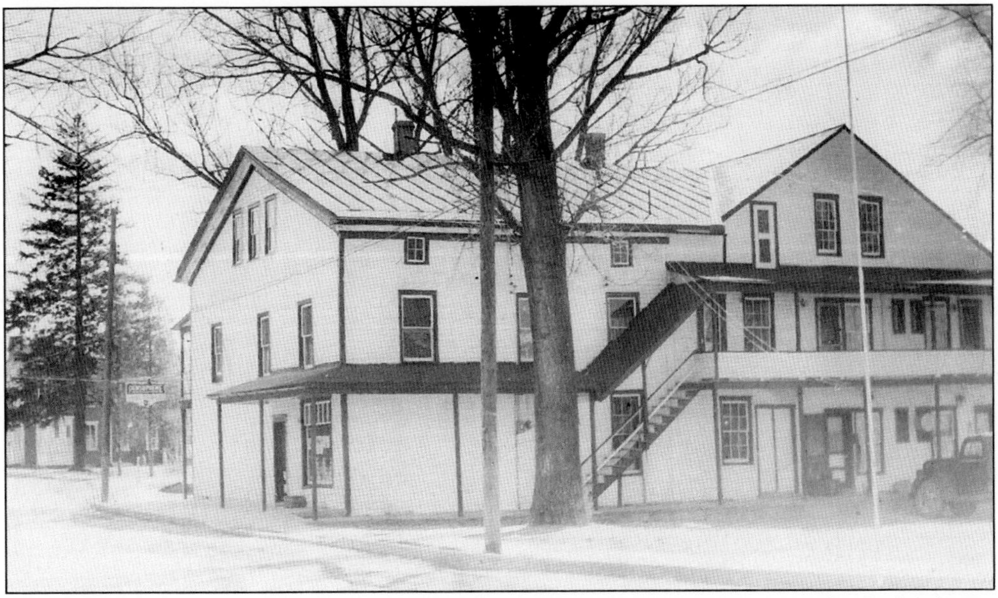

The name Sheetz as a convenience store and gas outlet is quite common in the mid-Atlantic states. However, to generations of Selinsgrovers, Sheetz meant an Isle of Que "fancy foods" store. Opened as a general store by Dr. Jacob Wagenseller during the canal days of the early 1800s, ownership passed eventually to James Burns, who in turn sold to Corbett Sheetz on July 21, 1936. The building, greatly damaged in the Agnes flood of 1972 and eventually dismantled, is pictured in 1942.

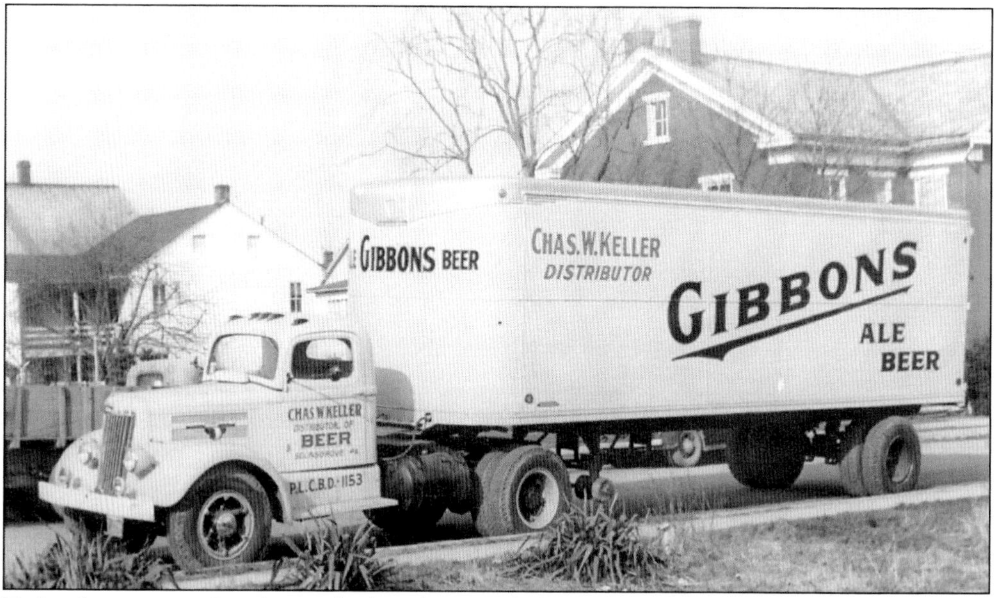

Today beer is produced mainly by about a half-dozen giant breweries, although many microbreweries dot the landscape. A family ice and beverage business for generations, Keller's distributed Gibbons ale and beer, along with other brands. Keller's is still in business today, although the Keller family is no longer involved. The distributorship was and still is located at the base of East Walnut Street where it intersects with Water Street. The yellow International Harvester truck is pictured in 1947.

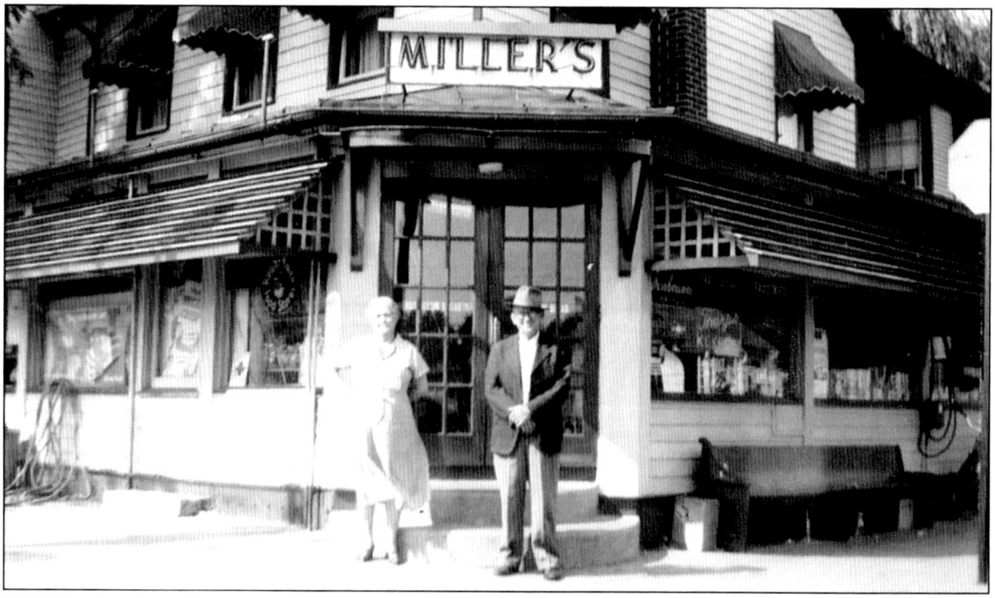

Not many are aware that what is now called We're Electric Dance Studio was Wallace Baker's bicycle agency in the 1890s. However, generations remember the Orange and Pine Streets property as Miller's grocery, as stated by the new neon sign above proprietors Elmer and Carrie Miller. Ownership was later passed to the Miller's daughter Anita and her husband, Roy "Flip" Harro. More than one local Susquehanna University student earned tuition dollars working part-time at the store, shown in 1948.

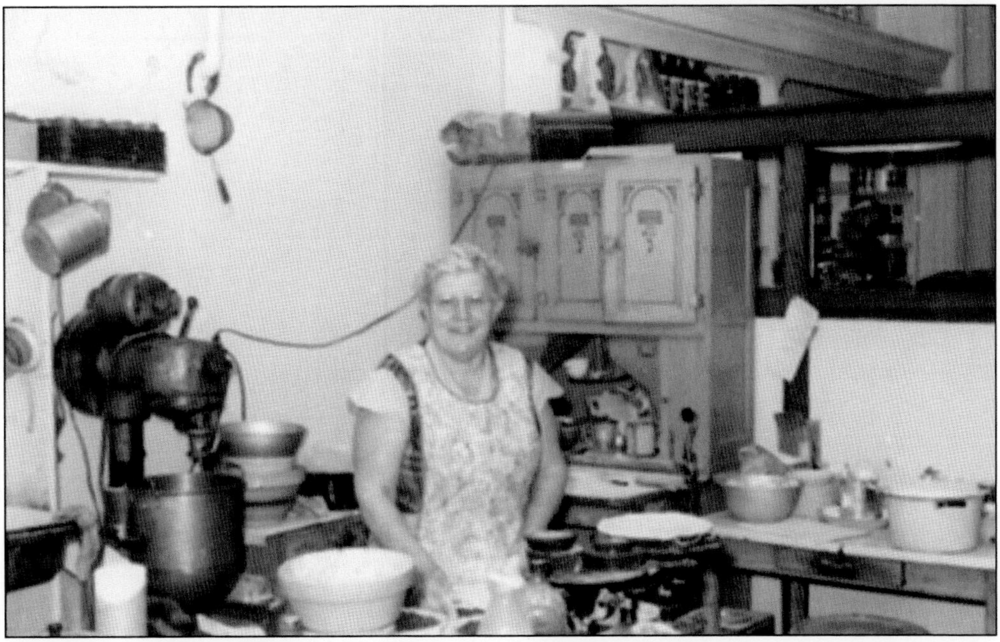

Through the years, Selinsgrove had as many bakeries as there were mom-and-pop grocery stores—about a baker's dozen. One was Miller's Home Bakery, operated by Roy "Rookie" Miller and his wife, Carrie (shown), from 1936 to 1939 on the Isle of Que and from 1939 to 1957 at Pine and Water Streets. The baked goods were of the highest quality. Baltimore Colts hall of fame tackle Art Donovan, by his own admission, attested to the tastiness of Miller's pastries.

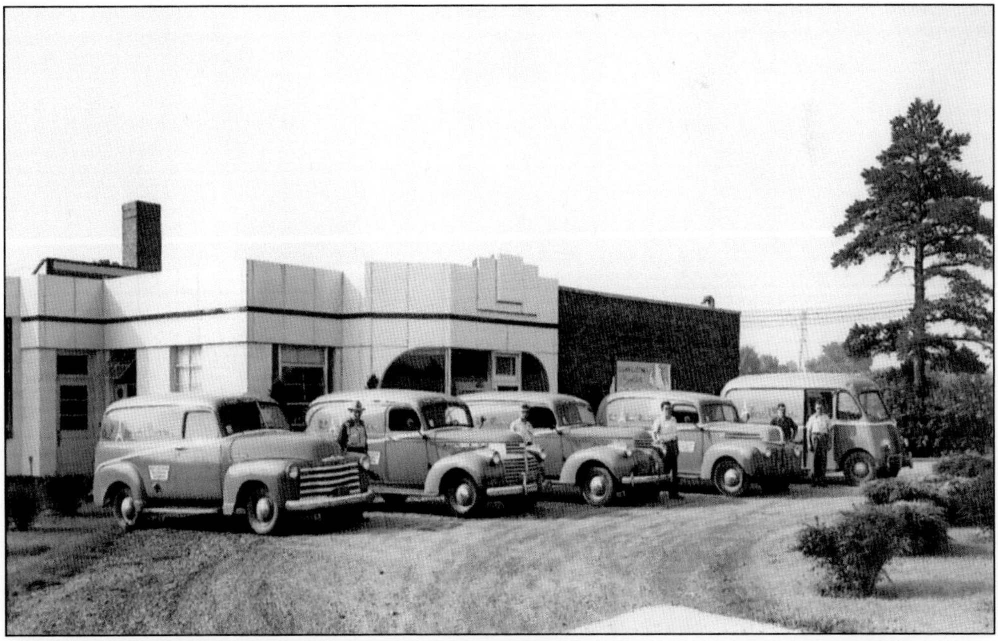

For many years, Real French Cleaners was a well-established dry-cleaning operation along Routes 11 and 15, where Hummels Wharf and Shamokin Dam meet. Henri Bouchard, a real Frenchman, was proprietor. Shown around 1953 in front of the plant is the fleet of pick-up and delivery trucks with their drivers. The business was located opposite the new Monroe Marketplace mall.

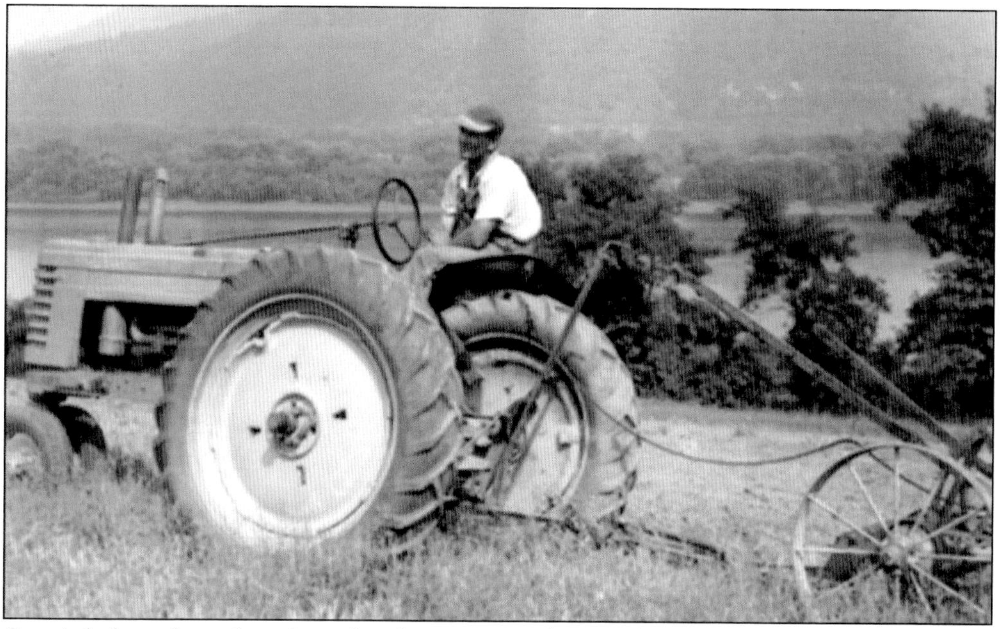

Certainly from the earliest days of settlement, agriculture or farming has been a very important vocation. In many cases, it was subsistence farming for the family. While Selinsgrove area families no longer raise and grow all their needs, a significant number still engage in farming as a full-time activity. With Mahanoy Mountain as a backdrop, Bernard Brown takes a break from working the land on a hillside near Port Trevorton.

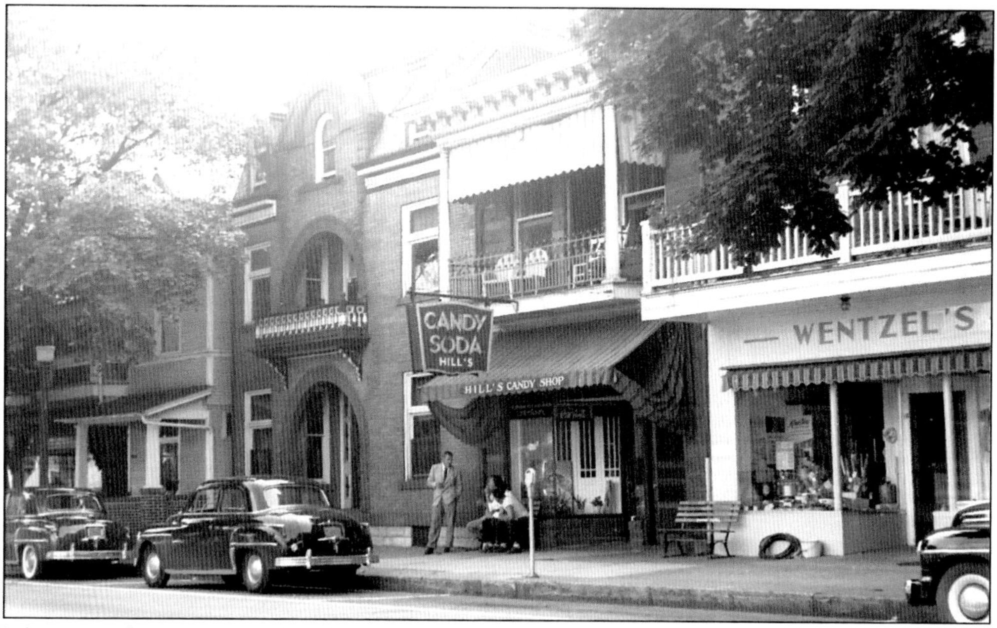

Like its predecessors—Reichley's and Taylor's—Hill's Candy Shop was a community gathering place, especially for youth. Selinsgrove youngsters, from junior high age through high school and college, all patronized the soda fountain, and there was never any friction between the diverse groups. This is a phenomenon worthy of a sociological study. A dapper Bob McFall chats with a pair of patrons in this 1949 photograph. Beverley's is now at the 12 North Market Street locale.

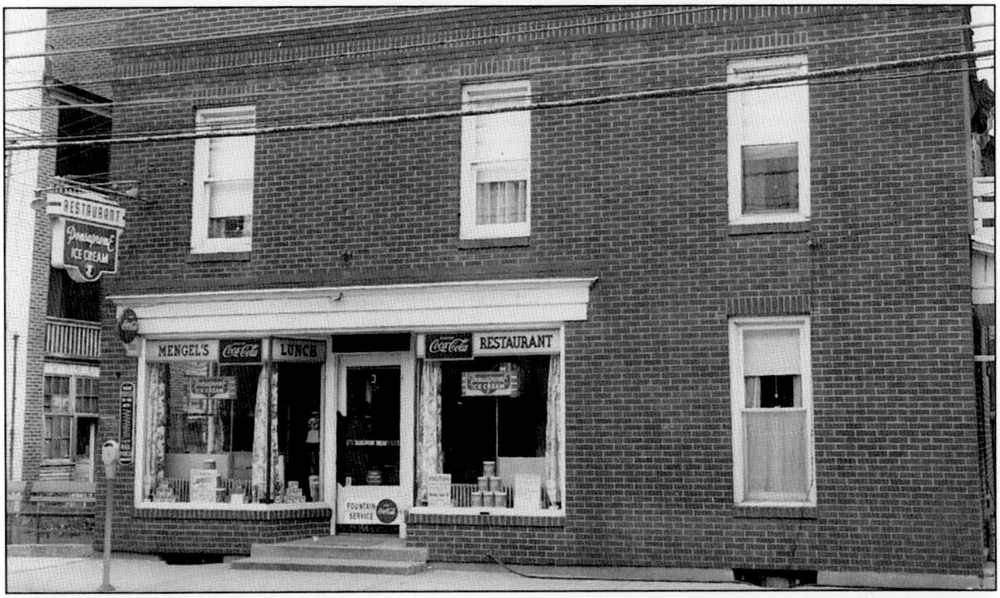

Selinsgrove's landscape was dotted with small but tasteful restaurants over the years. Many no longer exist. In 1947, Woody Mengel took over an eatery (shown in 1951) on West Pine Street, strategically close to the Pine Street School. While all the fare was excellent, Woody's French fries were without equal. A 25¢ grilled cheese, 15¢ fries, and a nickel Coca-Cola provided a substantial lunch for less than 50¢. The Bingaman family previously owned the restaurant in the building.

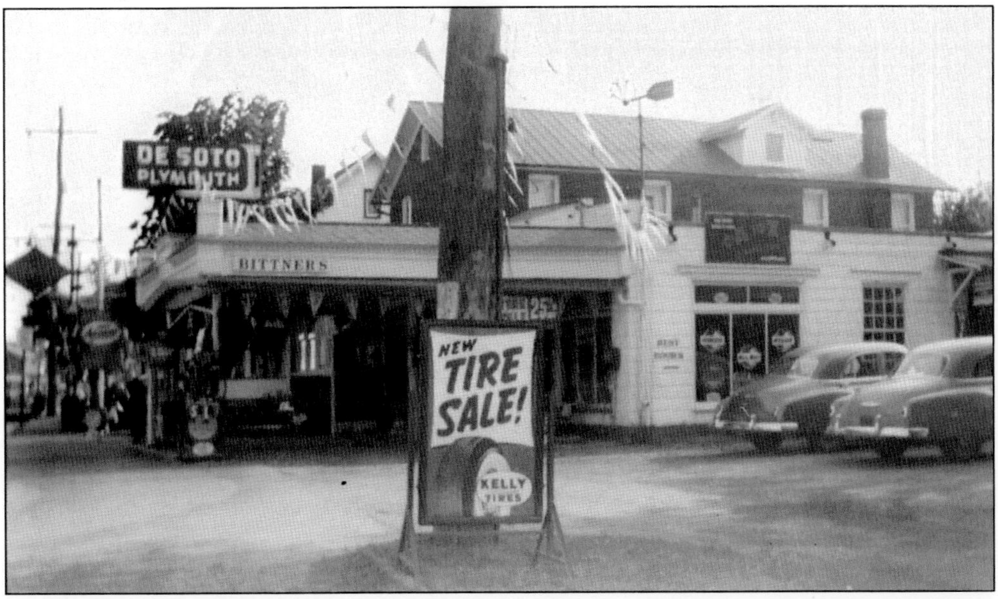

For decades, Selinsgrove was fortunate to have numerous garages, a garage being a place that repaired and maintained automobiles, pumped gas, and sold cars. Herb Bittner's, in the 800 block of North Market Street, was one such business, selling DeSotos and Plymouths. This photograph was taken in August 1955. In the background is the Bittner residence. Daughter Mildred graduated from Susquehanna University and was a respected Selinsgrove High School faculty member for many years.

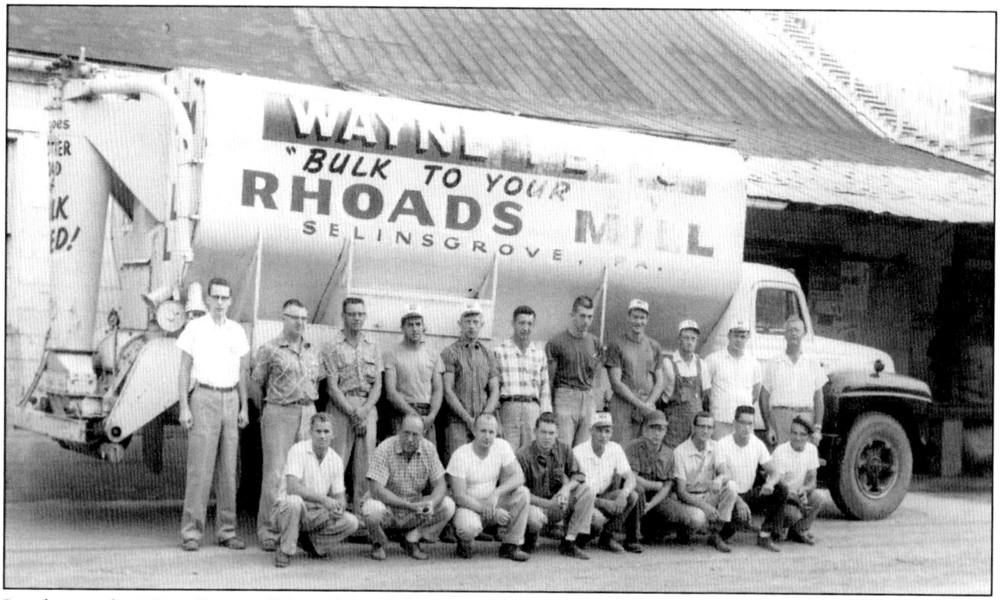

In the mid-1950s, Simon Rhoads and his employees posed beside a Wayne Feeds truck at the 200 block of the North Market Street location of the in-town mill. From left to right are (first row) George Ulrich, Jim Leeser, Don Musser, Carl Scholl, Andrew Snyder, "Red" Mattern, Neal Rhoads, Rick Bolig, and Jake Walters; (second row) Ed Rhoads, Clair Wochley, Charles Weiser, George Treon, Charles Culp, Harold Hummel, Laverne Longacre, Roy Dressler, Herman Goodling, Russ Goodling, and Simon Rhoads.

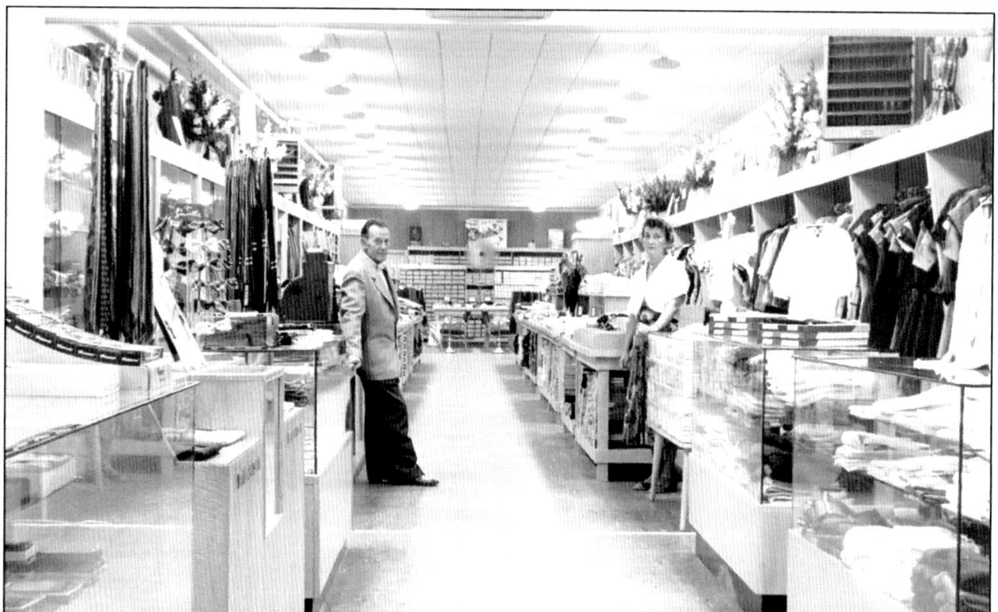

Lee R. Snavely's store came to Selinsgrove in 1930 and moved to its more-remembered location in the Benfer building (now the Mustard Seed) on South Market Street in 1935. Primarily a clothing and shoe store, Snavely's was ably managed for years by Harry Deckard (left). The woman is unidentified, but she might be either Helen Deckard or a sales associate. The neat and bright interior was photographed in 1954.

Seven

School Days

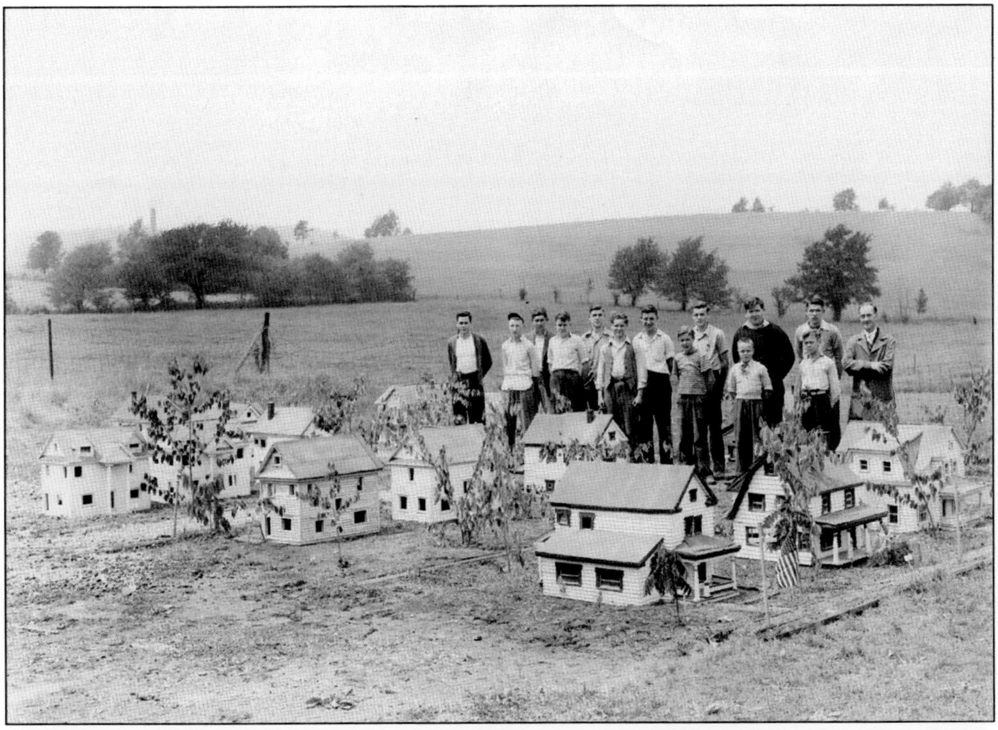

The photograph that serves as the cover for this book is a 1946 Selinsgrove shop class of Dave Perwine. These are not doll houses but miniatures. Pupils assumed the role of contractor and acquired the building materials, just as though they were constructing a to-be-lived-in home. From left to right are (first row) O. Long, S. Lenig, B. Thomas, J. Kratzer, unidentified, I. McCreary, and T. Picton; (second row) C. Klingler, R. Lenig, B. Herman, R. Klingler, H. Flanders, R. Hauser, and Perwine.

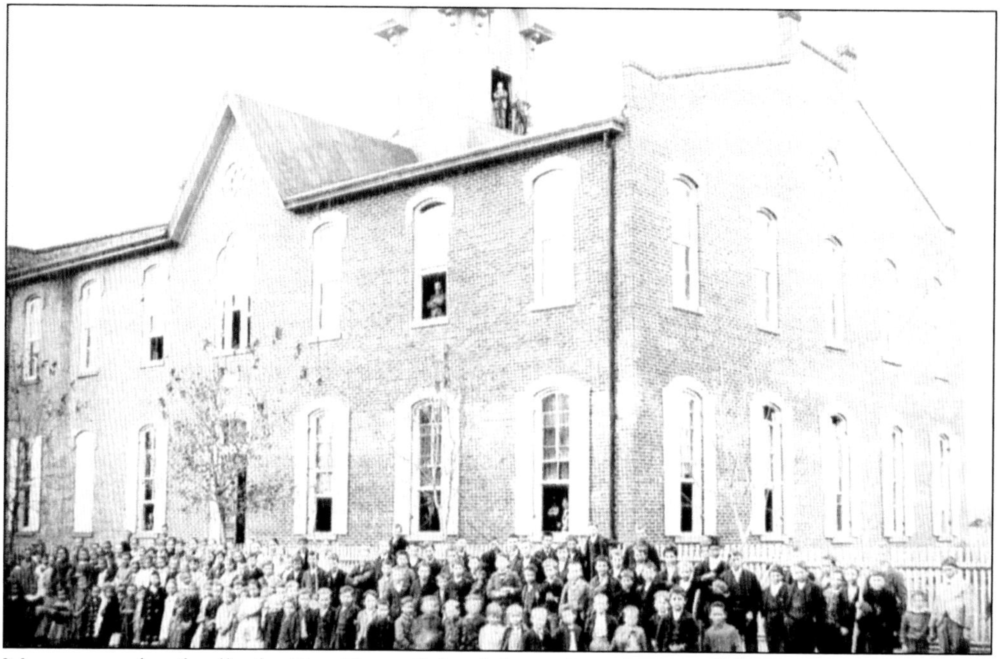

Many remember fondly the Pine Street School, located on the site of the town's present library at Pine and High Streets, but what is remembered, most likely, is the structure that replaced the original in 1928. This is the original school around 1885. It seems that the entire student body is posed in front of the building, and do not overlook the two youngsters up at the cupola.

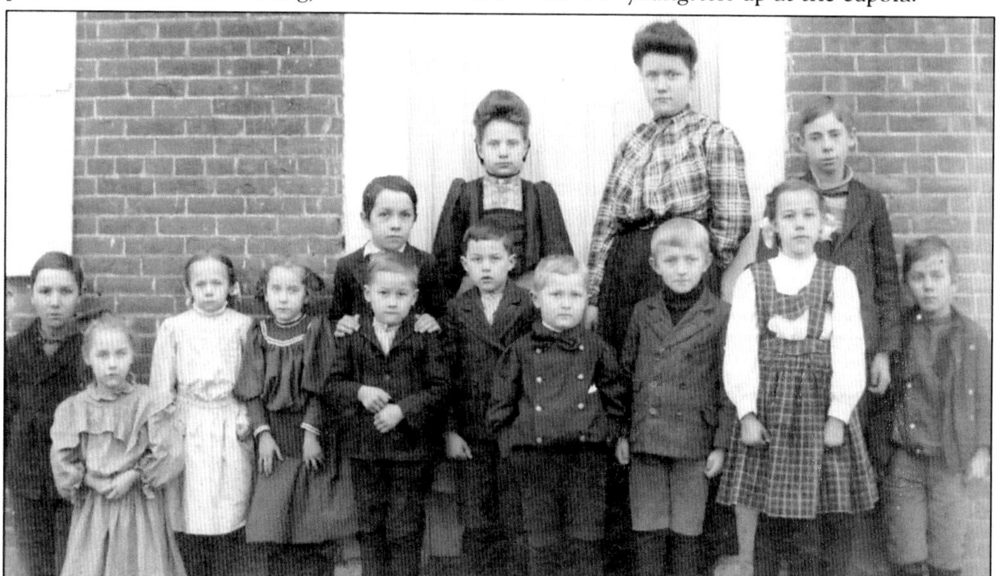

Vera Hummel, who later became the wife of Charles Fisher, taught at App's one-room school, located at the intersection of Mill and Airport Roads just outside of Selinsgrove. Shown in this 1906–1907 school year image from left to right are (first row) William Kratzer, Mary Kratzer, Theresa Moyer, Helen Goss, Elmer Reed, Charles Fisher, Guy Gable, Beulah Reed, and Murray Kratzer; (second row) Ralph Kratzer, Clara Musser, Hummel, and Robert Oswald.

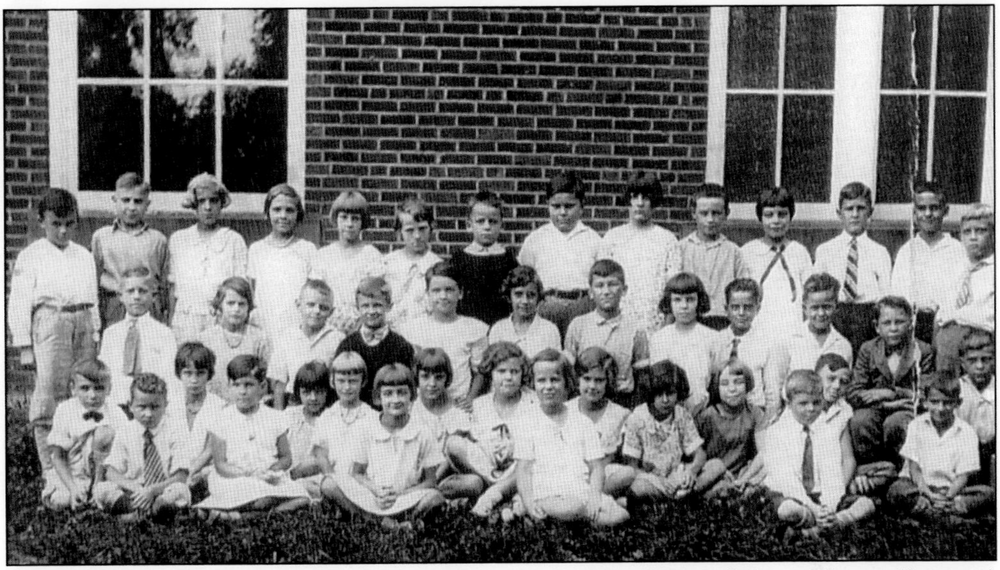

Jennie Miller's 1930 fourth graders pose at Pine Street School. From left to right are (first row) J. North, L. Bordner, D. Zechman, J. Killian, and M. Musselman; (second row) L. Newman, F. Spotts, unidentified, B. Stickle, unidentified, E. Row, A. Row, M. Reichley, A. Naugle, P. Sears, and W. Fritz; (third row) J. Wendt, C. Schnee, E. Aurand, R. Shafer, unidentified, H. Bogar, J. Rathfon, B. Smith, R. Mutchler, unidentified, R. Sechrist, and L. Musselman; (fourth row) H. Dreese, D. Stauffer, L. Trutt, P. Lentz, unidentified, B. Rhoads, C. Rathfuss, P. Coryell, H. Kern, L. Dreese, C. Bardell, R. Wilson, F. Gaugler, and W. Haas.

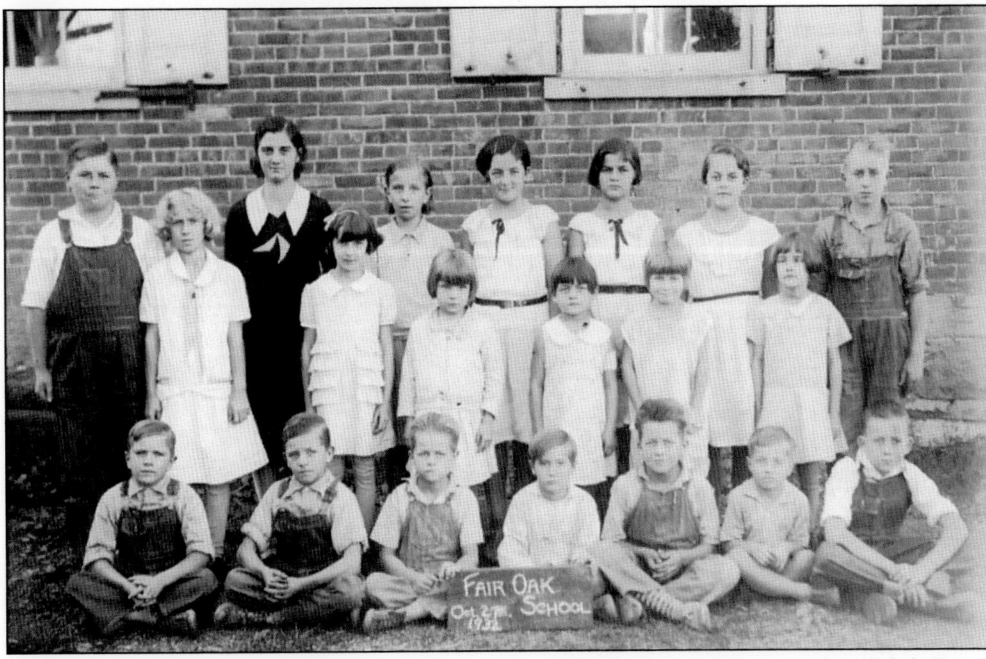

Picture day at the Fair Oak School on October 27, 1932. Shown with her pupils is Edith Boyer, who later married Percy Miller. Boyer's two sisters, Catherine and Hazel, were also teachers. The one-room school was located in the Salem area west of Selinsgrove. Identification of the pupils at the first through eighth-grade school was not provided.

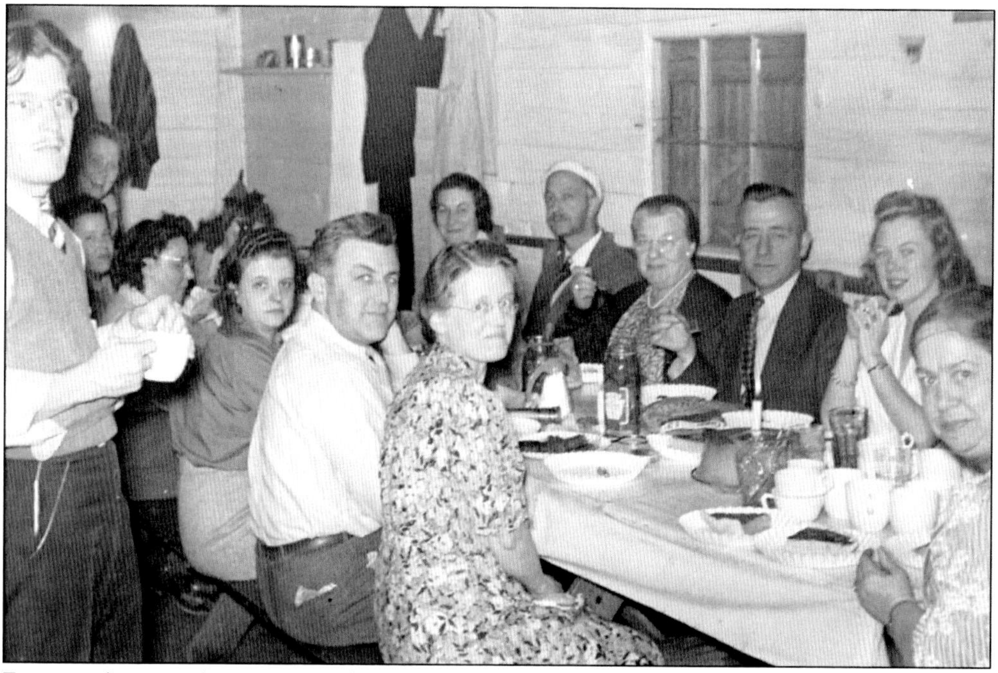

Even teachers need to get away from the classroom. Here Selinsgrove faculty are at a Heber Hendricks cabin retreat at Tall Timbers in September 1941. At the table from left to right are (first row) Dorothy Macfarlane, Mary Mitterling, Celia Marks, Kathryn Fasold, Albert Potteiger, and Elizabeth Scharf; (second row) Mildred Follmer, Harold Follmer, Anna Mae Frymire, Harry Frymire, Martha Manifold, and Elizabeth Hendricks. Standing is Paul Campbell.

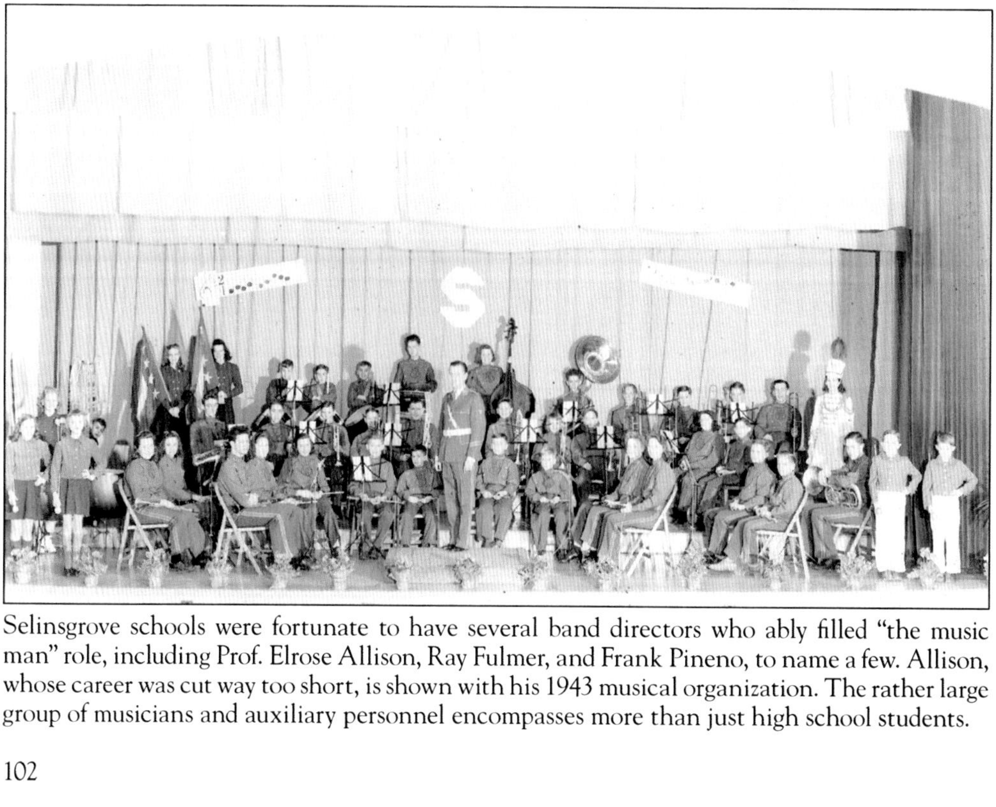

Selinsgrove schools were fortunate to have several band directors who ably filled "the music man" role, including Prof. Elrose Allison, Ray Fulmer, and Frank Pineno, to name a few. Allison, whose career was cut way too short, is shown with his 1943 musical organization. The rather large group of musicians and auxiliary personnel encompasses more than just high school students.

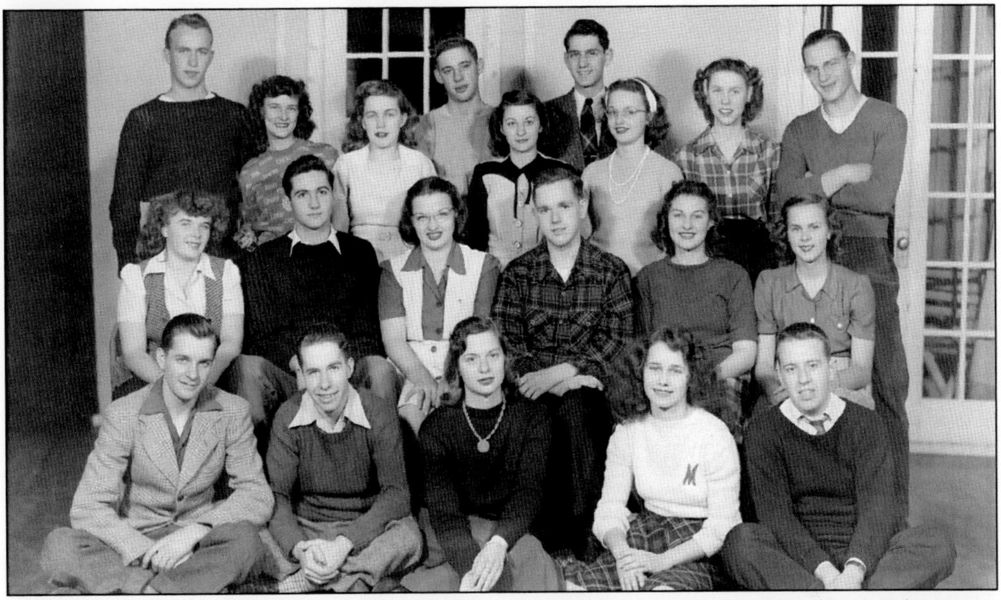

As usual, sisters Miss Phoebe and Miss Eva Herman directed the senior class play at Selinsgrove High School. In 1946, it was *China Boy*. From left to right, cast members are (first row) Ken Geist, Bob Laubscher, Ann Yorty, Mary Herman, and George Shaffer; (second row) Mae Evans, Ken McIntosh, Ruth Ruch, Charles Tyler, Louise Follmer, and Wilma Holtzapple; (third row) Don Fisher, Ferne Heintzleman, Jane Hersh, Charlie Gaugler, Jeanne Ludwig, Dave Bilger, Anna Belle Botteiger, Ethel Emery, and Bill Hummel.

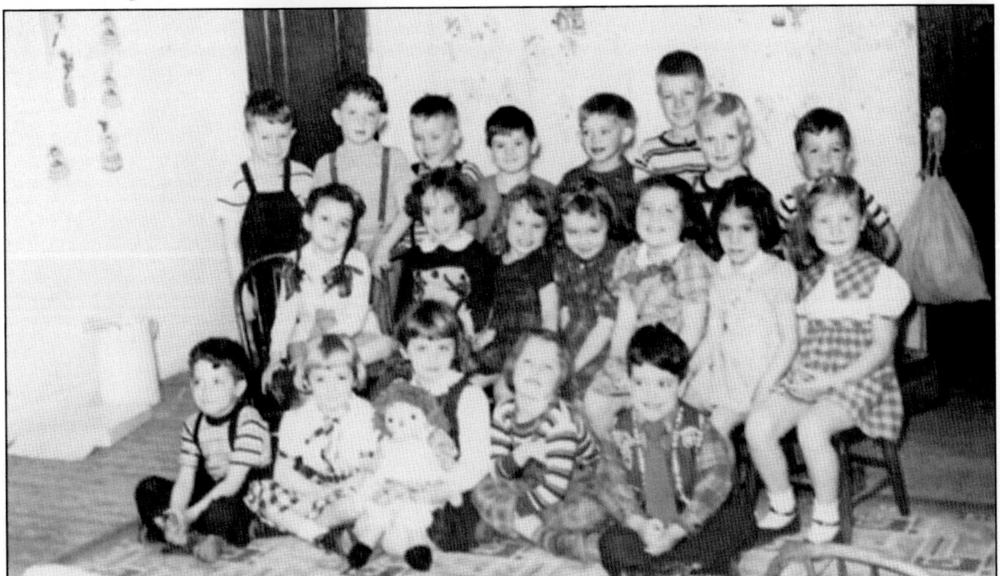

Ann Traher was named Selinsgrove's woman of the year in 1949. Her main contribution was the private Tiny Tot Kindergarten. Pictured in 1948 from left to right are (first row) John Troutman, Geraldine Heinbach, Tanna Burns, Priss Hall, and Craig Hummel; (second row) Letty Roush, Wanda Steffen, Maryon "Booty" Beck, Susie Fisher, Anne McGeehan, Sherrill Grugan, and Stephanie Franta; (third row) Pat Murray, Barry Kahn, Dave Rishell, Jimmie Stiber, Warren Bowersox, Bill Heim, Dale Miller, and Garner Traher Jr.

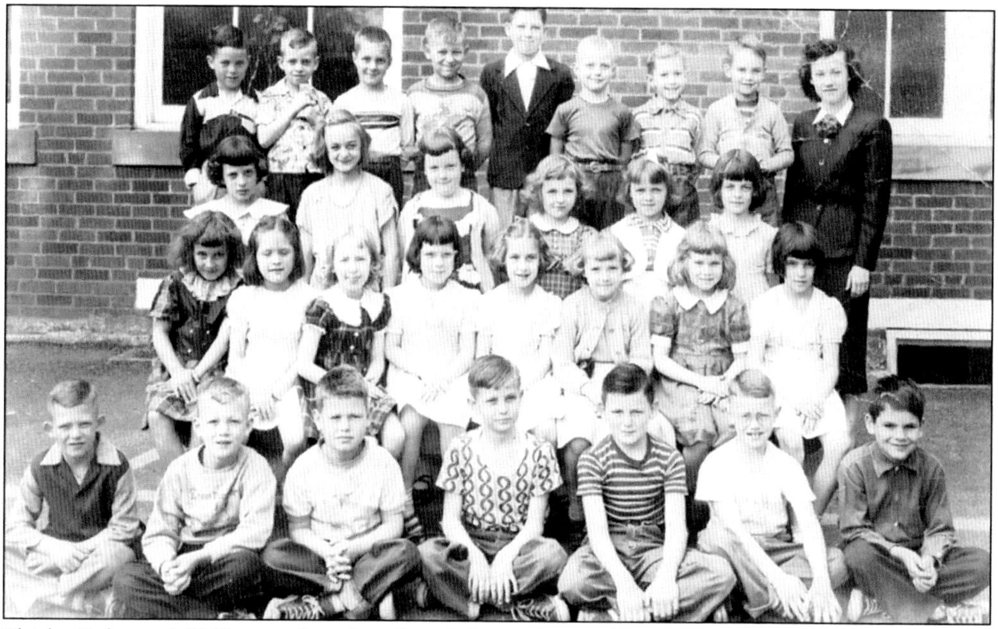

Shirley Solomon's 1951 second graders, from left to right, are (first row) G. Herrold, B. Zimmerman, T. Klock, F. Berkey, A. Kline, C. Greiner, and H. Christine; (second row) J. Bogar, P. Hall, B. Adams, M. A. Bolig, J. Bilger, D. Badger, B. Beck, and S. Grugan; (third row) J. Fisher, N. Willis, E. Fichter, S. Girton, C. J. Beaver, and D. Banney; (fourth row) J. Ludwig, K. Kinney, A. Bowen, J. Evers, C. Snyder, D. Miller, W. Bingaman, T. Conrad, and Solomon.

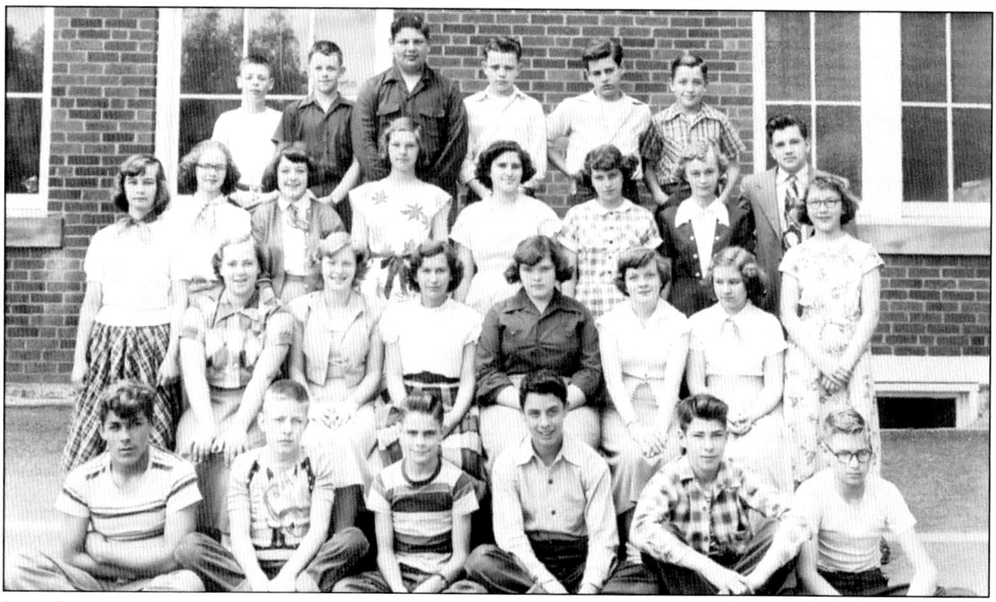

Ken Borst was the 8-1 homeroom teacher for the 1950–1951 school year. From left to right, his prize pupils are (first row) K. Krohn, D. Bowen, G. Aucker, J. Gaglione, J. Krohn, and K. Fahnestock; (second row) P. Parker, S. Heiser, H. Benner, F. Lewis, L. Kelly, C. Bedeaux, R. Frost, and L. Kratzer; (third row) D. Miller, G. Haddon, M. Aungst, J. Nace, C. Bingaman, D. Fisher, and Borst; (fourth row) J. Campbell, R. Forster, C. Bickhart, B. Benner, G. Christine, and B. Anderson.

Perhaps no one family had a greater impact on Selinsgrove's educational system than that of Dr. Percival Herman. Each of his three daughters graduated from Susquehanna University and had lengthy careers in education. Pictured from left to right in 1951 are Phoebe, Beatrice, and Eva Herman. Miss Phoebe and Miss Eva were icons at Selinsgrove High School for decades. Miss Beatrice chose the collegiate level. First she was at the University of Pittsburgh before returning to her alma mater as bursar for years.

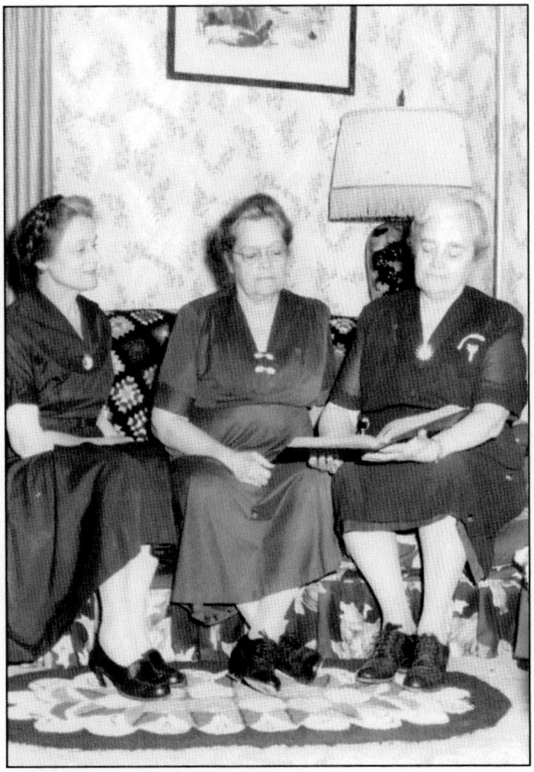

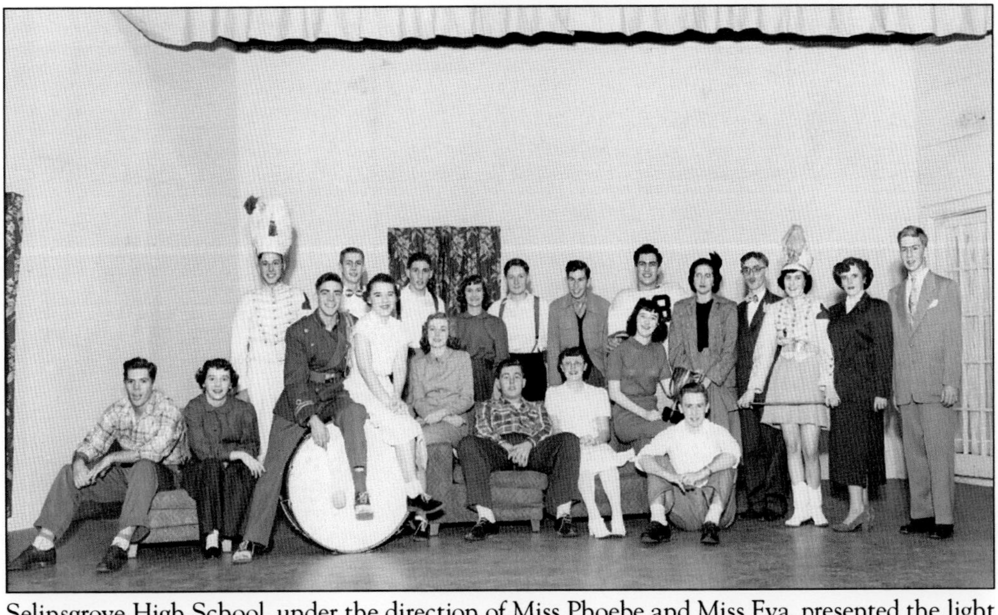

Selinsgrove High School, under the direction of Miss Phoebe and Miss Eva, presented the light comedy *The Beauty and the Beef* in 1951. From left to right, the cast includes (first row) N. Long, K. Koch, E. LeMay, N. Lepley, H. Redkay, D. Ritchie, M. A. Stauffer, D. Haddon, and R. Hepner; (second row) H. Lesher, D. Kretz, B. Rowe, D. Murray, G. Van Winkle, J. Taylor, Dale Booth, M. Feeher, J. Loudy, Jewell Hunt, L. Bailey, and B. Luck. Hunt was the beauty, and Booth was the beef.

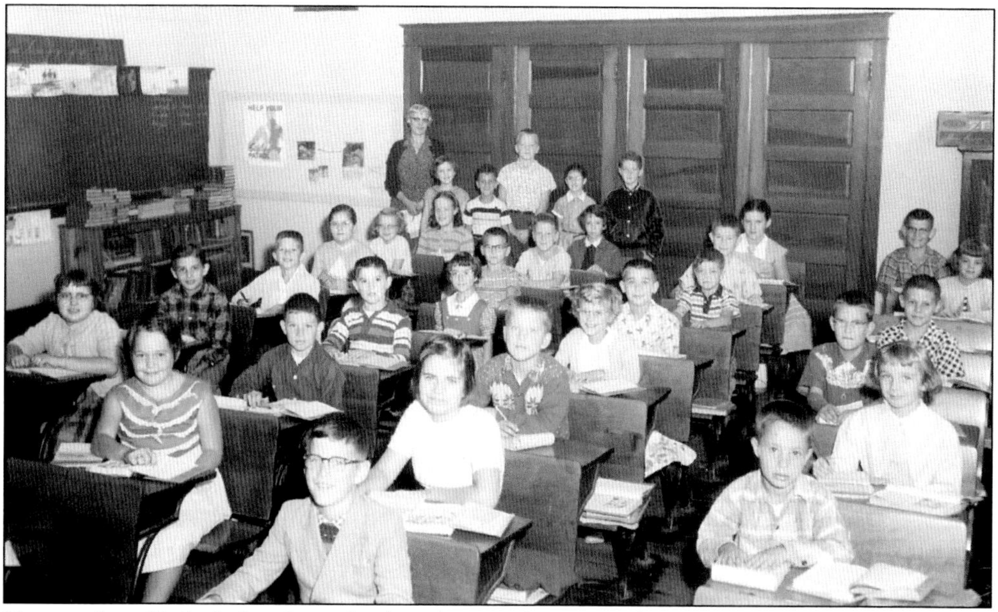

Here is Ann Bailey's fourth-grade class from 1956–1957. The students are identified by row from left to right and by seat from front to back. In the first row are K. Hoffman, C. Herrold, D. Lauver, H. Heimbach, H. Haas, and T. Fitzgerald; second row, J. Anderson, J. Fry, G. Hummel, L. Gemberling, D. Heiser, B. Bowen, and D. Wilt; third row, D. Adams, S. Ressler, D. Eichenlaub, D. Brouse, J. Goren, E. Cover, C. Aumiller, and C. Carvel; fourth row, S. Bressler, K. Bastress, P. Brouse, M. Gemberling, J. Aumiller, and T. Hoover. Standing from left to right are Mrs. Bailey, A. Zimmer, J. Kinney, J. Herbert, M. J. Harper, and J. Bingaman.

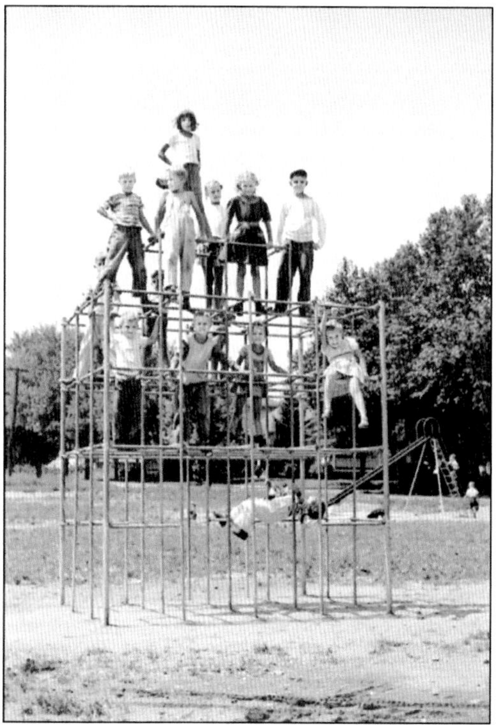

Once school is out, playgrounds are like kid magnets, as they should be. That was their purpose—to give kids a safe place to play. The LOOM playground at Mill and High Streets is a prime example, although some might question the safety of a jungle gym. Among those pictured are Dick Herbert, Harold Aucker, and Ann Lewis.

Eight

Fun and Games

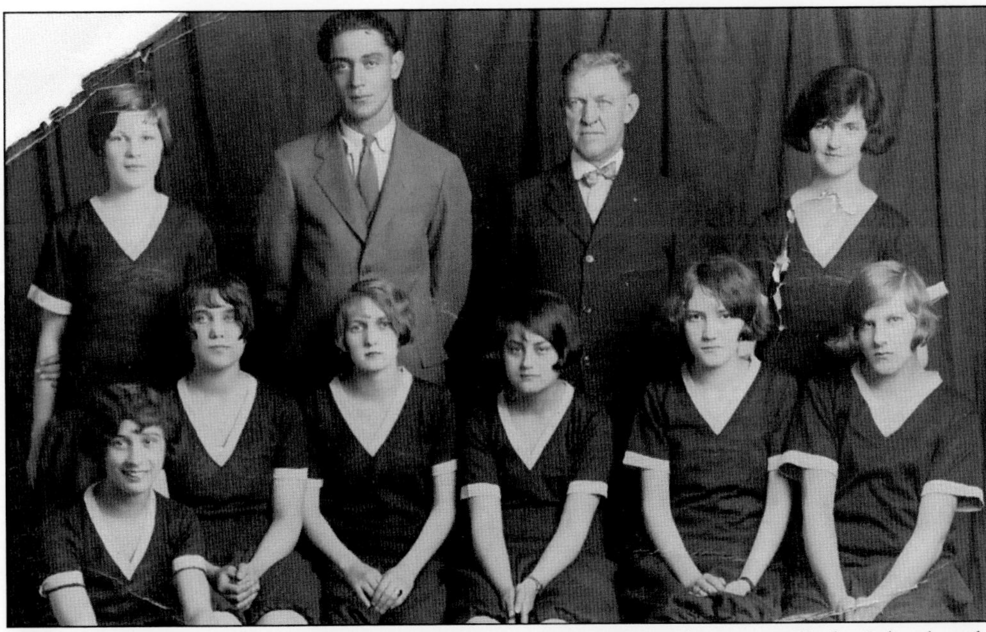

This somewhat shop-worn photograph of the 1925–1926 Selinsgrove High School girls' basketball team notes that the young ladies were "D.M.S. League Champions." No one has been able to determine what D.M.S. stands for. From left to right are (first row) Helen Kline, Gertrude Fisher, Mary Whiteley, captain Medora Coldren, Alma Bowersox, and Marion Bodmer; (second row) Elizabeth "Honey" Fisher, coach W. S. "Stew" Bannon, principal Heber Hendricks, and Cathryn Wagenseller.

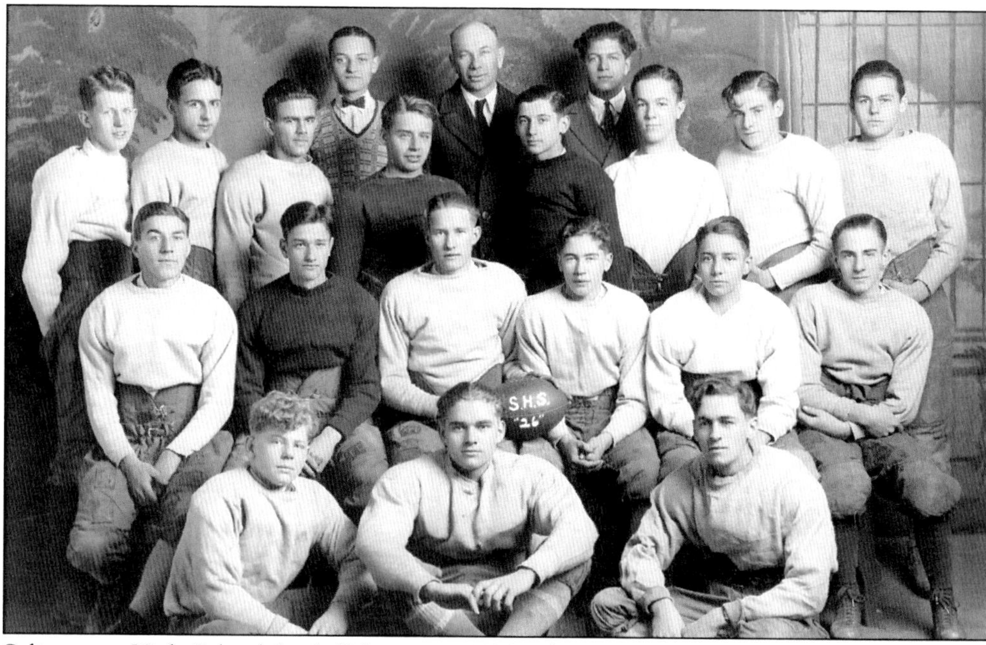

Selinsgrove High School football began in 1926, when Martin Beamenderfer formed a team for four games. From left to right, charter Seals are (first row) Fred Richter, Ralph Brouse, and George Detwiler; (second row) Ernie Rowe, Lance Bowen, John Salem, Lee "Skip" Rishel, Saylor Neiswender, and George Holtzapple; (third row) Seiler Phillips, Mark Lytle, Henry Fisher, Walter Groce, Manuel "Bud" Michaels, Rich Fisher, Warren Groce, and Howard Schnure; (fourth row) manager Ray Smith, coach Beamenderfer, and assistant coach Bruce Bendigo.

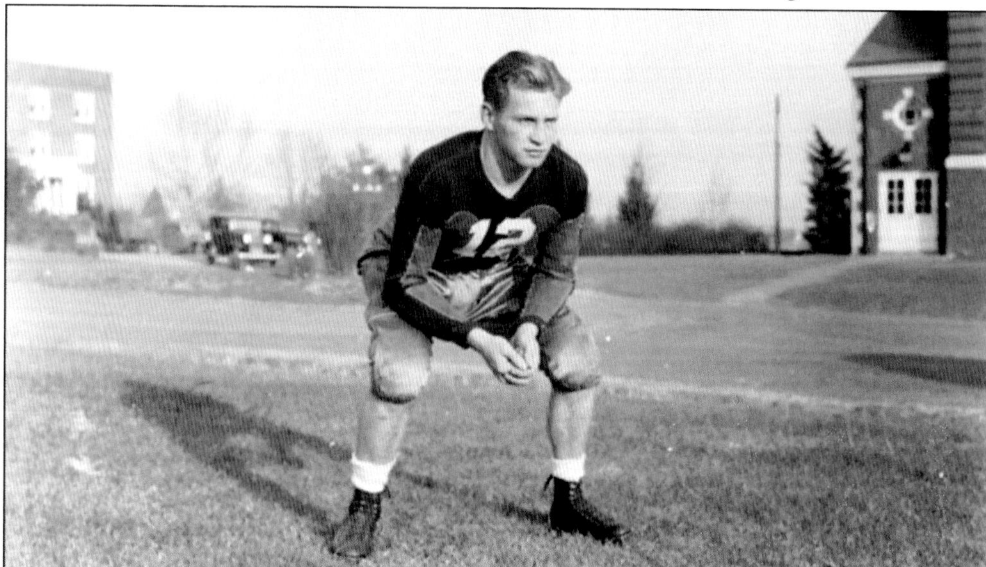

Selinsgrove High School star Paul Groce had a brief career at Susquehanna University. It was interrupted by World War II. However, it was a brilliant one. The slippery halfback was key in the Crusaders's unbeaten season of 1940. So effective was his open-field running in a 20-6 victory at the University of Buffalo on a sloppy, muddy field, that a New York sportswriter dubbed him "the Wizard of Ooze," a reference to the 1939 Oscar-winning film of almost the same name.

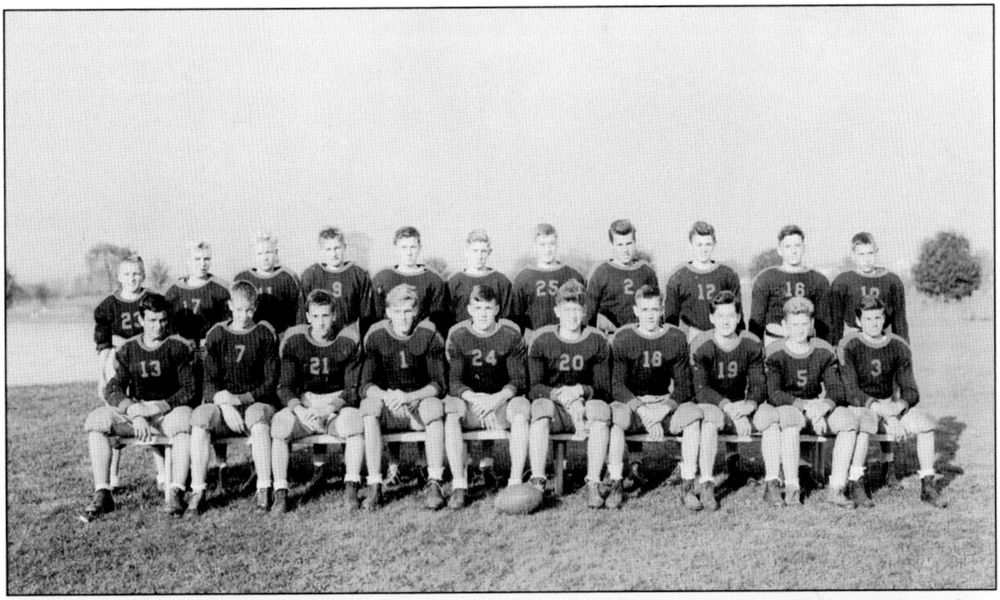

The 1944 Selinsgrove High School junior varsity team was made up of mostly 9th and 10th graders. Many starred for the Seals later. From left to right are (first row) Bill Van Buskirk, Clyde Bailey, Carl Dressler, Herb Schultz, George Hummel, Sherman Wolf, Paul Nolder, Bob Kuster, Glenn "Rip" Van Winkle, and Lear Wagner; (second row) George Sheetz, Charlie Farleman, Abie Fisher, Bill Bingaman, Marlin Young, Gene "Gus" Bodmer, Bob Shaffer, Wilson Foreman, Bob Pellman, John Finn, and Bob Musser.

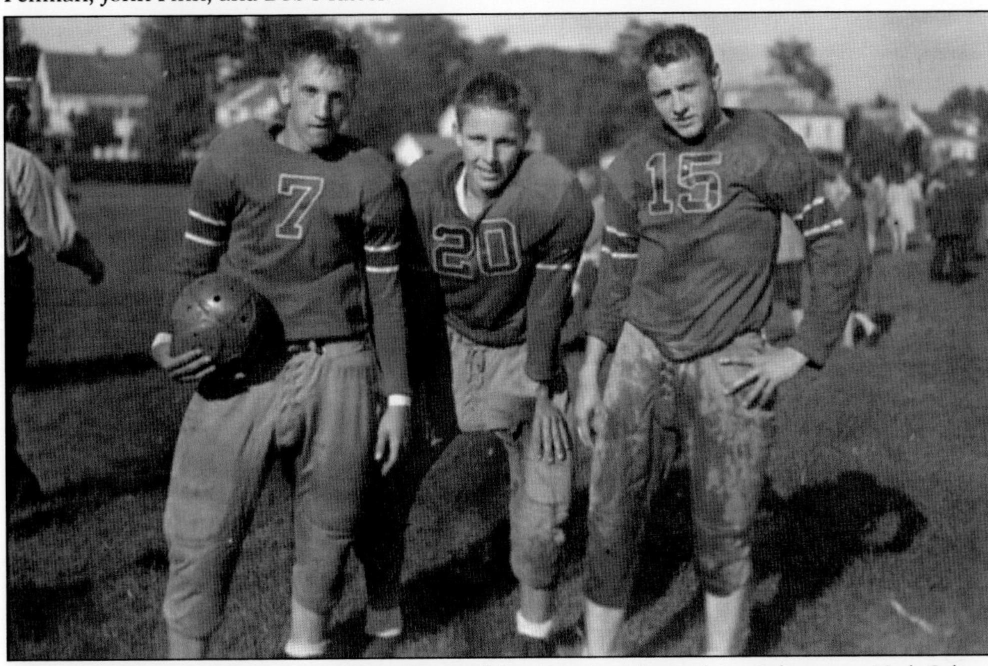

After a hard-fought 1944 game on Susquehanna University's gridiron, three Selinsgrove High School varsity players pose for a snapshot. The red jerseyed, leather-helmeted three amigos, from left to right, are Carl Dressler (who was later heroically killed in Korea), Wilfred "Bud" Duncan, and Wilfred "Wimp" Boyer. Those red jerseys were still being used by junior high teams in the mid-1950s.

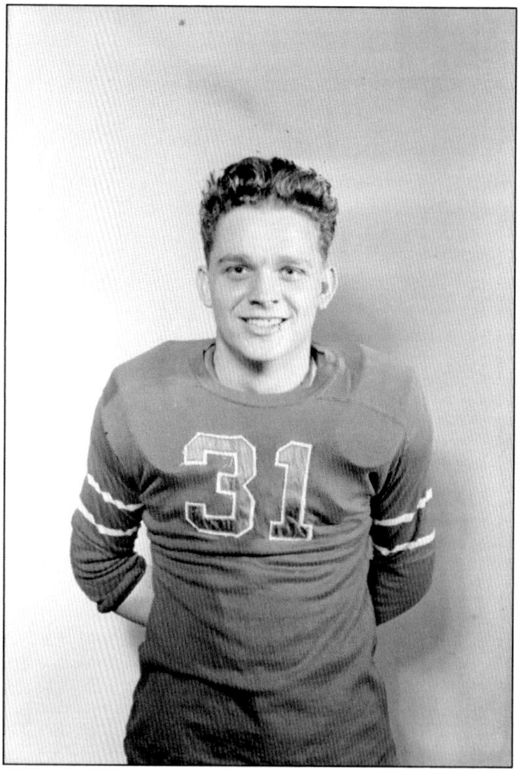

Any coach will say that games are won or lost "in the trenches," the battle along the line of scrimmage. To win, sturdy players not concerned with making headlines are needed. Lewie Rowe, a stocky guard, provided stellar line play for Selinsgrove High School under revered coach Tom Valunas during the World War II years. Fellow lineman included Wilfred "Bud" Duncan, Gene Leitzel, Bob Kuster, George Shaffer, Carl Dressler, George Hepner, and Don Fisher.

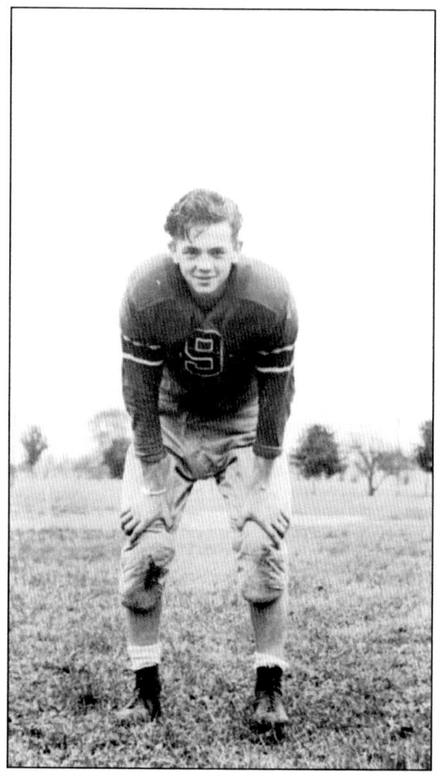

Jack Treas, a fine all-around athlete from the war years, was one of the Seals' backfield performers who benefited from the up-front work of Lewie Rowe and his mates. On the gridiron, Treas was truly one of "Saturday's heroes." Sharing backfield duties with him on coach Valunas's squads were Luke "Dick" Bogar, Al "Junie" Shaffer, Glenn Shaffer, and Wilfred "Wimp" Boyer.

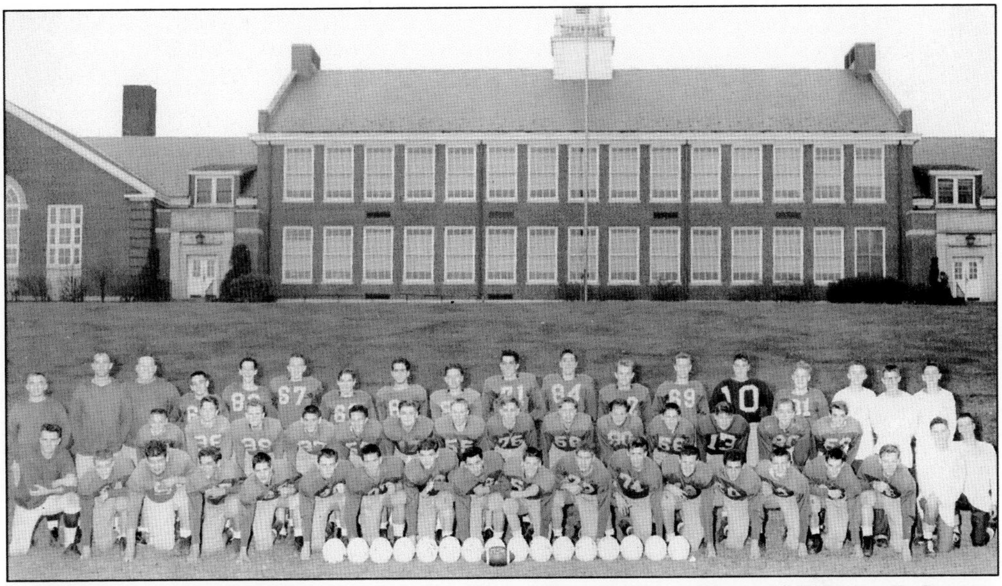

Football success in 1953 led to more in 1954. From left to right are (first row) T. Dean, D. Bowen, C. Bickhart, K. Krohn, M. Reed, R. Forster, M. Hoffman, D. Moyer, J. Gaglione, J. Campbell, K. Fahnestock, G. Snyder, W. Mengel, B. Hare, J. Wittes, D. Hane, I. Parker, T. Helvig, and R. Stauffer; (second row) C. Bowen, D. Thomas, A. Zerbe, D. Wendt, L. Nichols, Z. Wolf, C. Naugle, R. Naugle, R. Duncan, B. Fausey, C. Bailey, S. Leitner, L. Herrold, and M. Snyder; (third row) C. Rowe, J. Loudenberg, D. Smoker, L. Higgins, G. Walter, D. Heiser, J. Hartley, M. Herring, D. Mull, D. Booth, G. Hilbert, B. Gargie, P. Heimbach, B. Jarrett, J. Haines, G. Shotsberger, D. Troutman, and M. Inch.

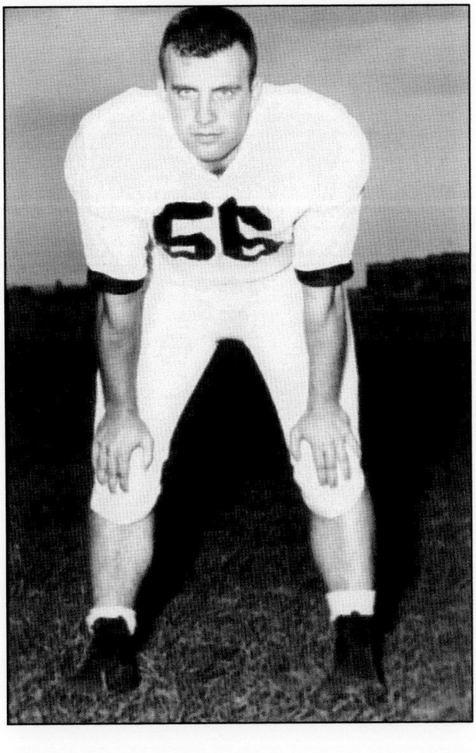

Earl Brown left Selinsgrove High School in 1950 and became a four-year starter at Lock Haven University. After graduation, he followed such legends as Joe Foss and Greg "Pappy" Boyington into Marine Corps aviation. While playing for a navy flight training team at Pensacola, Florida, he played for the service championship versus Fort Ord in the Poinsettia Bowl. A career officer, he flew over 100 sorties in Vietnam in an A-4 fighter. Many recall how later he would buzz Selinsgrove in his Marine Corps jet fighters.

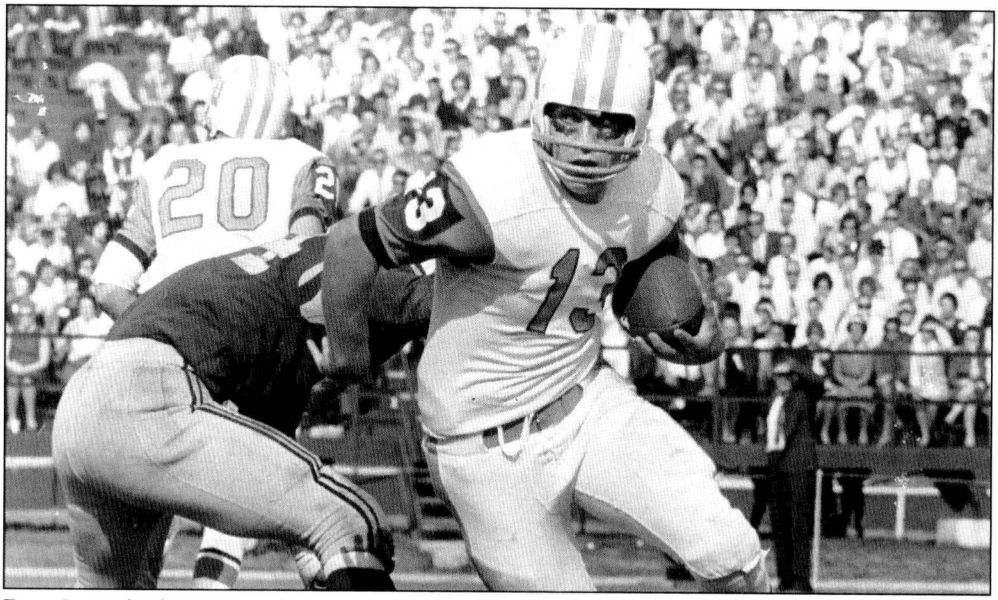

Don Green had no compunctions about wearing jersey No. 13. It was lucky for him and luckier for Susquehanna University. He stepped into the starting lineup as quarterback as a freshman. Green was the 35th overall American Football League draft choice in 1964, and the second choice of the Oakland Raiders. Over a decade later, Al Davis told a Selinsgrove resident, "Don Green could have played a long time for our club." At William Penn High School in Harrisburg, Green played for former Selinsgrove High School Seals coach Tom Dean.

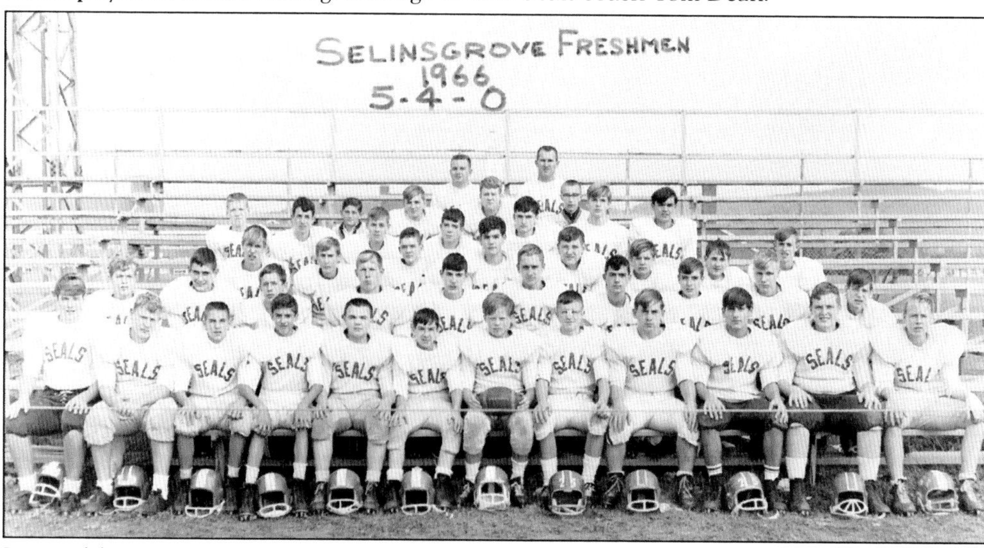

Pictured here is the undefeated 1966 ninth-grade team of coaches Ken Wochley and Gene Koehler. From left to right are (first row) B. Weston, C. Sampsell, D. Wendt, L. Greiner, F. Mease, T. Rowe, G. Bailey, J. Sassaman, K. Knapp, J. DeDay, B. Smoley, and J. Eisenhart; (second row) S. Troutman, C. Antanavage, D. Ferrari, R. Hummel, J. Reed, A. Antanavage, K. Kratzer, D. Kiess, R. Kissinger, and J. Dorak; (third row) F. Parker, R. Minnich, M. Marr, D. Pittenger, R. Nolder, C. Downs, B. Picton, and C. Beaver; (fourth row) K. Heaton, J. Inch, R. Rathfon, T. Kreitzer, D. Smith, J. Shadle, and B. Clouser; (fifth row) J. Renner, G. Wendt, R. Smoker, and R. Bolig; (sixth row) Wochley and Koehler.

The author was fortunate enough to be a sideline worker for the Pittsburgh Steelers, from 1970 to 1977. He told those who would listen, "Yeah, [Terry] Bradshaw and I were rookies together." One of his duties was organizing the starting lineup for pregame introductions.

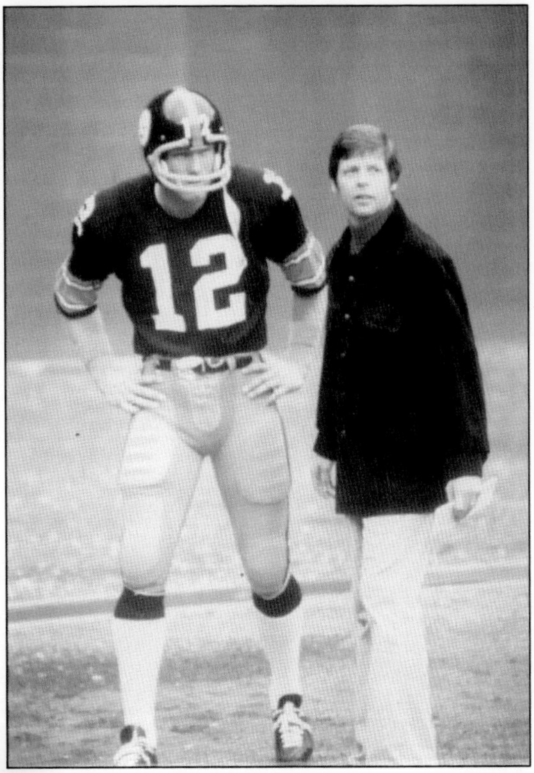

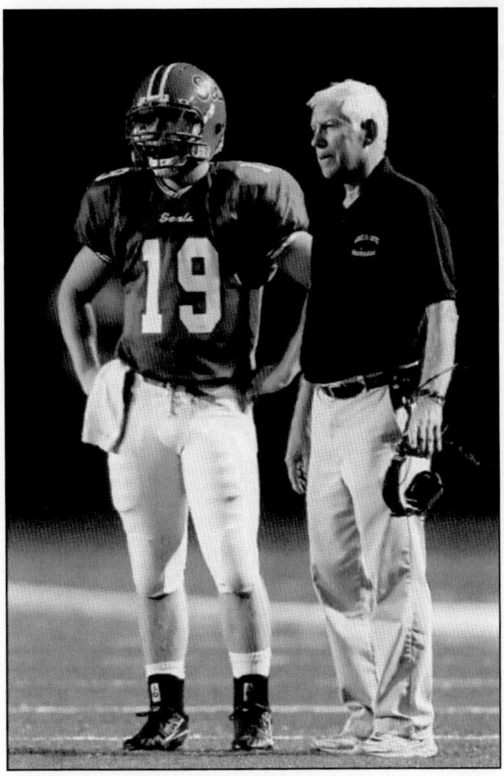

Selinsgrove High School has been fortunate to have a considerable number of successful football coaches over the long local history of the sport. With the possible exception of Pete Bolig, no one stayed and continued to produce winners like Bill Scott (pictured here with quarterback Eric Deckard). Scott coached the Seals for 36 seasons from 1972 to 2007. After medical issues during the summer that would have sidelined many, Scott earned statewide coach of the year honors for another fine season.

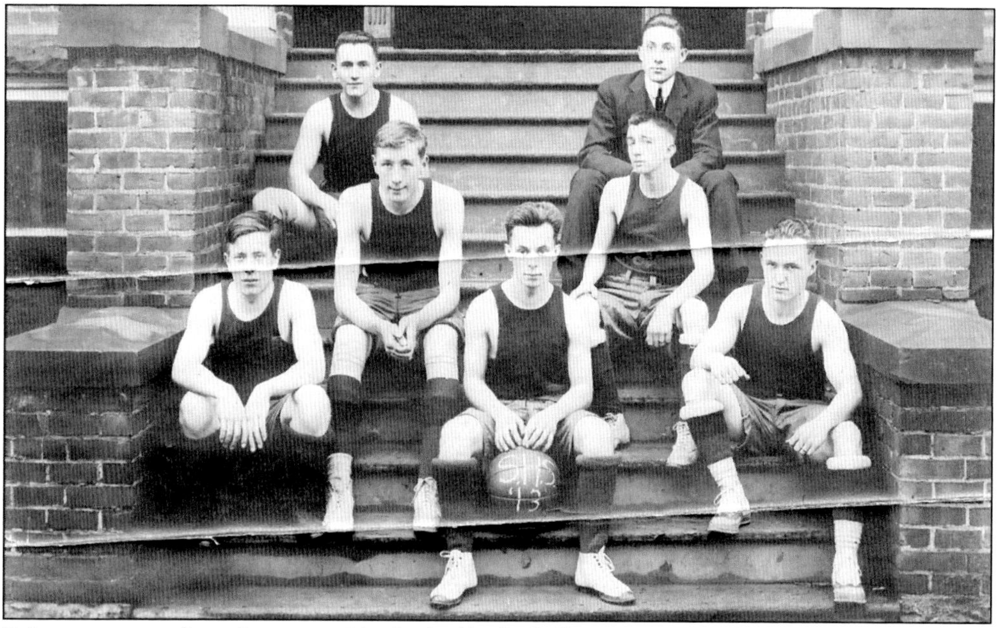

Selinsgrove must have been a real hotbed of basketball at one time. The game was invented in 1891, and two decades later, Selinsgrove High School already had a successful team. Without a gym of their own, the Seals practiced and played in Susquehanna University Alumni Gym. Posing on the gym's steps in their precursors to Air Jordans are Paul Houseworth in the first row, Brewster Schoch (second row, left), Ed Phillips (third row, left) and coach C. Fiske Brill (third row, right).

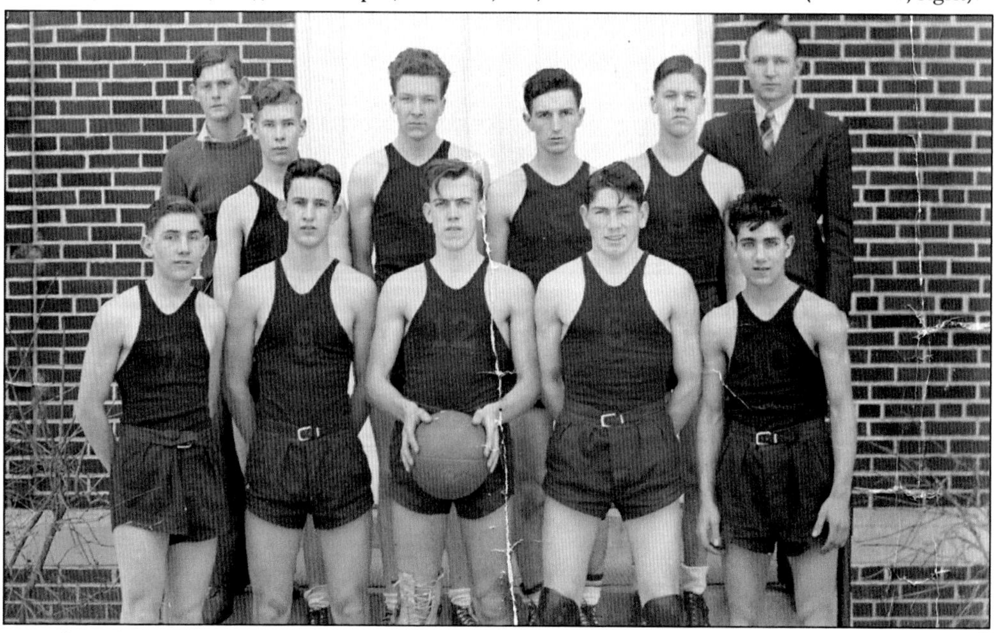

Not phased by the cold and snow, the Selinsgrove High School 1940–1941 "thin clads," as Bill Toland often referred to basketball players, pose in their abbreviated uniforms on the back steps of the school's gym. From left to right are (first row) Bob Keiser, Bob Bolig, G. Morris "Bud" Smith, John Dietzler, and Angelo Conti; (second row) Art Emery, Jack Hummel, Lee Steffen, and Jim Mowles; (third row) manager Ray "Red" Sanders and coach Tom Valunas.

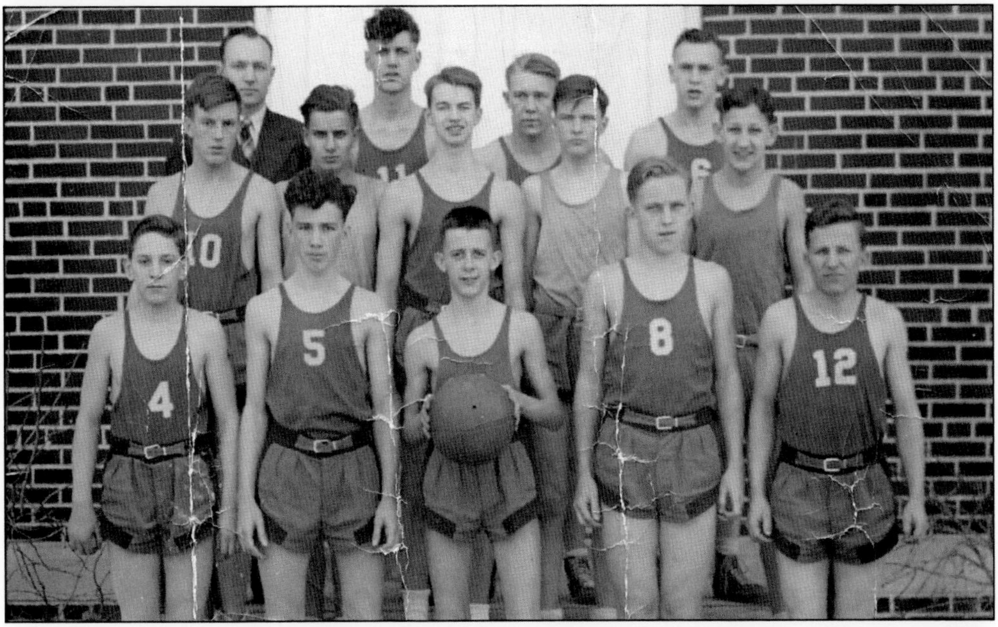

By the mid-1940s, this 1940–1941 Selinsgrove High School junior varsity team formed the nucleus of the varsity basketball team. From left to right are (first row) Danny Reitz, Stan Rice, Claire "Tee Hee" Spotts, Galen Troup, and Bob Lepley; (second row) John "Ducky" Snyder, Elmer Groce, Ralph Witmer, Dick Schuck, and Bob Bogar; (third row) coach Valunas, Ernie Renninger, Louie Reichenbach, and Marvin Hollenbach.

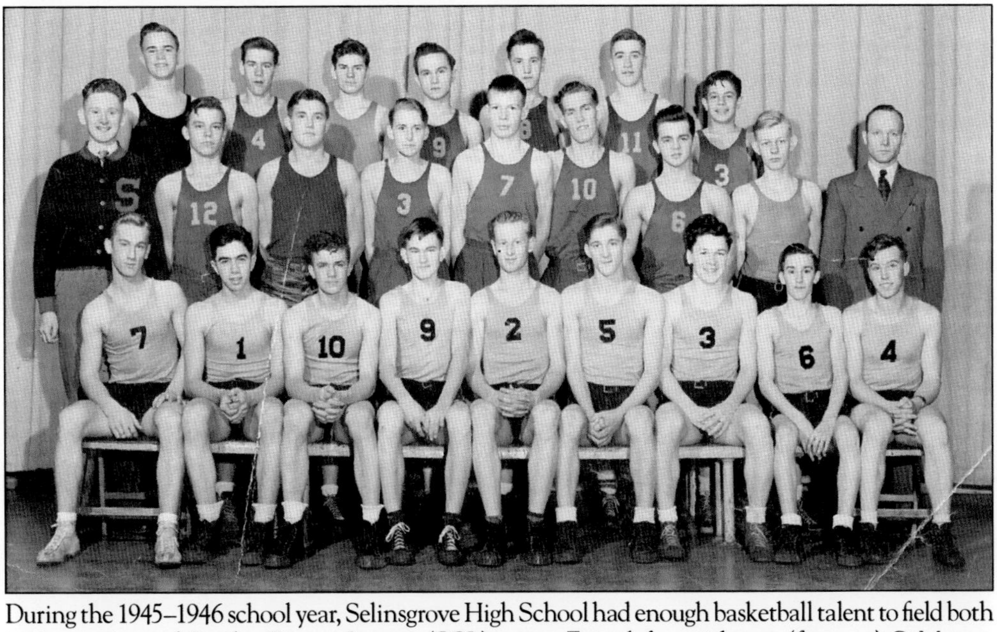

During the 1945–1946 school year, Selinsgrove High School had enough basketball talent to field both junior varsity and Snyder County League (SCL) teams. From left to right are (first row) C. Musser, G. Gaugler, S. Lenig, B. Reed, D. Ferry, R. Kline, A. Snyder, H. Fisher, and R. Walter; (second row) G. Van Winkle, J. Smith, G. Hummel, N. Walshaw, P. Bailey, H. Schultz, J. Treas, O. Kantner, and T. Valunas; (third row) M. Fisher, D. Foltz, L. Wagner, D. Day, C. Dressler, B. Shaffer, and M. Herman. The SCL players are in light shirts, and the junior varsity team is in the dark shirts.

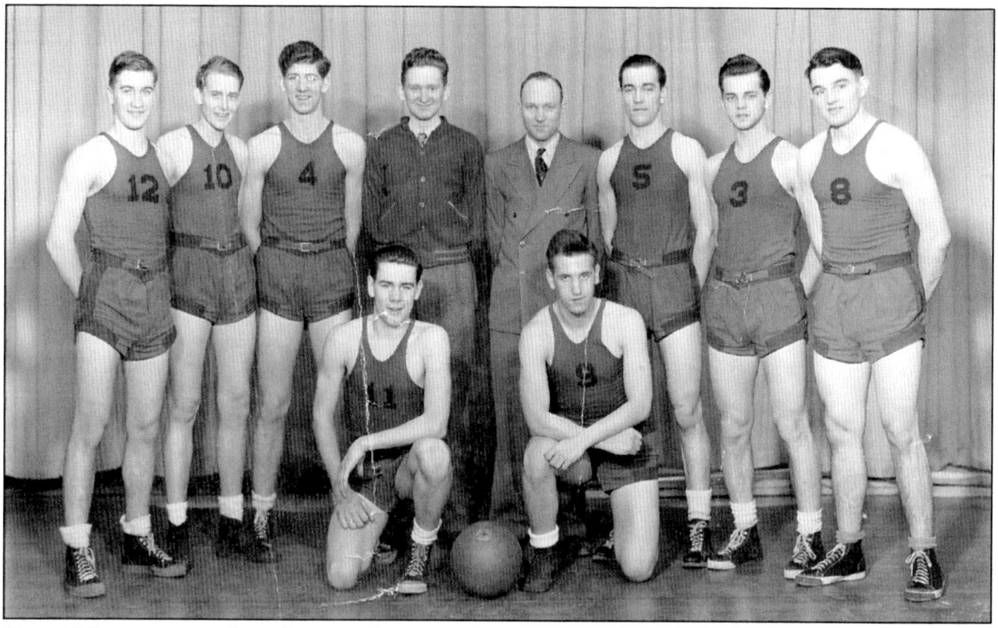

Tom Valunas, revered as few coaches ever are, mentored football, basketball, and baseball teams in the 1940s at Selinsgrove High School. Pictured is his 1947–1948 basketball team, or "dribblers"—another Bill Toland term. From left to right are (first row) Donnie Foltz and Carl Dressler; (second row) Bob Shaffer, Nick Walshaw, Sherman "Dasher" Wolfe, manager Glenn "Rip" Van Winkle, coach Valunas, Paul Nolder, Jack Treas, and Frank Heiser.

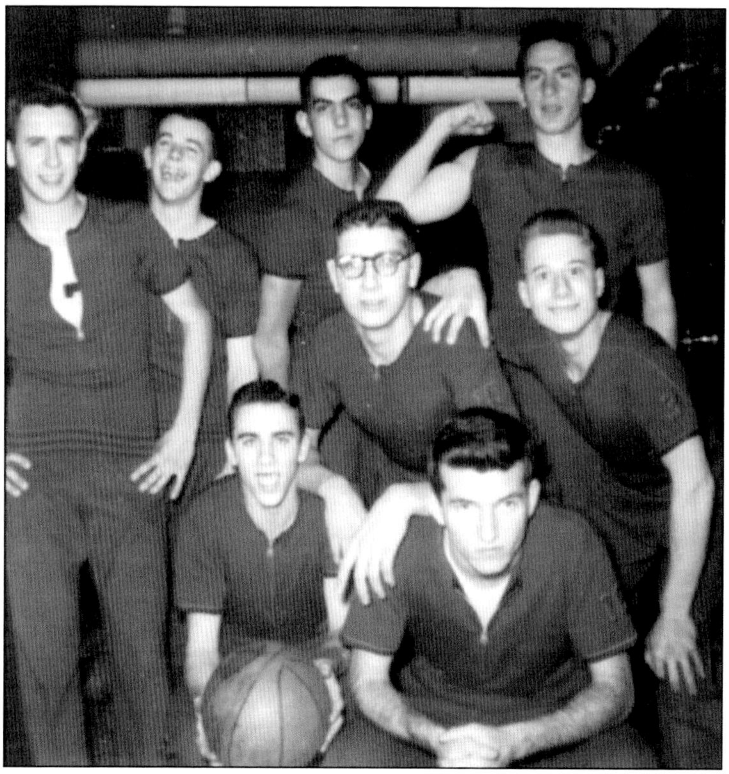

Selinsgrove High School's Blair Heaton, like football's Vince Lombardi, had a reputation as a strict disciplinarian. Just as a photograph exists of the 1963 Green Bay Packers goofing off for a team picture, the 1954–1955 Seals found time for high jinx. From left to right are (first row) Dave Davis and a serious Barry "Buzz" Siegfried; (second row) Karl Fahnestock and Jerry Rhoads; (third row) George Snyder, Ron "Rube" Forster, Dean Booth, and Mark Hoffman. Kidding aside, the squad contended for Susquehanna Valley League (SVL) honors.

Cara Vignone inherited athletic genes. Her mother, the former Becky Herman, was a fine swimmer and diver and officiated local meets for years. Her father, John Vignone, was arguably Susquehanna University's most versatile athlete, playing professional football and baseball. Without the benefit of a high school swim program, Cara became a standout diver at the University of Rhode Island. At Selinsgrove High School, she was a multiyear letter winner on the girls' basketball team.

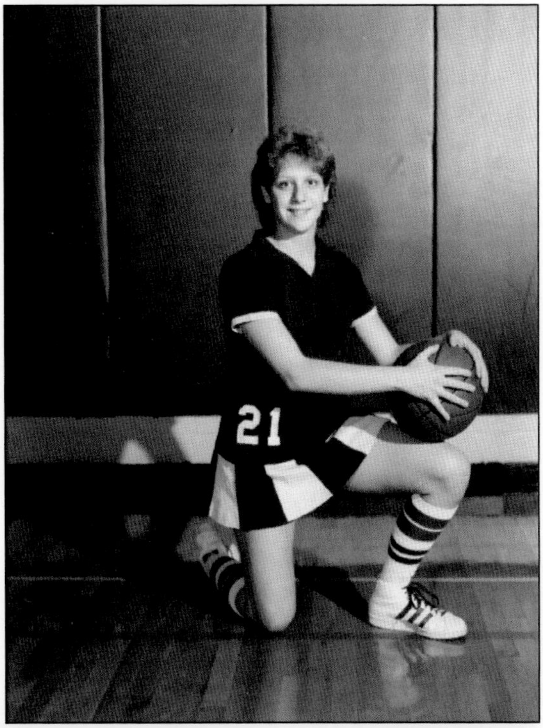

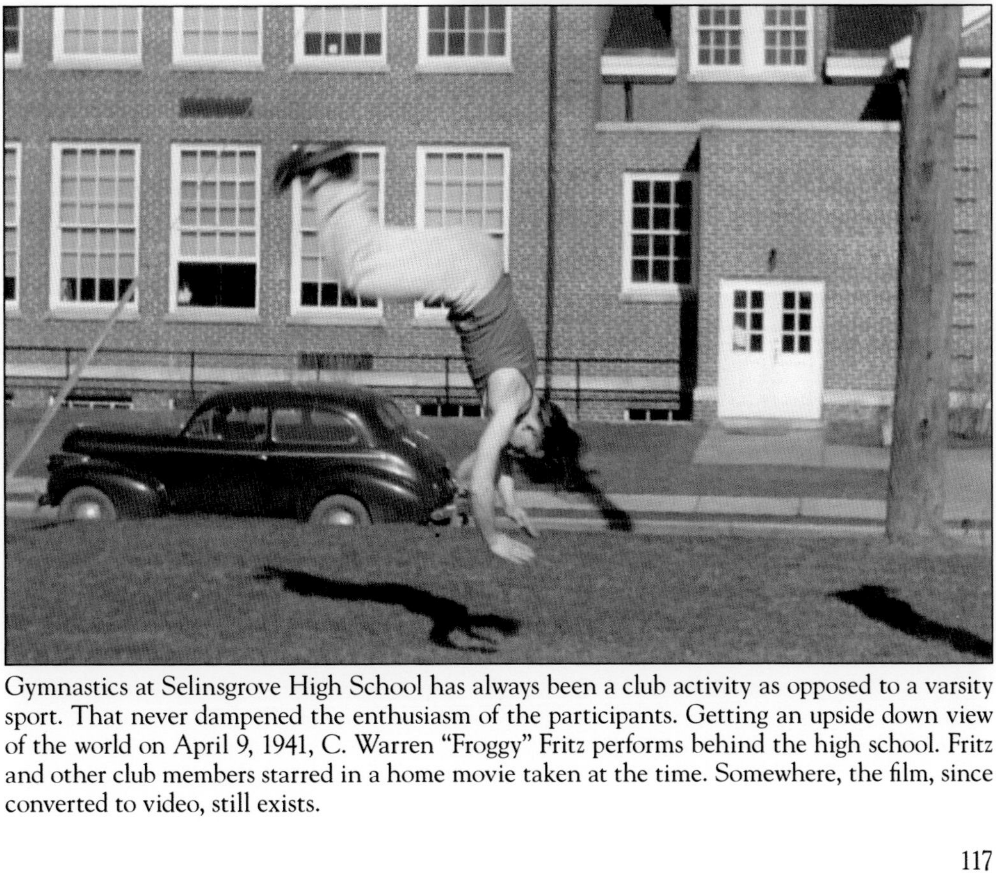

Gymnastics at Selinsgrove High School has always been a club activity as opposed to a varsity sport. That never dampened the enthusiasm of the participants. Getting an upside down view of the world on April 9, 1941, C. Warren "Froggy" Fritz performs behind the high school. Fritz and other club members starred in a home movie taken at the time. Somewhere, the film, since converted to video, still exists.

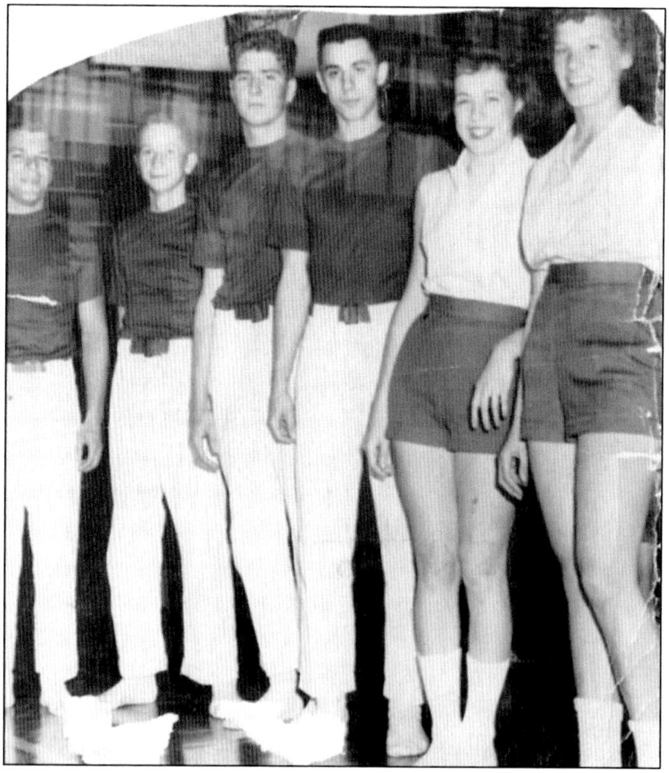

In 1954, under the direction of Bruce Wagenseller, Selinsgrove High School formed a trampoline team. Try finding a trampoline at a school these days. Somewhere along the way, they were deemed hazardous to one's health. Nevertheless, these five students enjoyed the activity. From left to right are advisor Wagenseller, Dale "Zeke" Thomas, Karl Fahnestock, Johnny Gaglione, Mary Ann Traher, and Ann Rowe.

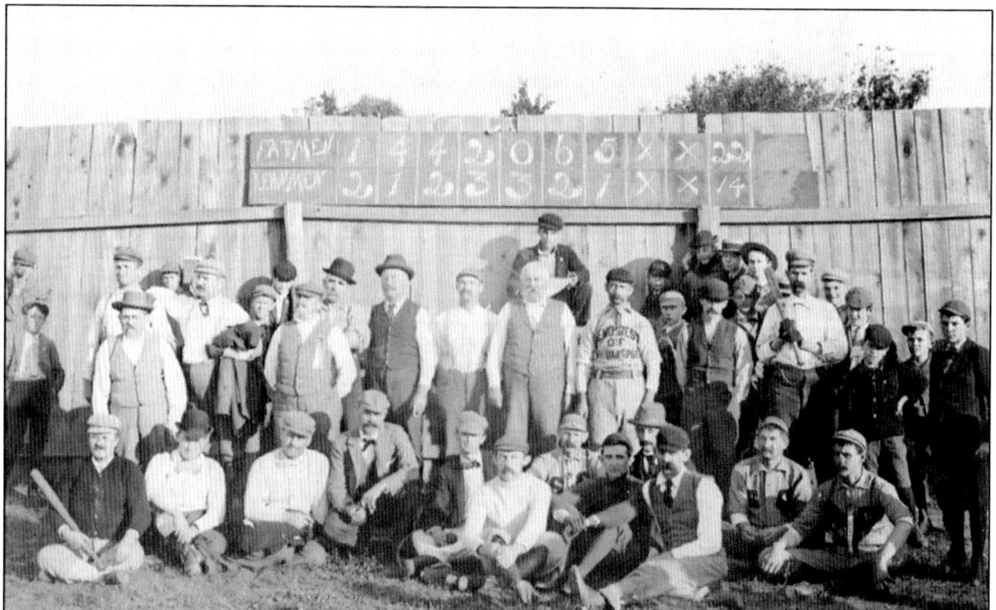

A fun time in Selinsgrove around 1900 was the annual benefit baseball game featuring the Fatmen versus the Leanmen. The Selinsgrove band was often the beneficiary of the charity game. This year, thought to be 1904, the heavyweights got the better of their thinner opponents. It is unclear if the game was scheduled for nine innings, but play was stopped after seven, with the Fatmen winning 22-14.

In his 1926 Selinsgrove High School *Cynosure*, Howard Schnure was described as "a combination of Babe Ruth and Red Grange," due to his prowess at baseball and football. After graduation, he prepped at Staunton Military Academy in Virginia. He then went to Duke University, where he became an ace pitcher. Duke was one of the first colleges to have a consistently good baseball program. It benefited from Philadelphia Athletics' manager Connie Mack paying tuition for several major-league prospects.

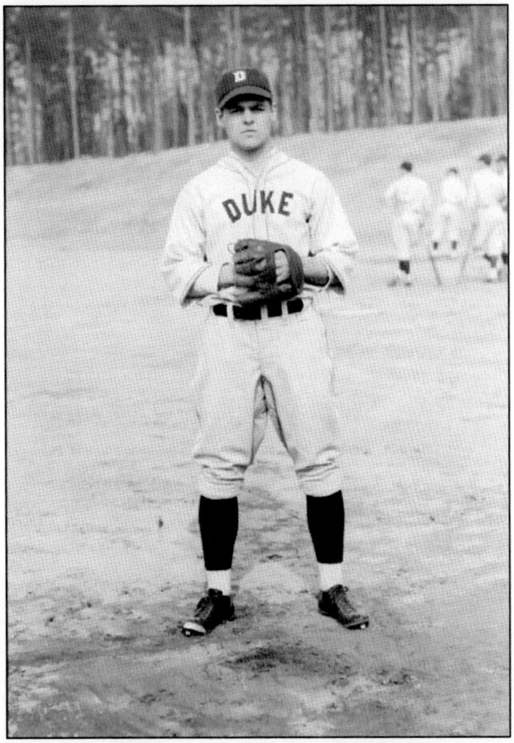

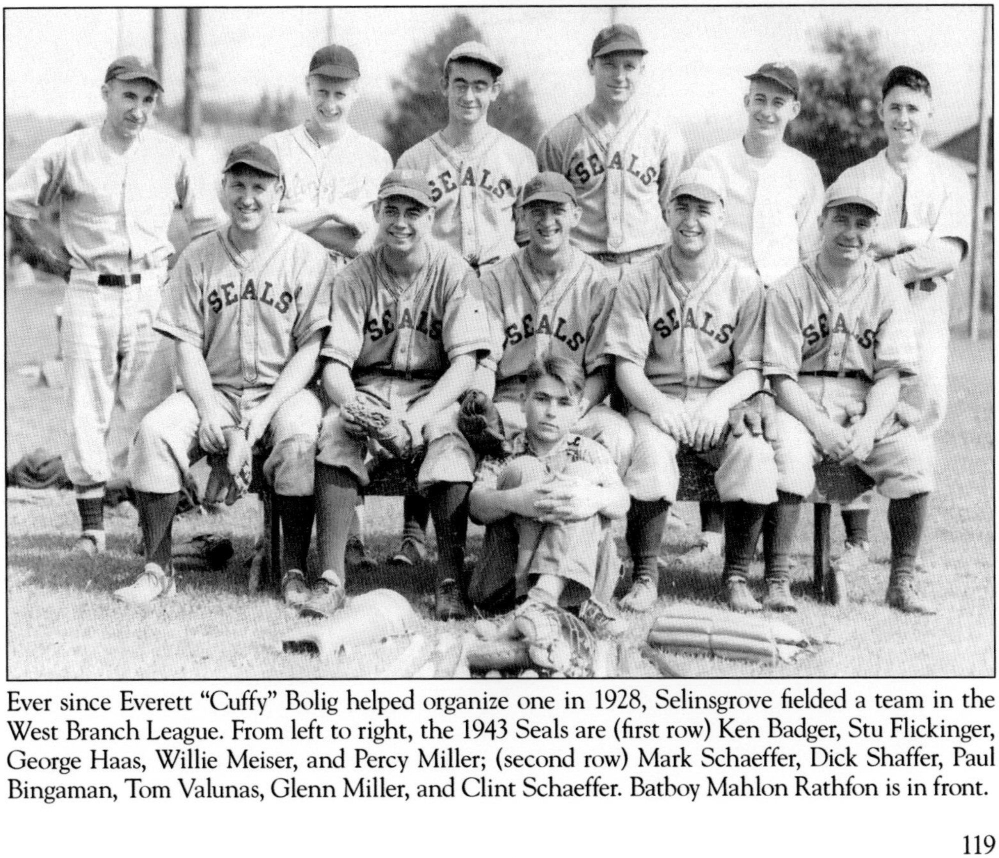

Ever since Everett "Cuffy" Bolig helped organize one in 1928, Selinsgrove fielded a team in the West Branch League. From left to right, the 1943 Seals are (first row) Ken Badger, Stu Flickinger, George Haas, Willie Meiser, and Percy Miller; (second row) Mark Schaeffer, Dick Shaffer, Paul Bingaman, Tom Valunas, Glenn Miller, and Clint Schaeffer. Batboy Mahlon Rathfon is in front.

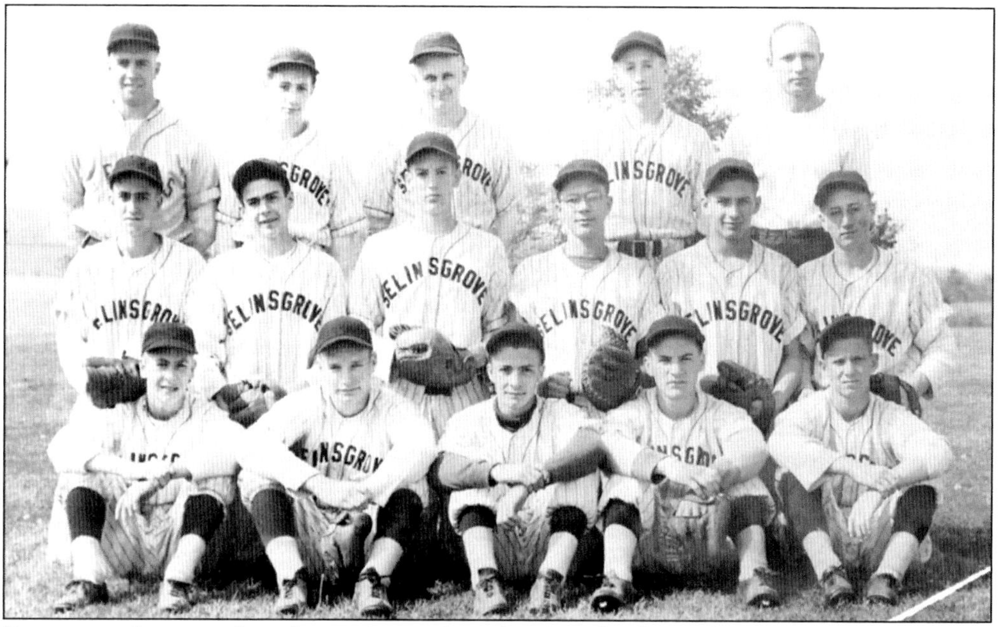

By necessity because of weather and an early end to the school year, high school baseball in this area is a short-season proposition. Nevertheless, the 1949 Selinsgrove High School Seals were a representative squad. From left to right are (first row) Dick Kretz, Davis Clark, Bob Riegle, George Gemberling, and Carson Miller; (second row) Johnny Robinson, Tommy Slayback, Jack Keller, captain George Wilhour, Bill Rowe, and Elton Kauffman; (third row) Earl Brown, Charlie Hoover, Jim "Peanut" Bolig, Roger Hepner, coach Tom Valunas.

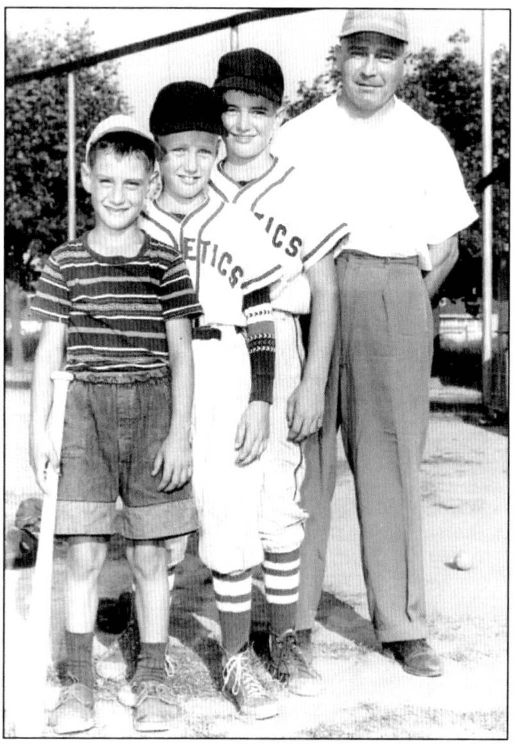

In 1953, Selinsgrove youth baseball was not very old nor was it officially affiliated with Little League Baseball. As is the case today, fathers and interested adults served as coaches. Percy Miller, himself an accomplished player, coach the Athletics, which included two of his sons as players, and another, still too young to play, as batboy. From left to right are Barry, Dale, Ken, and Percy.

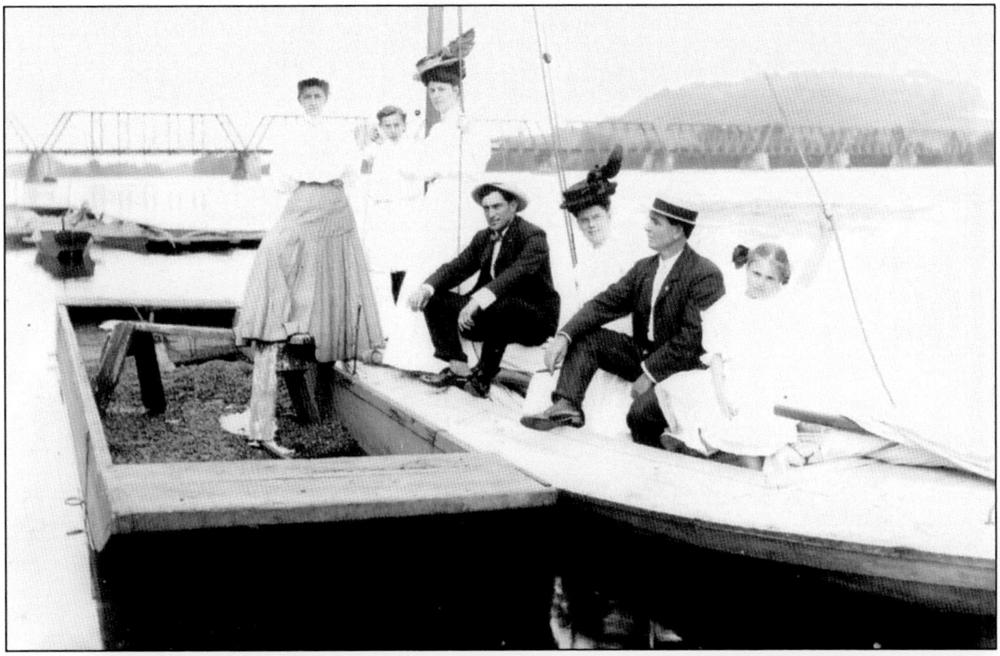

At the dawn of the 20th century, not all recreational activities were limited to ball games on dry land. There were boats and the Susquehanna River. One sport was yacht racing. A well-dressed group is readying its crafts at a spot in the river near Selinsgrove known as the Inlet. It was not too far from the railroad bridge, seen in the background. The photograph is from 1906.

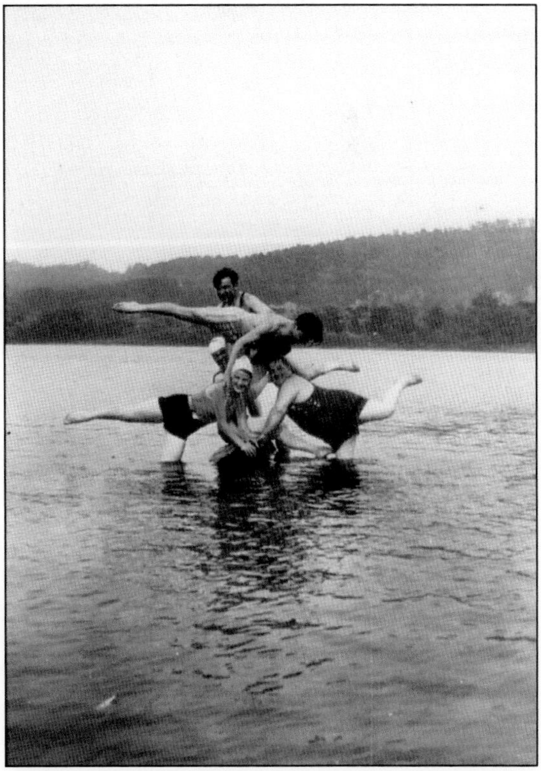

With the Susquehanna River forming the eastern boundary of Snyder County, it is an easy-access venue for water sports. On a summer's day in 1929, five members of Selinsgrove's Potteiger family form their version of a pyramid.

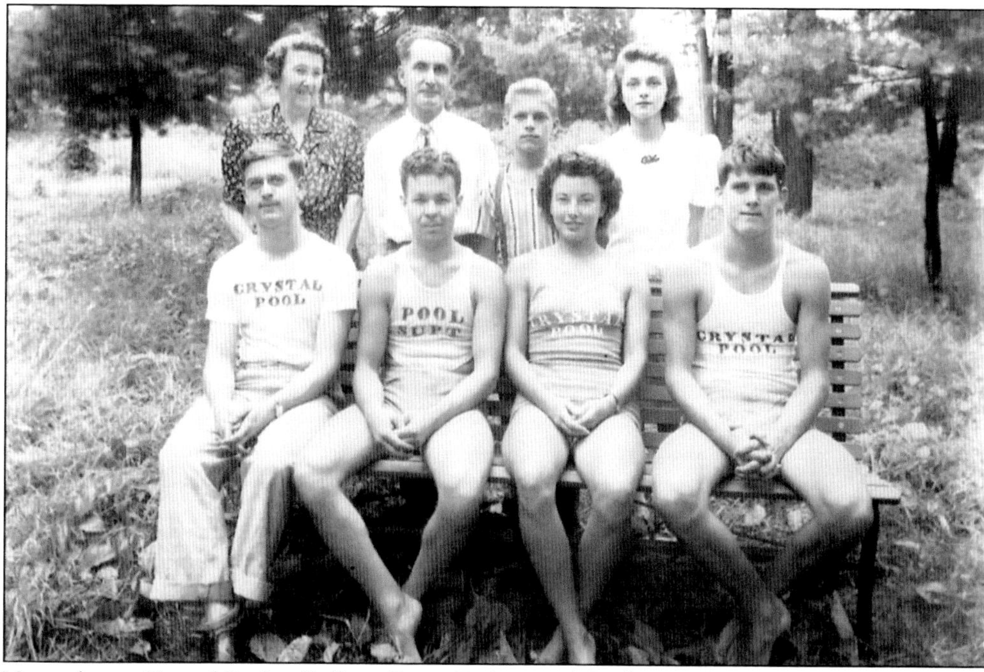

Not only was Crystal Pool at Rolling Green Park one of the first public swimming pools around, it eventually became one of the first with a modern filtration system as opposed to the old fill-and-draw method. In 1942, pool and park personnel posed for a picture. From left to right are (first row) John Leach, Henry Mitterling, Eleanor Benfer, and George Pollock; (second row) Carrie Clark, Roman Spangler, Bruce Wagenseller, and Lorraine Rowe.

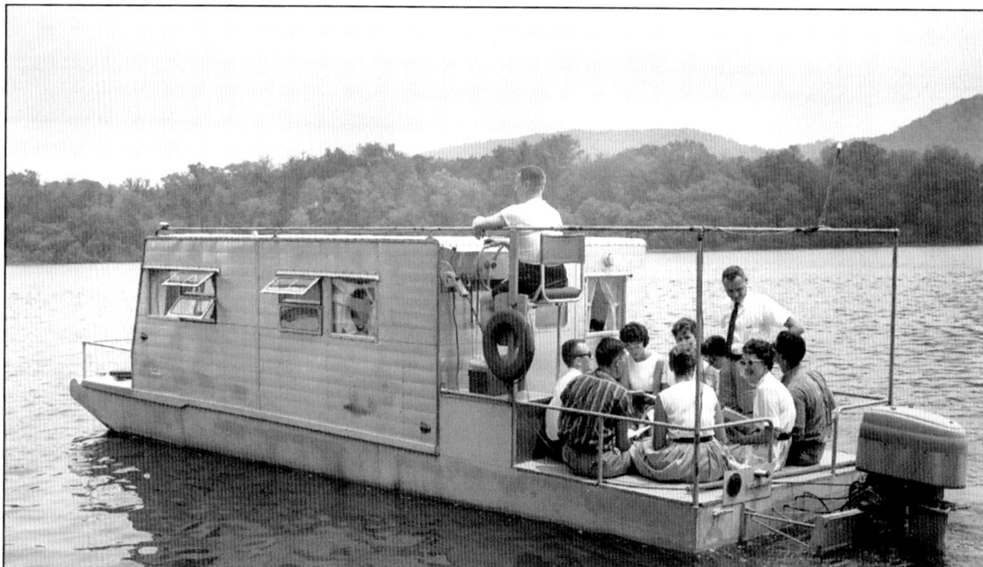

It may be a stretch to call this a sport, but there is a recreational quality to what is going on. Susquehanna University summer-school students of 1960 are pictured out on the Susquehanna River. The houseboat is owned by Prof. Fred Stevens, who often taught classes on the water. The photograph became a United Press International (UPI) wirephoto that received national circulation. UPI dubbed the boat a "scholarship."

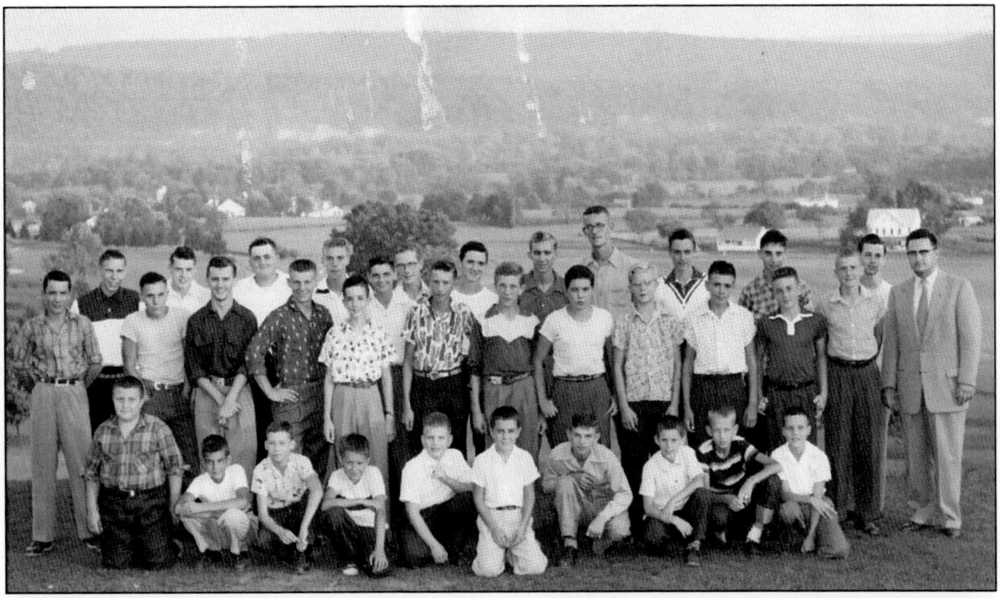

The Susquehanna Valley Country Club was a source of recreation and income for youngsters. From left to right, the 1954 caddies are (first row) R. Reichenbach, L. Herman, unidentified, J. Hendricks, J. Shadle, G. Traher, R. Hoover, J. Schuck, O. Zagars, and B. Nichols; (second row) B. Miller, C. Long, J. Snyder, K. Ludwig, unidentified, B. Clark, L. Heiser, L. Fox, S. Tyler, L. Boyer, K. Wochley, W. Starr, and professional Jim Dickenson; (third row) G. Slobodian, D. Inners, H. Pearson, A. Rowe, R. Zimmerman, J. Steigerwalt, R. Heiser, K. Ulrich, H. Powers, C. Herman, D. Bingaman, and W. Arbogast.

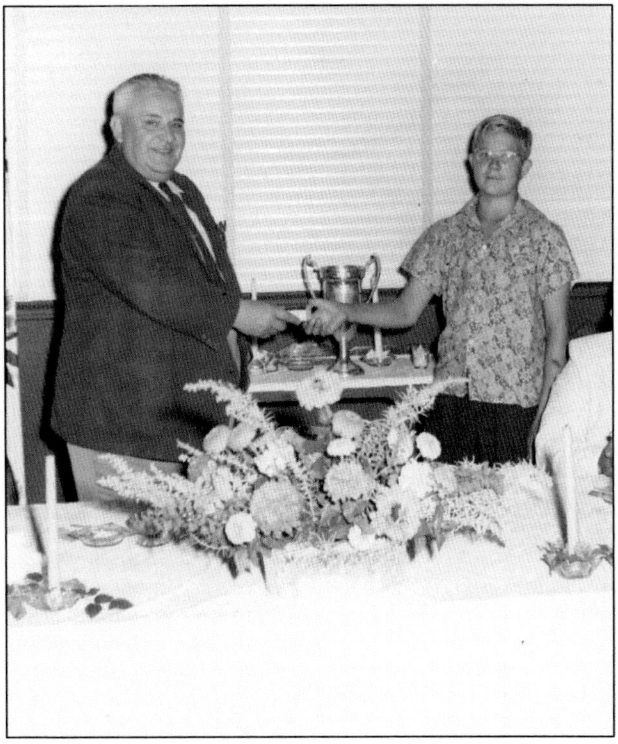

Caddying at the Susquehanna Valley Country Club was a great way to earn walking-around money when school was not in session. The country club was very appreciative of the contributions of the young caddies. The club allowed them to play on Mondays, sponsored a caddies' tournament, and hosted an awards banquet. Shown is Herman Noll (left), an officer of the club, presenting caddy Sam Tyler with an award earned by virtue of his putting skills.

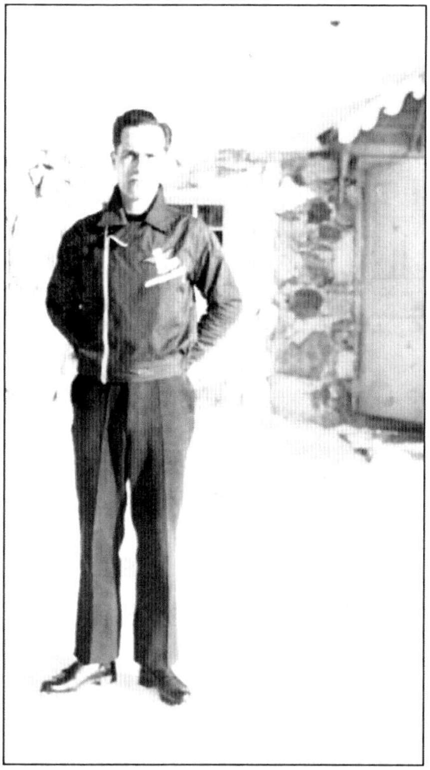

Grant Yerger was a man for all seasons, but winter was his favorite. As a figure skater, he cut a mean figure. He is shown on the ice at Selinsgrove's Little Norway in 1946, oddly enough, without skates. Not content to just skate locally, he was a member of the Harrisburg Skating Club, whose logo adorns his jacket. More than once, Yerger had the capital city skaters enjoy a Sunday afternoon at the local outdoor rink.

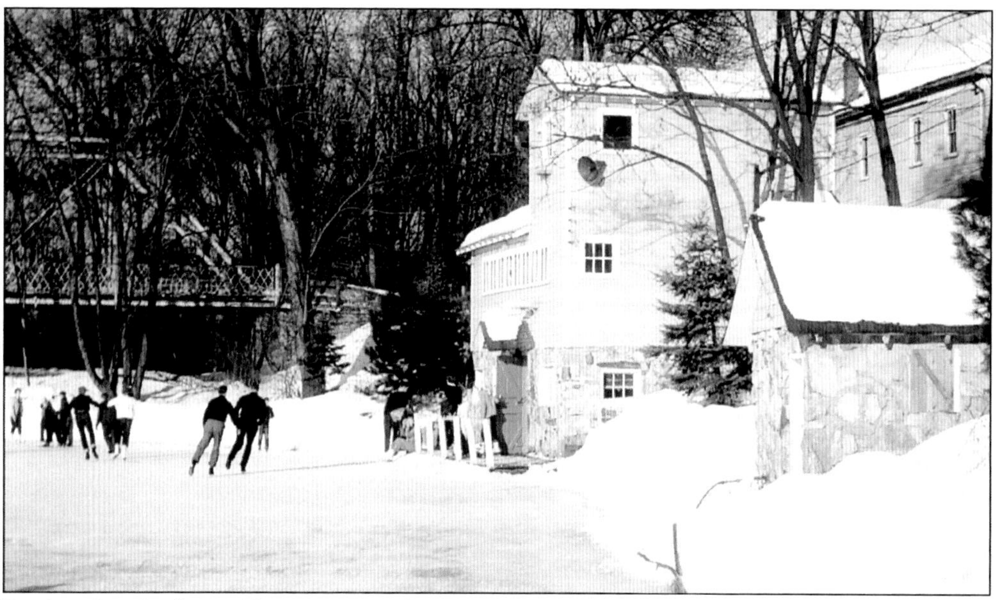

For four decades from 1938 to 1968, Little Norway was truly a winter wonderland. Operated most of that time by Selinsgrove's Burns family, it provided weekday evening and weekend daytime and evening skating. The wine cellar—early pictures show the chalet on stilts—was added in the 1940s. Accomplished skater Grant Yerger did much of the stonework. The building is yellow in this 1949 photograph. It was later painted red. Regardless of color, the fond memories linger to this day.

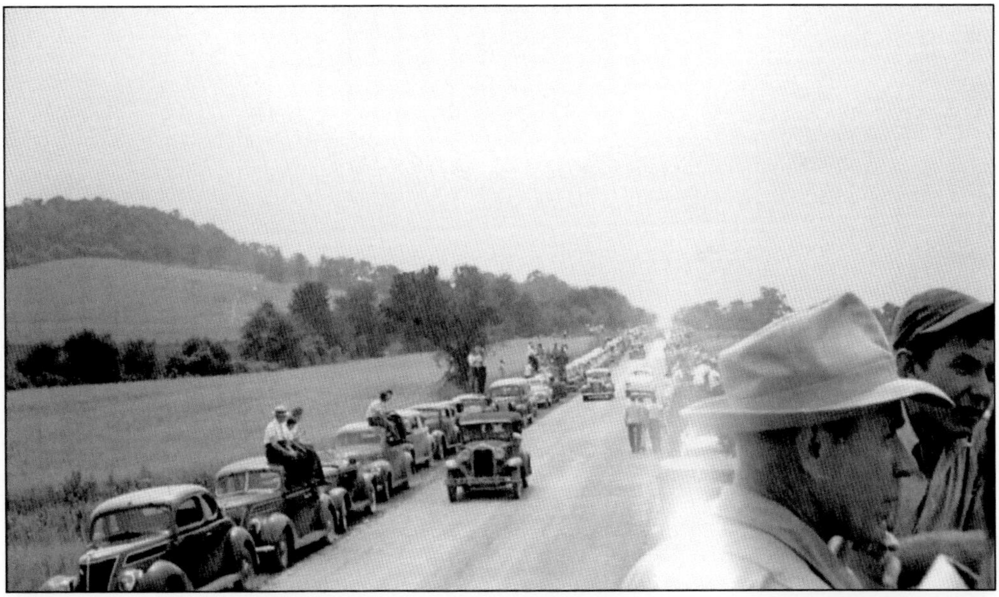

Laid out by renowned Native American racer and hell driver Joie Chitwood, the Selinsgrove Speedway quickly earned a reputation as "the fastest half-mile dirt track in the East." The track's first race, promoted by Buster Keller, was on Saturday, July 20, 1946, during fair week. Not everyone chose to gain entry to the speedway. A long string of cars, many of them prewar models, lined Route 35, the Freeburg Road. Bill Holland won the inaugural race. He also won the Indianapolis 500 in 1949.

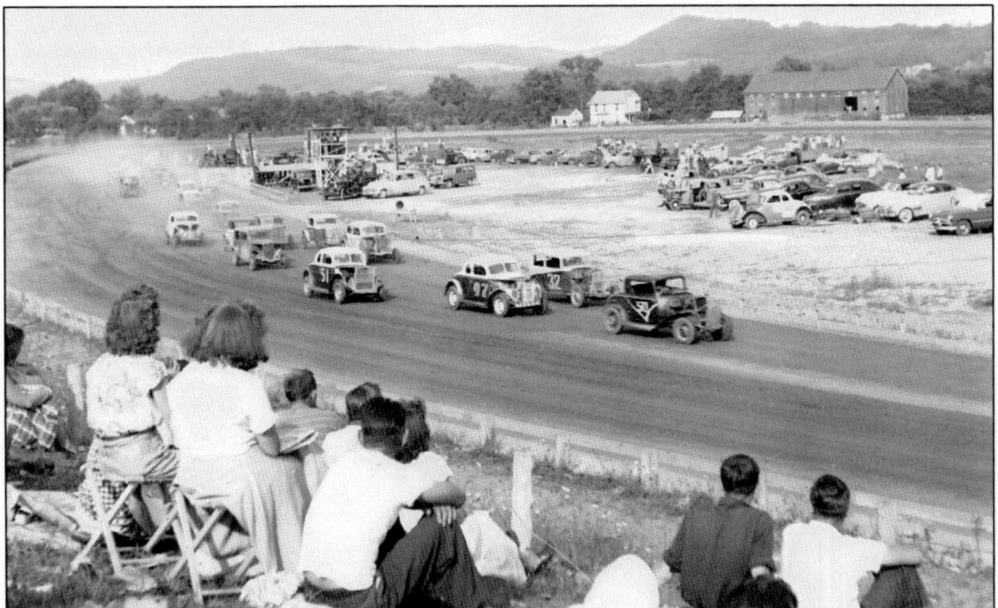

Sprint car races have become a Saturday-night tradition at the Selinsgrove Speedway. Top drivers and top purses attract a top crowd. Racing was not always under the Saturday-night lights. In 1951, as seen, it was a Sunday afternoon event, and the cars were stock. Early favorites from the era were drivers Merlin "Blackie" Balliet, Vic Nauman Jr., Wilbur Reese, Johnny Crawford (in his "Craw-Ford"), Al Fisher, and Harlan "Cat" Fisher.

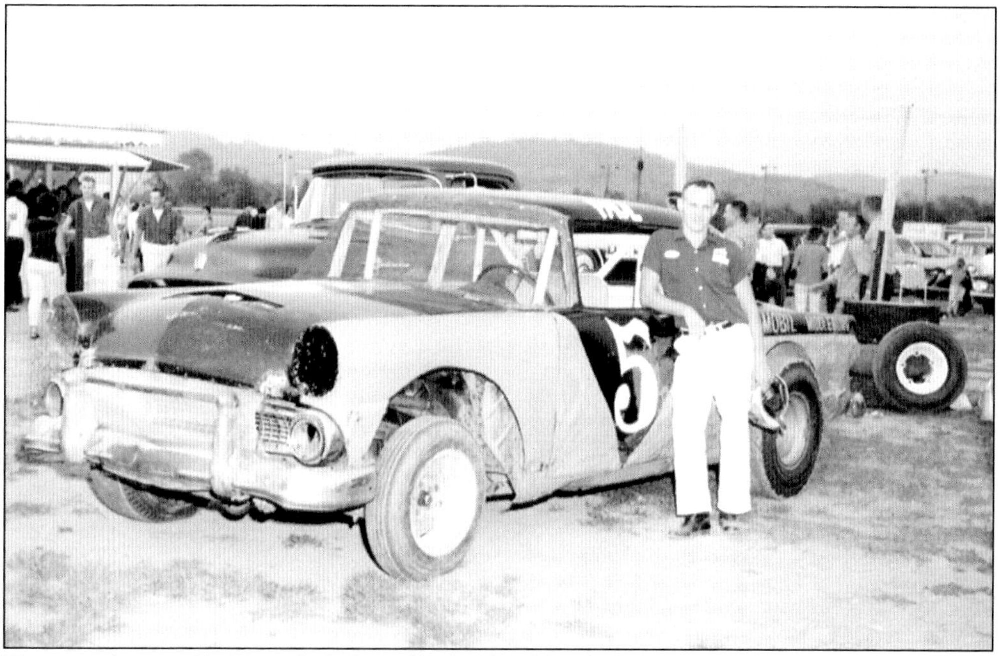

Texas can keep its Friday-night lights of high school football. Central Pennsylvanians prefer the Saturday-night lights of the Selinsgrove Speedway. Over the years, many drivers have become local favorites. One of the most admired was driver Paul Long of Middleburg. Shown here in the early 1960s is a young Long in the days before Selinsgrove Ford sponsored his ride.

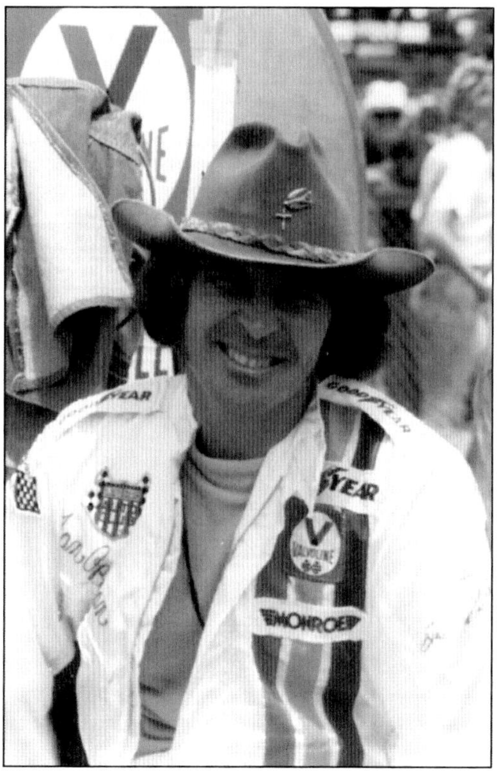

It can be safely said that no Selinsgrove Speedway driver was more successful nor had a more devoted following than Jan Opperman. His flat-out driving captured the imagination and admiration of nearly all. His Bogar's Special got the attention of spectators and competitors alike. Opperman not only raced the local speedway but also raced the top NASCAR circuit. Many from the area trekked to Pocono Raceway to see him. This photograph was taken there in 1976. He also drove the Indianapolis 500.

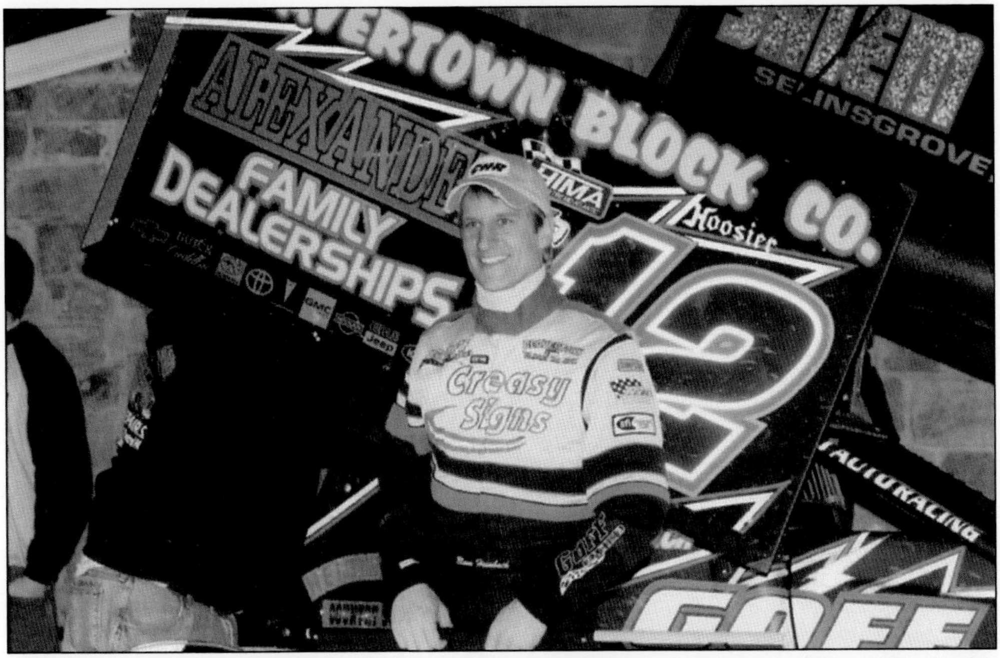

This page represents current and future Selinsgrove sports luminaries. Blane Heimbach's pedal-to-the-metal style of sprint car driving has won the young driver a legion of fans. He has captured the Selinsgrove Speedway sprint car championship numerous times. Although still in is 20s, Heimbach has a long history of racing, starting out with go-karts at an early age.

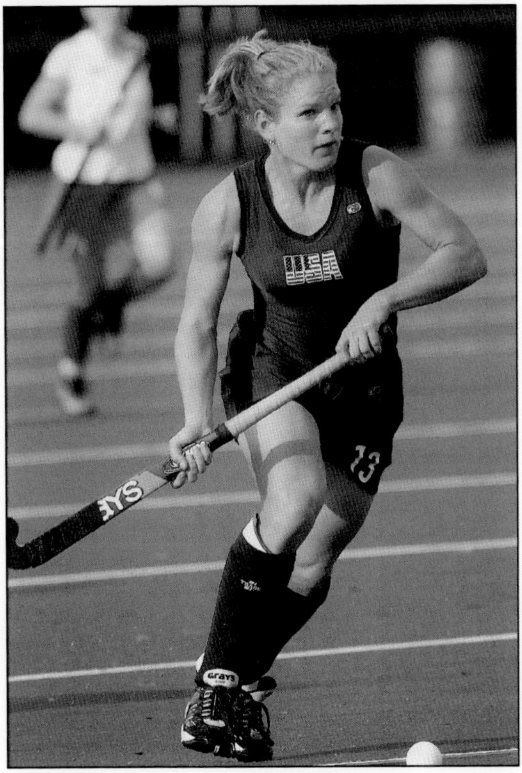

Kelli Smith is another who inherited great athletic genes. Her mother, Sharon Smith, was a fine high school athlete. Her father, Neal Smith, went from walk-on to consensus All-America safety at Pennsylvania State University. After a legendary Selinsgrove High School career, Kelli made All-America and was on an NCAA championship field hockey team at the University of Maryland. Pictured in an international tournament in 2004, she later helped her United States national team make the 2008 Olympics, becoming Selinsgrove's first-ever Olympian.